MARCUS GARVEY

ANTI-COLONIAL CHAMPION

DATE DUE

In memory of my mother
Lettice Monteith-Lewis 1918-1957.

MARCUS GARVEY
ANTI-COLONIAL CHAMPION

by Rupert Lewis

Africa World Press, Inc.

P.O. Box 1892

Trenton, NJ 08607

P.O. Box 48

Asmara, ERITREA

Africa World Press, Inc.

P.O. Box 1892
Trenton, NJ 08607

P.O. Box 48
Asmara, ERITREA

First American Edition 1988
Second Printing 1992
Third Printing 1998

Cover design: Ife Nii Owoo

Typeset by Typehouse of Pennington, Inc.

Library of Congress Catalog Card Number: 87-72598

ISBN: 0-86543-061-6 Cloth
0-86543-062-4 Paper

Contents

Acknowledgments

This study is long overdue. Completion is in large measure due to the encouragement and assistance of my wife, Dr. Maureen Warner-Lewis who has not only read, edited and typed different drafts of the manuscript, but has also assisted me in the use of oral accounts from Garveyites in Cuba, Panama and Jamaica.

Special tribute has to be made to the late Mrs. Amy Jacques Garvey who stimulated my interest in her husband's work and for her own inestimable contribution to my knowledge of Garveyism. While I lived at her home in the early 1970's, I had full access to her papers and to her vivid memory of what it was like to have embarked on such a course. She is adequately described by the Guyanese revolutionary, the late Dr. Walter Rodney, as a Black revolutionary fighter in her own right. Amy Jacques Garvey was not only anti-colonialist but also anti-imperialist and made me realise that as far as Garveyism is concerned there is a continuity between the two struggles.

I acknowledge the assistance of Garveyites in Jamaica, the United States, Trinidad, Panama, Cuba, whom I have interviewed throughout the years. Special thanks are due to Rev. Scarlett of Colón, Panama who facilitated my contacts there, and to Richard Hart for his helpful comments on this text, I am grateful to the following institutions: the National Library of Jamaica, where a lot of the library research was done; the Island Record Office in Spanish Town, The Library of the University of the West Indies, Jamaica, the Schomburg Collection in New York; the Ministry of Culture in Cuba which made possible my research at the José Marti National Library in Havana, to the international collective at World Marxist Review in Prague where I was able to learn much about the early communist movement of the 1920's, the Lenin Library in Moscow from which I received valuable information, the Public Records Office, the British Museum and the Library of the Institute of Race Relations in London. A special thanks to the first year students in politics at the University of the West Indies, Jamaica between 1972-1982 whose questions on Garvey further stimulated my own work and to civic and community groups who invited me to speak on different aspects of Garvey's life. Thanks also to the Institute of Social and Economic Research which financed the typing of the manuscript, to Mrs. Rosalie Bernard who typed it, to Denzil Kerr who helped with the proofing of the typescript.

Key to Newspapers

B	*Blackman*
BM	*Black Man Magazine*
CA	*Commercial Advocate* (Jamaica)
DC	*Daily Chronicle* (Jamaica)
DN	*Daily News* (Jamaica)
DG	*Daily Gleaner* (Jamaica)
FWI	*Free West Indian* (Grenada)
Herald	*Herald* (Jamaica)
Heraldo	*Heraldo de Cuba*
JA	*Jamaica Advocate*
JG	*Jamaica Guardian*
JT	*Jamaica Times*
Nation	*The Nation* (Trinidad)
NJ	*New Jamaican*
NN	*The Northern News* (Jamaica)
NP	*Nigerian Pioneer*
NW	*Negro World*
People	*The People* (Trinidad)
POp	*Public Opinion* (Jamaica)
PP	*Planters' Punch* (Jamaica)
PT	*Plain Talk* (Jamaica)
POSG	*Port of Spain Gazette* (Trinidad)
SGM	*Sunday Gleaner Magazine* (Jamaica)
SGd	*Sunday Guardian* (Trinidad)
Sg	*Sunday Gleaner* (Jamaica)
TG	*Trinidad Guardian*
WP	*Worker and Peasant* (Jamaica)
WICR	*West Indian Critic and Review*

Marcus Garvey

Introduction

This study focuses on Marcus Garvey's struggles against racism and colonialism. His work has had an impact on the history of this century and forms an important part of the historical legacy of African people. As was the case in his life, Garvey's work has been the subject of much controversy. His impact, especially in the United States in the early 1920's, was positive and dynamic, and it was from the streets of New York that the cry of African people for self-determination reached millions scattered throughout the globe and acted like yeast to the diverse anti-colonial forces.

Garvey's development as a mass leader was made possible by a number of factors. His early years, with its peasant Afro-Jamaican ambience, were a school of preparation for him. His character-formation as a young lad showed him possessed of a determination to overcome the circumstances of his birth not only for himself but for his community. These too were the years of his budding intellectualism. As a rural boy in a colony with severely limited avenues for formal education, intellectualism was expressed through wide and voracious reading, mental curiosity, keenness to join clubs fostering social and cultural activity, as well as the cultivation of written and oral language skills, including logic, debate, rhetoric and elocution. These years, therefore, prepared him to be the articulate spokesman, journalist and organizer he was to become.

The circumstances of the post-World War I years were propitious to Garvey. These were years when Black soldiers from the United States and the Caribbean who had fought for democracy in Europe returned with a determination to fight for their own democracy, to reject second-class citizenship in the U.S. and the Caribbean, and to vigorously oppose the apart-heid-like conditions in many parts of the USA. These war veterans had seen many of their own die in Europe and they were now prepared to make this ultimate sacrifice for themselves. Then, there was the impact of the Russian Revolution which the more politically conscious Blacks, particularly those from among the intelligentsia, saw as a breakthrough in the armour not only of international capitalism but of international colonialism. These were integrally connected. Another factor that was favourable to Garveyism was the demographic change in the United States brought about by mass migratory movements to the Northern states. Urbanization, proletarianization and population density made people more open to radical ideas and broader perspectives.

Furthermore, Marcus Garvey appeared at a time when there was a vacuum in Black leadership in the United States. He responded to that call for leadership in a manner which was in keeping with the possibilities of the time and developed an international organization of Black people under the banner of African Redemption, anti-colonialism and civil rights.

He had to find his own way in a colonized world where the odds were against him in one sense, but in which the historical process which he envisioned and which most could not comprehend was moving towards the realization of his ideas. Garvey's achievements were also enabled by that foresight and drive which allowed him to launch an international organization, to publish newspapers and develop an arsenal of opposing political and cultural institutions geared to defeating the dominant colonial system. Impractical schemes, poor management, idealistic conceptions, and corruption meant that many of his organizational schemes did not endure. However the UNIA and African Communities League set an example which later mass movements and political parties in the Third World have followed.

Through his work Garvey showed that he was an intellectual of a new type, one whose efforts embodied the aspirations of millions of colonial peoples. He was no bookish academic. For him, knowledge had to be pursued in order to assist in the process of liberation from racism and colonialism. His intellectual capabilities are evident in his speeches and writings which were a form of communion between himself and his people and were characterized by a profound knowledge of the circumstances under which they lived, of the historical reasons which accounted for their condition, and the certainty that they could overcome these conditions through their own efforts. He articulated ideas about self-reliance, about the relationship between oppressed peoples throughout the world regardless of colour, about the relationship between the working class movement in Europe and the colonial peoples, about the Russian Revolution and the anti-colonial movement, about the condition of Blacks as an international problem, and he put forward ideas which are central to the process of decolonization. This formidable agenda required great self-confidence and foresight at a time when it seemed that it was impossible to break out of the apparently impenetrable colonial fortress in which so many millions of non-white people had been trapped, a structure of servitude they had been forced into erecting.

In fact, Garvey was the opposite of a traditional colonial intellectual. The formally trained intellectual in Jamaica at that time would have graduated from a teacher training or theological college. These institutions were founded by the colonial authorities and were therefore colonial in their orientation. Their graduates would return to the rural towns as cultural emissaries of the British, denying the vigorous Afro-Jamaican and Caribbean cultures, despising their own people, frustrating their efforts towards freedom, arguing that slavery and colonialism were blessings in disguise, and that Africa was heathen, dark, and uncivilized.

But for Garvey Africa was central. Its redemption was necessary, its sovereignty imperative for the future of Africans "at home and abroad". He did not in fact preach the philosophy of mass exodus to Africa. Instead, his words and deeds indicate that whilst the liberation of Africa was central to the future of Blacks in the modern world, the struggles in the United States, the Caribbean and other areas of the diaspora were equally important. The emphasis that I have placed on Garvey's later Jamaican years, particularly 1929-34, bears out this point.

As its structure indicates, this book is not a biography. Part I looks at Garvey's Jamaican colonial origins, the movements which influenced him, and shows the early stage of his political evolution.

Part II deals with Garvey's radicalization during the years of World War I in the U.S. and how conditions led to the mass emergence of the UNIA. It goes on to examine the specific organizational forms and ideological expressions of an anti-colonial movement in the 1920's which had its headquarters in New York, with growing influence in the U.S., Africa, Central America and the Caribbean. In this section the relationship between the early national liberation struggles and the young international communist movement is also examined. The question of the relationship between the national liberation movement in the colonies and the international working class movement is not of purely historical interest but continues today into the second stage of national liberation when the colonial system has virtually collapsed, but when neo-colonialism has developed as a powerful successor. This section also shows Garvey's real contribution to the anti-colonial movement in Africa.

Part III looks at Garvey as one of the pioneers of Jamaica's social-political advancement. Here we see him in his own national and Caribbean setting. The struggles between the colonial and anti-colonial forces here are presented as closely as possible in relation to historical events, thus enabling other generations living and working at the end of this century to see more clearly the legacy of this outstanding fighter against racism and colonialism.

Of course, given the scope of the Garvey movement, its social composition and subsequent differentiation, some Garveyites adopted neo-colonial positions. However, examining the Garvey legacy in its true historical perspective we can reject what in it is now anachronistic or weakens the struggle against imperialism and we can look toward developing the positive, which in any case, represents the main thrust in Garveyism.

Part I

Process of Political Maturing

Chapter One

Origins

Garvey's Parentage

Marcus Mosiah Garvey was born at 32, Market Street in the northerly sea-port town of St. Ann's Bay, Jamaica, on August 17, 1887. (Rose, 3). Garvey Snr. is said to have fathered three sets of children, making a total of eleven. Marcus was a product of his father's last union, that with Sarah Jane Richards. (Hill d I, 16, fn. 3)

Garvey's father was a mason by trade, and both his stone and brick work on houses, churches and tombs were well known in the parish of St. Ann where fields were separated by low grey stone fences. However, Garvey's father was not only a master-mason. He was a deacon of the Methodist Church and was also regarded as a 'village lawyer', who settled disputes, wrote letters, and gave advice to the peasants. He loved reading, had a small library, and subscribed to several local newspapers. He was to bequeath his son not only a persistence of character, but also his love of books, and his intellectual abilities.

Temperamentally, Sarah and Garvey Snr. were quite different. Sarah, as her son later described her, was "a sober and conscientious Christian too good and soft for the time in which she lived," while his father, whom even Sarah, in Victorian fashion, called "Mr. Garvey," was "severe, firm, determined, bold and strong, refusing to yield even to the superior forces if he believed he was right." (Garvey a, 71)

Mr. Garvey Snr. appears, in fact, to have been cast in the mould of the self-righteous, autocratic male family head perceptively analyzed in respect of Trinidad society.(Braithwaite, iii passim) This character-type seems to have been created by an amalgam of cultural and social influences. One of these is likely to have been the tradition of dominant male family and clan-heads in many African societies. That cultural pattern was reinforced by the male chauvinism of European societies and exemplified in the Christian, Victorian family code. In the colonies, however, the male personality nurtured by these codes through domestic example, the Bible, the Church, and formal education came to feel its self-confidence, its pride in achievement, its consciousness of intellectual worth, its social, financial, and cultural aspirations thwarted by legal and racist restrictions on "the native". Such a personality, innately strong and proud, felt its strength challenged and crushed, and its pride dishonoured. These positive character traits thus became distorted, finding outlets in petty contentiousness, wilfulness, moodiness, and social withdrawal.

These tendencies can be gleaned from the following episode about Garvey Snr. One Mr. Gall, a newspaper publisher in Kingston, had been sending Garvey copies of his newspaper over the years. When Gall died his executors sent Mr. Garvey a bill for thirty pounds — a very large sum in those days — which he refused to pay.

He was sued, contested the case, lost, and still refused to pay claim and costs; so by court order one of his properties was attached and sold for much less than its value.

He became more irritable, as he felt that he was unjustly dealt with. He quarrelled with a neighbour about a boundary line of a few feet, with another about cutting down a cedar tree which he claimed, and so he was in and out of court, losing each time as costs piled up against him, until he lost all of his lands, except just a house spot. (Jacques Garvey a, 4)

The Garveys had long since moved from the wooden house in which Marcus was born to a property Garvey Snr. had purchased on Winders Hill from Cloisters as the Methodist Church property was called. Here he built "a Spanish walled house", and continued in his craft while cultivating his property and the adjacent Church lands. (Rose, 3)

By the time Garvey was in his teens, his father had become morose and withdrawn. His mother, for her part, consoled herself with church and children, and fell back on a convenient home industry to make ends meet: she baked cakes and boiled confectionery for sale. She had to come into the town-centre from the outskirts where they lived to make her sales. But here too, colonial injustice placed obstacles in the way of the poor. In the mid 1880's, a new market was built to accommodate the higglers who came down from the hills with their foodstuff on Wednesdays and Fridays. But the planters who dominated the Parish Council were more concerned with the revenue from market fees. Market women had to pay high fees and even those who sold biscuits and sweet-cakes had to pay for a license to do so. Indeed, the Parish Council records for the latter part of the 19th century show that market fees and trade licenses together constituted the largest sources of parish revenue. Much of this money was spent on the repair and construction of major roads adjacent to large estates and some on poor relief.

Another pen-sketch of the life and fortunes of one of Garvey's relatives illustrates the stifling conditions of colonial existence for those who either had nothing, or had just enough to escape poverty. Garvey himself related the following story at a public meeting in Kingston in 1929:

> "I can remember a man by the name of Pratt in St. Ann. He had a large property. He rented about 25 acres of it to my uncle; and my uncle was a hard-working Christian. When he was not reading his Bible he was working in his field. He worked and plantd out 25 acres of land in canes, ground provisions and every imaginable agricultural produce you can think of . . . . He had one farm that brought him an income of about one hundred pounds per year. He had up to his mule sending his bananas to market on Mondays, and he was expanding and he was intelligent and he was able to educate me because my father would not do it. I helped to keep his books and so at the week-end I got a commission of 13/- for selling bananas some of which I got honestly and some I stole (laughter). I used to go to Sunday school and when the girls were looking, threw 4/- in the collection plate (laughter). I used to go around with money in my pocket so as to attract the girls (laughter).

But my wife is here and I want to announce that I have stopped my bad ways. But this is the story: that uncle of mine, one morning when he went from his home town to the farm he found one hundred cows in his field. Pratt had instructed his headman to set the cows in so that he could drive him out of the place and when my uncle went up to his residence he could drive him out without any recompense and turn my uncle off his piece of land. My uncle never recovered until he died." *(B,* 12 Sept. 1929)

This episode reflects an essential factor in the life of the people, that is, the arbitrary action of the large landowners, who, backed by British colonialism, made life a hell for the masses. It is experiences like these which helped to shape Garvey's consciousness and spurred him on from early to public activity.

Education and Childhood

Garvey attended infant school, and then elementary school at St. Ann's Bay Methodist. From all reports, including his own, he was an intelligent pupil. As a senior, he on occasion deputized for the teacher.

The chief subjects learnt were Reading, Writing from dictation, and Arithmetic. Other subjects were Religious Knowledge, General Knowledge, Grammar and Composition, Geography and History, Handwriting, Singing, Organization and Discipline.

Garvey had private tuition which contributed to his development as an outstanding pupil. This private tuition he got from his godfather, Mr. Alfred E. Burrowes who, from 1892, ran a printery. Burrowes "was godfather to a lot of young people in the town who went to his printery not only to learn about printing but also about life." *(SGM,* 16 January 1983, 3)

Garvey was friendly with the children of the white Wesleyan minister, Pastor Lightbourne, who lived on the adjoining property. The clergyman had three girls and two boys. In an autobiographical essay, Garvey wrote,

"We romped and were happy children, playmates together. The little white girl whom I liked knew no

> better than I did myself. We were two innocent fools
> who never dreamed of a race feeling and problem. As a
> child I went to school with white boys and girls; like all
> other Negroes then. I never heard the term used once
> until I was about fourteen.
>
> At fourteen my little white playmate and I parted. Her
> parents thought the time had come to separate us and
> draw the colour line. They sent her and another sister to
> Edinburgh, Scotland, and told her that she was never to
> write or try to get in touch with me, for I was a 'nigger'."
> (Garvey h, 125)

This was Garvey's first lesson in racism. Racial separation,
racial prejudice, and the denigration of African peoples were
characteristic of colonialism. Sooner or later Garvey was bound
to experience them. Unfortunately, some Blacks regarded it as
their lot and justified colonial oppression on Biblical grounds.
But this was not representative of the dominant trend in the
social thinking of the Black population which aspired towards a
better life, free from the shackles of colonialism.

In 1901, when the white clergyman's children were advancing
their education in Scotland, Garvey's formal schooling was
approaching its end. At fourteen he became a printer's appren-
tice under his godfather, Mr. Burrowes, whom he described as
"a highly educated and alert man" from whom he learnt a great
deal. He quickly mastered the trade, learning "on a heavy iron
foot-pedal machine" (*SGM*, 16 January 1983, 3), but continued
regular reading and discussions with the many people who
stopped to talk politics and social affairs with Mr. Burrowes. As
such, Garvey was pupil, discussant and teacher at the same
time. An ex-school mate gave this description of Garvey's
deportment at the time:

> ". . . . all the time when I meet him he wear jacket and
> everytime, his two jacket pockets full of paper, reading
> and telling us things that happen all over the world. How
> him know, I don't know, but him telling us. He was very
> interested in world affairs." (Rose, 4)

Garvey left school in Sixth Standard around 1903. The end to
his school education was the usual fate of most Jamaican
children who could obtain a continuous period of schooling.

Many never had the opportunity of learning to read and write, because of poor health, lack of facilities, and lack of funds, because of their parents' need of practical help at home, in the fields, and at market, or because of the limited perspective of uneducated parents who felt that nothing practical was to be gained by irrelevant brainwork. After all, one was "slated to be a cowhand or labourer, a blacksmith or shoemaker . . . ." (Garvey in *BM*, December 1937)

Colonial education was limited. It could not take the pupil very far from plantation skills and the plantation mentality. School-children were taught to accept British rule and love it. There were pictures of the British sovereign in all schools; the children sang the British national anthem and British songs, and were taught to revere the Governor of the island who represented the British Crown. The Governor himself lived in Kingston in King's House which was the central point of the official social life of the planters, merchants, and high colonial officials. As such, the life of the colonial ruling class was fundamentally different from that of the ordinary Jamaican.

For example, Sir Henry Norman, who was appointed Governor of the island in 1883, gained this position as a result of having faithfully served British colonialism in India. He had held several military and civilian posts in the Indian colonial administration. He had been Acting Adjutant-General of the Bengal Army, Secretary to the Government of India in the Military Department (1862-1870), Military Member of the Council of the Viceroy of India (1870-1877) and a member of the Council of India (1878-1883). Other members of the colonial hierarchy had seen service in Africa. To them, Jamaica was a minor colony to be governed in Britain's interest.

So that even though through formal education, children got to know more about Britain and imperial achievements than about the Caribbean or Africa, all the same, in this socio-political context, many Blacks looked to education as a means to social advancement to some minor clerical job in the colonial administration, to teaching, or a career as a minister of religion. But whatever one's profession, a colonial education was intended to inculcate subservience. White-collar work drew the awe and admiration of the plantation worker and part-time peasant.

While the colonial system wrought political, social, economic, cultural, and psychological damage on the people, natural disasters also wrought their own forms of havoc. In 1903, A hurricane hit St. Ann with full force. Many houses were destroyed and farmers lost tons of produce. Hurricanes not only inflicted immediate damage on life and property but the flooding caused by torrential rains led to the pollution of water supplies and food contamination. It also took a heavy toll on animal stock so necessary to the peasants.

Garvey would have experienced the 1903 hurricane which blew down the Methodist Church where he had attended Sunday School, (Rose, 4), and he also lived through the 1907 earthquake which nearly destroyed Kingston and killed more than eight hundred people. Nature and colonial society seemed to conspire to make life hard.

St. Ann's Bay, a small sea-port town with a population of only two thousand people, did not offer much scope for Marcus. Although a sea-port in shipping contact with other Jamaican ports and the outside world, and therefore, more exposed to change than inland rural towns, it still offered little opportunity to young people. It was, for instance, over-shadowed by Port Maria which, with four shipping companies operating there, was the hub of the banana trade controlled by the United Fruit Company. Port Maria was, therefore, in direct contact with Boston, U.S.A., by sea, and the United Fruit Company maintained its own reliable telephone links with important Jamaican towns. Port Antonio was next in significance on the north coast and was reputed to be even bigger than Kingston. (Scarlett)

So after some time spent in the employ of his godfather (Rose, 4), Garvey moved on to Port Maria in the company of another of Burrowes' students, one Cottrell, who was setting up a printing press there. (Scarlett)[1]

Then, around 1906, Garvey went to Kingston. There he worked at the Government Printing Office for some time (Rose, 4; Scarlett), and later as a compositor in the printing section of P.A. Benjamin Ltd., a firm of manufacturing chemists which at that time had a good export trade with Central America, Cuba and other West Indian islands.

The Garvey of those years has fortunately been described by his friend and associate J. Coleman Beecher:

> "He was fiercely proud of being black. He carried a pocket dictionary with him and said he studied three or

four words daily, and in his room he would write a paragraph or two using these words." (Jacques Garvey c, 34)

De Leon said:

"He had a mature mind from the time he came to Kingston in his teens. He was always busy, planning and doing something for the underprivileged youth. Uplift work we called it, and he had us in the shaft with him." (idem.)

For instance, there was

"a man in Kingston named Tom Prang, a big fat fellow. When any of the waterfront workers went to speak hard to the managers, the employers would get Tom Prang to beat them. Marcus called Tom Prang and told him must stop it, because did he think any white man would beat him friend for a nigger? Tom Prang did stop it. He leave Kingston and go to MoBay (Montego Bay) . . . ." (Rose, 4)

Alexander Bedward under armed guard

Chapter Two

Turn of Century Ambience

Robert Love's Influence

Garvey was born twenty-two years after the 1865 Morant Bay Rebellion. The conditions which spawned that rebellion and its several hundred peasant martyrs still continued. But the fighting spirit of the people had taken a beating after the suppression of the rebellion. British imperialism was at the end of the 19th century, in its heyday. After the 1880's, the partitioning of Africa among the capitalist powers of Europe had been completed and Britain had secured a huge slice of the continental 'cake'. It was this experience which led the anti-colonial fighter, Dr. Robert Love to write:

> "Africa has been the carcass upon which the vultures of Europe have descended and which they have sought to partition among themselves, without any regard whatever for the rights of the Africans." *(JA,* 20 Ap. 1901, 2)

Garvey was later to acknowledge that "much of my early education in race consciousness is from Dr. Love. One cannot read his *Jamaica Advocate* without getting race consciousness . . . . if Dr. Love was alive and in robust health, you would not be attacking me, you would be attacking him . . . ." (Letter, *DG,* 17 February 1930, 12)

Discussion of Love's work in Jamaica is important to show that anti-colonial politics was alive and that black spokesmen such as Love set an example for Garvey. There is a direct line in post-emancipation black political struggle from George William Gordon and Paul Bogle, to Bedward the evangelical leader, and to the secular spokesman, Dr. Robert Love. This, of course, reflects the progressive movement in Jamaican politics which Garvey's work continued.

Love was born in Nassau, the Bahamas, in 1835, and died in Jamaica in 1914.[1] As a young man, he emigrated to the United States where he studied for the Episcopalian priesthood and worked as a clergyman in the South. Love then turned to medicine and by the end of the 1870's he had completed his course at the University of Buffalo. He then travelled to Haiti in 1880 where he was employed to the Haitian government as an army doctor before settling in Jamaica in 1889. Love emerged as the most prominent radical figure in Jamaican politics at the turn of the century and his activities were often the subject for memos and despatches of concerned colonial officials to the British Colonial Secretary.

Love is best remembered for his militant journalism in the *Jamaica Advocate* (1894-1905), which was a tribune anticipating Garvey's American and Jamaican periodicals. Love was also involved with the Jamaica Cooperative Association (1897), and the People's Convention (1898). At the first Conference of the People's Convention, a discussion was held on the "Distribution of Land to the Peasantry." The Chairman of the People's Convention was Alexander Dixon, who in 1899 won a seat to the Legislative Council.

Love himself had been a main organizer for black representation in the colonial legislature, which was dominated by white planters, merchants, and colonial officials.

In an editorial published in the *Advocate* in 1895, Love listed several black men whom he said should put themselves up for election, including Alexander Dixon. Love argued:

> "And these black men can no longer hide themselves without being guilt of treason to the best interests of their race and to the hopes which the race have a right to entertain of them." (*JA*, 7 December 1895, 2)

He furthermore pointed out:

> "Let no Negro allow any man to deceive him by saying that there is no class feeling against him. That is a falsehood. He must, therefore, work out for himself and have nothing to do with that man . . . . Let the Negroes look around them in their own parish, for a representative Negro, gather around him, help him, and send him to the Legislative Council . . . ." (idem.)

This was also Garvey's perspective, not only for Jamaica but for the English-speaking Caribbean which was then under colonial rule. In Love's writing as well as in Garvey's, "race consciousness" is used in its positive sense. "Race consciousness" was an anti-colonial concept. It asserted the humanity of a race of people, regardless of class, whom capitalism oppressed and exploited and branded inferior. In this context, racial oppression and class exploitation stemmed from the same source. Therefore, race consciousness in Love and in Garvey was very often both the national cry of a people and also a class cry, but the latter was not the cry of one class, but of several classes linked by a common yoke of suffering.

Love's electoral struggles were bitterly opposed by whites and mulattoes. Most of the black population was disenfranchised. But Love obviously intended to make use of certain limited reforms that had been introduced in 1895. In that year, the number of elected members was raised from nine to fourteen and the franchise had been extended by lowering the property qualifications and removing the literacy restriction. Voter registration consequently rose from two thousand in 1884 to forty-three thousand two hundred and sixty six in 1894-5. (Knox, 144) As a result, Love was elected to the Kingston City Council in 1898 and to the Legislative Council in 1906. In these bodies he continued to defend the oppressed colonial population.

Love was an advocate of land reform. He agitated for the distribution of Crown lands to the landless peasantry on terms which would bring their possession within the reach of all. (*JA*, 29 February 1896, 2). He called for the abolition of certain landholding taxes which severely affected the peasantry, and also for a stop to the heavily subsidized importation of East Indian labour introduced largely to depress wages and to coerce black labour into accepting the conditions of plantation toil. As one scholar has written:

> "many whites believed that the plantation was a vital agency for civilizing the black masses and ought to be kept alive irrespective of economic considerations." (Knox, 149)

This was, of course, a racial justification for the plantation system. In the *Jamaica Advocate*, the plantation system was described as a profit-making institution that kept the labourers "dependent, poor, ignorant, unclean, contemptible and miserable." (idem.)

Love's newspaper also served the migrant labourers in South and Central America, exposing the injustices meted out to them, which in several cases were particularly outrageous. Love's work, therefore, naturally brought him into conflict with the planters and the colonial rulers in Kingston and in London.

Love concerned himself with all aspects of colonial life. In the *Advocate* he exposed police brutality, called for the appointment of black school inspectors and generally the integration of qualified Blacks into the colonial bureaucracy. He also discussed health, education, and the question of black women and their role in society. About black women, Love wrote,

> "the destiny of the Negro Race depends upon the elevation of the women of the race,"

and added that

> "the conditions in which the black people of the B.W.I. (British West Indies) are found today is due to the fact that no effort has been made to lift the black women up and to put her on the plane that woman ought to occupy in society." (*JA*, 14 November 1896, 1)

Of course, the conditions of black people were due to more profound social, economic, and political reasons, but the fact of Love's attention to the role of black women in the struggle is itself an achievement. He lectured in a rural town on "Phyllis Wheatley, the African Poetess." This was done in aid of the contemplated establishment of a high school for girls to be named after Phyllis Wheatley. Love was well known for his public lectures.

Of significance was his series on the Haitian Revolution and Toussaint L'Ouverture which were published in the *Advocate* between July and September, 1898 and which created wide public discussion. The Haitian Revolution evoked the same response at that time as the Cuban Revolution did and continues to do among imperial interests and the local ruling classes. And to mark the centenary of the Haitian Revolution, Love warned Haitians against imperialism's several facets:

"Keep clear of United States greed and avoid German
brutality." (*JA*, 2 January 1904, 2)

In 1896, he suggested that a public memorial be put up to
mark the memory of George William Gordon. Love made this
suggestion thirty one years after Gordon's execution for his
links with the 1865 peasant revolt led by Paul Bogle. Governor
Eyre, who had ordered Gordon's execution, was at the time in
comfortable retirement in England. Moreover, this was done at
a time when one of the major assumptions of the colonial
political system was that the revolt of 1865 could be repeated.
The law enforcement agencies, especially the local consta-
bulary force (established 1866-1867) and the courts acted on
this assumption. (Knox, 160)

Love's influence on Garvey must be seen not only as an
introduction to early nationalist politics in Jamaica but also to
the Pan-Africanist ideas articulated by Afro-West Indians,
Afro-American, and African intellectuals. In a very real sense,
Love was a DuBois-type intellectual. In his writings there are
references to the works of Paul Lawrence Dunbar, Phyllis
Wheatley, Booker T. Washington, W.E.B. DuBois, Alexander
Crummell, John E. Bruce, H. Sylvester-Williams, J. Albert
Thorne, Frederick Douglass, Edward Blyden and J. Casely-
Hayford. In fact, it was the partnership of Dr. Love and H.
Sylvester-Williams which launched a Pan-African Association
in Jamaica in April, 1901.

The establishment of such an organization was a consequence of the Pan-African Conference held in London from
July 23-25, 1900, which was attended by twenty four delegates
from the Caribbean, the United States and Africa. H. Sylvester-
Williams, a Trinidad-born barrister (who was George Padmore's uncle), became the organizing Secretary of the Pan-
African Conference and was mainly responsible for convening
the meeting. And W.E.B. DuBois, who later organized four Pan-
African Congresses between 1919 and 1927, was Chairman of
the Resolutions Committee and also Regional Officer for the
U.S.A. (Geiss, 726)

Just before Love's People's Convention met in August, 1900,
the *Advocate* informed its readers about the London Conference. The brief item read:

"The Pan-African Conference composed of black men is to meet and to deliberate in London during the present month. Its object is to bring before the people and government of Great Britain the circumstances, claims and desires of the black populations incorporated in the British Empire." (*JA*, 28 July 1900, 2)

The Conference also received the support of another Pan-Africanist figure, J. Albert Thorne, who was, from a political point of view, in the Booker T. Washington mould. Thorne was born in Barbados and taught for many years in Jamaica. He was not a radical but he had ideas about resettling Blacks in Africa. (Lewis a, 8-18)

In March, 1901, Sylvester-Williams arrived in Jamaica to organize the Pan-African Association. As part of the publicity, the *Advocate* published documents from the London Conference, including the "Address to the Nations of the World," written by DuBois, and which sets out the early progressive ideological orientation of Pan-Africanism.

Some success attended the efforts of Sylvester-Williams. Within a month, membership in the Jamaica Pan-African Association reached five hundred and there were groups in Kingston, Annotto Bay, Porus, Port Antonio, Black River, Mandeville, and Yallahs in St. Thomas.[2] Love and his newspaper performed a vital role in the development of this short lived Association.

The objectives of the Pan-African Association as set out at the first meeting of the Kingston branch were:

1. To secure the Africans and their descendants throughout the world their civil and political rights;

2. To ameliorate the condition of our oppressed brethren in the continent of Africa, America, and other parts of the world, by promoting efforts to secure effective legislation;

3. To encourage our people in educational, industrial and commercial enterprises;

4. To foster friendly relations between the Caucasian and African races;

5. To organize a bureau as a depository for collections of
    authorized productions, writings and statistics, re-
    lating to our people everywhere;

6. To raise a fund to be used solely for the forwarding of the
    above. *(DG,* 11 April 1901, 7)

These were, in a sense, modest objectives, but they represent
the beginning of the mass anti-colonial torrents of later decades.

The Governor, Sir Augustus Hemming, opposed the Pan-
African Association. He had been asked to give his patronage to
a concert to raise funds for the Association, but he refused,
citing three reasons. First, he said, there was no need for
organization; secondly, it was aggressive; and thirdly, he would
have to submit the matter to Mr. Chamberlain, the Secretary of
State for the Colonies. *(JA,* 20 July 1901, 2)

Love replied in his very incisive manner:

> "Sir Augustus Hemming, the man, sees in the African
> Race, a people subject and to be kept in subjection,
> even though they are called 'British subjects'; and
> consistently enough, he refuses to sympathize with their
> aspirations and aims.... Sir Augustus Hemming cannot
> arrest the tide of aggression. It is the law of the world
> and if the African, like others, is to be progressive, he
> must be aggressive. And he is not to ask leave of Sir
> Augustus Hemming in the matter." (idem.)

Hemming replied, repeating his position and arguing with
crass hypocrisy that "in British Colonies like Jamaica" there
was

> "one law for black and white, and that law is impartially
> administered, without fear, favour, or prejudice." *(JA,*
> 27 July 1901, 2)

Love's reply is well worth quoting at length as, with a touch of
his characteristic irony, it cuts through and exposes the class
and racial realities that determined how the law was exercised:

> "There is one law for black and white," is a convenient
> phrase frequently employed in Jamaica and elsewhere,

as a vehicle to convey a false impression as to the prevailing conditions of the various classes, positively and relatively. It has become the stock formula under which the plausible sound of which a subtle deception is veiled. 'There is one (constitutional) law for white and black', in the United States, yet black citizens of the United States are publicly shot, hanged, and burned at the stake and thousands are disenfranchised, in spite of that 'one law'. The letter of the law and the spirit of the rulers are very different things. His excellency says: 'in Jamaica there is but one law for black and white, and that law is impartially administered without fear, favour or prejudice,' but in spite of this, we are left to ask, where is the black man whom His Excellency has appointed member of any Public Board? Although almost all the prisoners in the island are black men, where is the black man whom he has ever appointed on the Board of Visitors of either the Prisons or Reformatories . . . . In Jamaica 'there is but one law for black and white' yet by that very law, the black masses are made to pay more taxes than the white classes . . . . We do not deny that in Jamaica, 'there is one law for black and white' but we do deny that a spirit of impartial justice gives value to that law; and after all the latter is the main point." (idem.)

It was this very issue of a class and race-prejudiced judiciary which Garvey was to take up twenty years later and which led to his imprisonment in Jamaica.

Under other circumstances, Love continued to engage the exponents of colonialism and racism. Joseph Chamberlain was reported to have said:

" . . . . as the dominant race, if we admitted equality with inferior races, we would lose the power which gave us our dominance." (*JA*, 30 July 1904, 2)

Love's *Advocate* replied fiercely, attacking colonialism:

"It is with this principle that they vex the Africans with 'punitive expeditions', and destroy the Indians with famine and oppression. It is thus minded that their Governors and officials and under-strappers come to these isles. But Englishmen will wake up some day to find they are making a great mistake . . . . The subject races will not always be governed by that spirit. They were not always thus governed. The Indian will some day repel the assumption, the African will do the same thing, the Egyptian and Burmese, etc., will vindicate their individuality, and will prove that temporary dominance is not evidence of constitutional superiority." (idem.)

This line of anti-colonial struggle was directly continued in Garvey's work. Love's was an important orientation that preceded Garvey, a legacy of ideas and battles that he could draw on, a platform of views and aspirations to which he could attract a mass base. Love was a fighter, but he was largely alone; he really had no mass following.

West Indians had a 'paternalistic' attitude to Africa. Some had gone via the colonial route to work as teachers, missionaries, and skilled craftsmen. The perspective of the *Advocate* was that West Indians must qualify themselves "to assist in the enlightenment of neglected Africa." (*JA*, 8 August 1896, 2). At the same time, the *Advocate* did its best to use views and information from the West African colonial press. Newspapers like the *Sierra Leone Weekly News*, the *Lagos Weekly Record*, the *Lagos Standard*, the *Lagos Echo*, the *West African Mail*, and the *Gold Coast Leader* were frequently referred to in the *Advocate*. There is even reference to the *Advocate* having a Special Correspondent in West Africa. (*JA*, 12 July 1902, 3)

In 1897, the *Advocate* published a series of articles by Dr. Scholes on European imperialist policy in Africa.[3] Scholes was a Jamaican who authored a number of scholarly books critical of imperial policy and racism. In addition to Scholes, the *Advocate* reproduced the writings of Dr. Edward Blyden and J.E. Casely-Hayford. Indeed, the attitude of the *Advocate* towards African political development is summed up in the comment:

" 'Africa for the Africans' is the new shape of an old cry . . . . this cry will waken the so-called civilized world to a consciousness of the fact that others who are not accounted as civilized, think with regard to natural rights, just as civilized peoples think . . . ." (*JA*, 20 April 1901, 2)

The *Advocate* also dealt with the struggle by Afro-Americans for civil and political rights against racism.

Booker T. Washington was at this time the acknowledged leader of the Afro-American population. Love described him as the "Negro Apostle of Industrial Education for the African Race." (*JA*, 2 November 1901, 2). The *Advocate* in 1903 published a comprehensive report of the 12th Tuskegee Conference and between November and December of 1901 a series of articles also appeared on "The Race Question in the United States" which dealt at length with Washington's activities. (*JA*, April 1903, 3 ; 30 November, 7 and 14 December 1901, 2). However, Love was critical of Washington's apparent acquiescence to the racism of the American South. Instead, Love paid more attention to the more radical Afro-Americans, like John E. Bruce, the radical journalist who later worked for Garvey's *Negro World* newspaper. Love in an attack on American racism, quoted extensively from Bruce's protest pamphlet "Blood Red Record" dealing with the lynching and burning of Blacks in the United States.

These are some of the political positions adopted by Love which makes him significant in any study of Garvey's early life and work. Clearly, Garvey had been privileged to hear Love lecture, no doubt especially around the period of the 1906 election, and he was certainly a reader of the *Advocate*. As a matter of fact, one of Garvey's co-workers at the Government Printing Office, Kingston, Enos J. Sloly, knew Love personally, and Sloly not only travelled to Costa Rica when Garvey went there around 1910, but was to be one of the founding members of the UNIA. (Scarlett)

Socio-Religious Ferment - Bedwardism

While Dr. Robert Love represented the secular form of anti-colonialism, there was also the religious form which manifested itself, especially in Bedwardism. Throbbing at the heart of Bedwardism was the restless frustration of the down-trodden and displaced peasant masses who looked to God for salvation and saw in Bedward, his representative in Jamaica.

Bedwardism took the name of its founder, Alexander Bedward (1859-1930), a Native Baptist preacher who had been a cooper on Mona Estate, St. Andrew, and in Panama. (Brooks;

Pierson) The Native Baptist movement of Bedward goes back
to the peasant activity of the 1840's which culminated in the
'Great Revival' of 1860-61, (Curtin, 170), and in the Morant Bay
Rebellion of 1865. During the 1880's in the parish of Hanover,
there had also been another significant Revivalist Movement.
(*DG,* 7 June 1921, 6)

The crucial years for Bedwardism were from the 1890's to the
1920's. Bedward was well aware of the historical tradition of
peasant struggle from which he emerged. He, in fact, identified
himself with Paul Bogle, a fact which set the stage for a repeat
of the Morant Bay repression that followed. (Pierson, 72)

Bedward is reported to have proclaimed:

> "There is a white wall and a black wall, and the white
> wall has been closing around the black wall; but now the
> black wall has become bigger than the white wall. Let
> them remember the Morant War . . . ." (*in* Roberts)

Characteristically speaking in parables as so many Jamaican
working people do, Bedward was challenging the colonial state.
This was a seditious statement defiantly uttered in the tradition
of Paul Bogle which bore testimony to the fact that the black
militancy and rebellious spirit of elements among the down-
trodden peasantry had not been snuffed out in 1865. The
colonial officials had not forgotten how Bogle had ordered the
black constables sent out to arrest him, to join their own colour
and "cleave to the black." (1866 Commission, 32-33). Bedward
was too ominous a reminder of Bogle and the 'Morant War' to be
left alone.

A contemporary white Jamaican police inspector wrote in his
memoirs:

> "It should always be borne in mind that although under
> normal conditions there is no racial animosity in evi-
> dence, any riot which is not promptly and ruthlessly
> suppressed at once tends to develop into a race war; or
> rather, I should say, a class war: for the people of mixed
> race, and even the well-to-do negroes themselves, would
> in such an event fare no better at the hands of the mob
> — consisting as it does of the lowest and most danger-
> ous elements of the population — than the 'buckra' who
> stands at the top of the social scale." (Thomas, 28-29)

Thomas paints for us a vivid picture of class and racial alignment. With the sharp class sense characteristic of a veteran of the armed sector of the colonial state, he realized the threat from the lowest as being the most dangerous, and that such a threat had to be "ruthlessly suppressed." Thomas' position was the norm of ruling class sentiment in the colonies. Beneath the Whites were the people of 'mixed race' and 'well-to-do negroes' who were often more vitriolic in their hostility to radicalism than the Whites. This difference was not because the latter were more disposed to the Blacks than mulattoes or middle-class Blacks, but rather it was because it was prudent for others to do their dirty work, and it was a role that the colonial-minded middle sectors could be relied on to carry out.

The elements represented in Love were not the same as those represented in Bedwardism. Bedwardism attracted the most oppressed section of the poor peasantry and semi-proletarian masses out of which Rastafarianism later came. Love reflected the middle-peasantry — the better-off Blacks — whom advance in all areas — professional, mercantile, social, cultural, and political — faced the stonewall of colonial racism.

The source of disaffection which fed Bedwardism was the bitter struggle waged by the plantocracy and the colonial government to continue the enslavement of the peasants to the estates. As Dr. T.E.S. Scholes in a contemporary analysis of the late nineteenth century points out:

> "In order to make the peasantry more dependent on the estates, the Sugar Interests pursued the policy of withholding its lands from that portion of the community." (Scholes, 368)

Evidence of this process is seen in the fact that between 1894 and 1901, one hundred and twenty-eight thousand acres of land had been reverted to the Crown. By 1912 this figure reached two hundred and forty thousand three hundred and sixty-eight acres. (Eisner, 222) This situation primarily affected the poorest peasants. They faced intensified impoverishment and demoralization, and sought outlets by leaving for other plantations in the Americas, or by abandoning the countryside to settle in Kingston and St. Andrew. This rural-urban drift was certainly one of the streams feeding the rise of Bedwardism during the 1890's.

The Bedwardites, in turn, found an outlet in religion. The followers of Love, for their part, were spokesmen for their class and sought to develop a political movement with an anti-colonial platform. From the standpoint of colonial and racial oppression the two streams needed to be brought together into a mightier force. The possibilities for this were not realized in Love's time and when Garvey attempted it severe strains were imposed by the strength of the colonial system itself and the inconsistency of the middle class Blacks, especially those influenced by colonial values and pressures: because the little they had acquired in property and social standing, they did not want to lose.

Bedward, like Garvey and Edward Blyden, often referred to the passage in the Bible which reads: "Ethiopia shall stretch out her hands unto God" (Psalm 68:31). (Pierson, 72) Used by these men to people who used the Bible to understand the world, their condition and their future, this verse acquired an anti-colonial meaning. That Bedwardism, with all its religious mysticism, was also a form of nationalism, was recognized by his contemporaries and is evident in this despatch by a correspondent to the *Jamaica Times* weekly newspaper who wrote:

> ". . . . for if the heads of church and state take up the uncompromising position (negro inferiority ever; and negro progress never) then what DuBois, the educated American Negro Teacher, and Booker T. Washington and Frederick Douglass and Dr. Love strive for will come not by the peaceful wand of the school-master but by the juggernaut car of strife . . . . Therefore, I conclude that Bedwardism is a manger of Black Ideals . . . . from which will spring the menace of black progress." (*JT* 6 July 1907, 4)

Alexander Bedward was a target for the colonial authorities because he was a religious leader of the masses who in his church and on the banks of the August Town river preached against British colonialism. On January 21, 1891, Bedward was arrested and charged with sedition. He spent four months in jail before being summoned for trial. He was judged insane. Bedward nevertheless continued his religious work. He was finally put into the mental asylum after an attempted protest march on Kingston in April 1921, when six hundred and eighty-five of his followers were arrested and two hundred and eight convicted. (*DG*, 28 April 1921, 1 and 8; 2 May 1921, 1)

That march included casual labourers, cultivators,, carpenters, wharf labourers, butlers, and shoemakers. From this social class came, in fact, a number of Bedwardites who were drawn to Garveyism or who retained dual allegiances. Just one example of the latter tendency was Roman Henry of August Town who was active in both the Bedwardite and Garveyite movements at the same time. Garvey himself realized the link between his work and Bedward's when he publicly stated in 1927 that the colonial authorities would have a hard time putting him in the asylum as they had done with "poor Bedward." (Nembhard, 117)

The colonial authorities were supported by the *Daily Gleaner*, which waged a journalistic battle against Bedwardism, maligning the religious practices of the group and calling constantly for their repression. During the early 1890's, Joshua DeCordova, proprietor of the *Daily Gleaner*, described his newspaper's policy toward Bedwardism in the following way:

> "The *Gleaner* set itself by reporting and sarcasm to kill the folly and ridiculed it out of existence . . . ." (*DG*, 13 September 1934, 4)

This was however not the truth. Sarcasm and ridicule were minor aspects of a broader policy. In 1921, official policy was to destroy Bedwardism by force. The determination to crush Bedwardism is clearly evidenced in the instructions from governor, Sir Leslie Probyn, to Resident Magisrate Sam. C. Burke, to pre-arrange the charges under which Bedward would be arrested on the day in April he and his followers attempted to march from their August Town camp into Kingston. Plans were also made and effected by the police to ambush the march at Matilda's Corner. Many of Bedward's followers were subsequently arrested and sentenced to hard labour on trumped-up charges. (J.H.S.) The *Gleaner* argued that "the only way to smash up the gang" was to compulsorily "acquire the lands in the village." (*DG*, May 2 1921, 6). This was supported by letters to the press. In one of its characteristic racist comments, the *Gleaner* stated:

> "We must choose now between tolerating West African
> survivals on a gigantic scale and preserving the name of
> Jamaica as a civilized country." (idem.)

What we now know as 'psychological warfare' has a long
history as the newspapers in the hands of the colonial press
barons were used alongside the gun in the hands of the soldiers
and police. The *Gleaner* resorted both to ridicule and the
advocacy of force, using each according to their assessment of
the threat represented by the Bedwardites. These tactics were
to be very ably used by the leader-writer of the *Gleaner*, H.G.
DeLisser, against the Garvey movement in the 1920's and 30's.

Garveyism insofar as its Jamaican origins were concerned,
reflected the two currents headed by Love and Bedward which
were in conflict with the colonial system.

J. Robert Love

Chapter Three

Initial Political Involvement

Trade Union Exposure

In November 1908, workers in the printing trade organized by the Jamaica branch of the Typographical Union of America went on strike. (*JG*, 24 November 1908 7) The young Garvey was by that time employed in the printing section of the P.A. Benjamin pharmaceutical firm in Kingston, and had become vice-president of the compositors' branch of the Union. (Hart a) He joined the strikers in spite of the fact that he had been offered an increase in wages. (Jacques Garvey a. 5)

The strike was not successful. Differences emerged between the printers and the older Jamaica Trades and Labour Union which had been organized in 1907. (*JT*, 24 October 1908, 19). The JTLU disputed the affiliation of the local Typographical Union to the American Federation of Labour, claiming prior and sole association with it. (*JG*, 29 December 1908, 6). On the other hand, the demands for increased scales of pay, and an eight-hour working day among other things were completely rejected by management. Moreover, some workers did not join the strike. The strike inconvenienced some newspapers, but the employers soon got the better of the workers, isolating the militant ones. The strike fizzled out in mid-December.[1]

Richard Hart points out that "members of organizations participating in ordinary trade union activities could have been prosecuted for criminal conspiracy in restraint of trade. This was not merely the old common law principle, but was supported by local statutes in the various colonies prohibiting 'combinations'. Jamaican Law 15 of 1839 stated that

> ".... all combinations for fixing the wages of labour and
> for regulating and controlling the mode of carrying on
> manufacture, trade or business, or the cultivation of any
> plantation .... are injurious to trade and commerce ...
> . and especially prejudicial to the interest of all who are
> concerned in them . . . ." (*in* Hart d, 62)

However, the ruling class did not prosecute the Printers'
Union but used other means to defeat the efforts of the printing
workers. Hart, for example, points out that the reason given by
the Gleaner newspaper company for refusing to recognize the
printers' union was that it was affiliated to an American
organization rather than a British one. (idem.)

Garvey's connection with the trade union movement was
overall a positive one. He was involved from the outset of trade
unionism in the island in the first decade of the twentieth
century though trade unionism was not to be the main area of
his battles.

The National Club

As regards his early political activities, Garvey later recalled
having published a short-lived journal called *The Watchman*
and also having participated in the campaigns of two politicians,
H.A.L. Simpson, who later supported Garvey's work, and Jacob
Wareham. (*DG,* 22 January 1935, 16)

Garvey's involvement in the National Club during the first
decade of this century, can be described as his practical
introduction to anti-colonial politics. In March, 1909, the
National Club was formed by S.A.G. Cox, a near-white city
barrister, who had been discriminated against in the Civil
Service, (*JT,* 6 March 1909, 15) and who was said to have been
influenced by the Sinn Fein movement. (Hart c) The Club
called for "self-government within the Empire" similar to that
of Canada and Australia. *(Our Own,* 14 August 1910, 7) Cox
had, prior to the founding of the National Club, been active in
the Montego Bay Citizens Association. The National Club grew
out of a number of Citizens' Associations in towns like Kingston
and Spanish Town, as well as towns in Trelawny.

The Club was most active from 1909 to 1911, and Garvey was
elected a secretary of the Club in April 1910. Other noteworthy

members were S.M. DeLeon, later representative of the UNIA in London; J. Coleman Beecher, Circulation Manager of Garvey's Jamaican *Black Man* newspaper, and the nationalist figure of the forties, W.A. Domingo. *(JT,* 30 April 1910, 22 Jacques Garvey b)

Although primarily based in Kingston, the Club's influence extended to Central America where Cox was reported to have addressed five thousand labourers in Panama, in December, 1910. *(DN,* 17 December 1910, 3) From time to time, the Jamaican press also published a number of letters from migrants supporting the politics of the Club. *(JT,* 28 May 1910, 3)

Cox won the seat for the parish of St. Thomas in a bye-election to the Legislature in 1909, *(JT,* 23 October 1919, 12), and was re-elected in the 1911 General Elections. The Club secured two seats in the Legislature as H.A.L. Simpson was also elected. *(JT,* January 21 1911, 16). Cox was later disqualified as he failed to meet certain residential requirements for the parish of St. Thomas which he was representing. Shortly after losing the appeal, he announced his departure from Jamaica for the United States. *(DN,* June 2 1911, 1). The Club was re-organized by Alexander Dixon and S. DeLeon in 1913, however it never regained its popularity. *(JT,* 25, January and 15, March 1913)

Despite the Club's short life-span, the issues raised in its journal continued the democratic positions of Robert Love,[2] which were to be developed by Marcus Garvey in the early 1930's.

Cox published a fortnightly journal called *Our Own* between July 1909 and July 1911 which had a circulation figure of three thousand. *(Our Own,* 1 December 1910, 12-13) In this journal, Cox attacked the Crown's policy of subsidizing the importation of East Indian labour, arguing that the tax burden fell on the peasantry which was paying out money to ensure their further exploitation by the planters. *(JT,* 19 June 1909, 14) He was also severely critical of racism in the colonial bureaucracy. *(DN,* 29 June 1911, 7) He called for trade unions to be legally recognised and for Crown Lands to be made available to the landless peasantry. *(Our Own,* 1 May 1911, 11-15) In defence of this plea, he quoted, in one of his articles, figures to show that the Government had increased by nearly five hundred per cent (500%), the price of Crown land per acre to the peasantry. *(Our Own,* 15 April 1911, 1-11; 1 June 1911, 18-21) In other articles, he protested against legislation to suppress wakes and other forms of peasant religious and cultural practices.

Needless to say, the Club attracted the hostility of the *Gleaner* who referred to its leaders "as a gang of men who had already openly avowed their decision to make things hot for the Government and the large landed proprietors." *(Our Own,* 1 October 1910, 7)

In the final issue of *Our Own,* 1 July 1911, Cox indicated a direction, which though never developed in the National Club's politics, was to become central to Garveyism. Cox wrote:

> "The coloured and black people in Jamaica can only hope to better their condition by uniting with the coloured and black people of the United States of America and with those of other West Indian islands, and indeed with all Negroes in all parts of the world."

Not much is really known of Garvey's activities within the National Club, but its orientation indicates the general democratic direction he took. As such, this period forms an important part of Garvey's initiation into political theory and practice.

Political Agitation During Early Travels

Garvey's participation in the activities of the National Club was restricted by the fact that from late 1910, and into 1911, he travelled in Central America. He seems to have travelled first to Costa Rica where his uncle got him a job as time-keeper on a plantation. The conditions faced by the migrant workers outraged him. He protested to the British Consul but was told "that nothing could be done by him as Consul; he could not change conditions in Costa Rica." (Jacques Garvey a, 7) Garvey also worked as editor of a paper called *La Nación* with one Simon Aguiléria. *(DG,* 8 June 1921, 13)

From Costa Rica, he went to Bocas del Toro in Panama, where the racist treatment and savage exploitation meted out to his people further led him to political and journalistic activity.

While in Panama, he again became involved with a newspaper, this time called *La Prensa*. According to Amy J. Garvey, he also travelled to Guatemala, Nicaragua, Ecuador, Chile, and Peru. At this stage, he was travelling in search of work.

Around 1912, he travelled to England. (Hill a) The next two years further added to his personal and political development. He attended lectures at Birbeck College in London, worked as a journalist, met people from other parts of the Empire, and was able to meet English working people and gain a better idea of the political realities at the centre of the British Empire.

Referring to this first English experience, Garvey said twenty years later:

> "We of ourselves, who are not coloured but black, found no difficulty in securing lodgings. We secured lodgings not only in London but the different cities we visited, as also in different places in Scotland. We were even offered employment during the time .... however, when we made our third visit in 1928, we were astounded to be confronted with a pronounced prejudice that shocked our concept of things English . . . ." (Hill a, 38-39)

Garvey in 1912 was not, of course, the Garvey of 1928 who had the rich political experience as leader of a mass movement with international organization. In a real sense, Garvey during his first London years had not yet developed past the Booker T. Washington type of reformism despite the influence of Love and his work in the National Club. At the same time, the ideas which he was later to develop were expressed in discussions with other people and in articles that he wrote.

These were lean years for Garvey. His only surviving sister, Indiana, had paid his passage to England and she helped him during his stay as she herself then lived there. "He worked around the docks of London, Cardiff and Liverpool and gained a wealth of information about African and West Indian seamen." (Jacques Garvey c, 35). His experience as a black working man in England, his main academic interests, which have been described as "Law and Philosophy," and his relationship with the Egyptian journalist, Duse Mohammed Ali, made him more aware of the common problems faced by millions of colonials. While in London, he worked on the *African Times and Orient*

Review published by Ali. The latter had made a reputation for himself with the publication of his book, *In the Lands of Pharoah,* "reputedly the first history of Egypt written by an Egyptian and a work that was critically well received." (Hill a, 41) Duse Mohammed later served as Foreign Affairs editor of the *Negro World* newspaper. *(NW,* 3 June 1922)

The African Times and Orient Review first appeared in July 1912 as a monthly journal and ceased publication in 1919. (Geiss, 731). Its main interest was said to have been West Africa and in fact it was saved from going out of print during an early period of financial difficulties by a group of West African nationalists, among them, Casely Hayford. (Geiss, 730-1) Duse Mohammed, who had attended the First Universal Races Congress (also attended by W.E.B. DuBois) in London in 1911, outlined the direction he hoped to pursue in the following way:

> "The recent Universal Race Congress . . . . clearly demonstrated that there was ample need for a Pan-Oriental, Pan-African Journal, which would lay the aims, desires, and intentions of the Black, Brown and Yellow Races . . . . within and without the Empire — at the throne of Caesar." (Geiss, 730)

Although the journal focussed on West Africa, it concerned itself with developments in the "German colonies in Africa, Egypt, Morocco, the West Indies, Afro-Americans in the USA, Japan, China, Persia and Turkey." (idem.)

The African Times and Orient Review was a precursor of 'Third World' journals. It was known in Kingston as it was distributed through the Jamaica Times store and was well advertised in the *Jamaica Times* newspaper. *(JT,* 6 September 1913). Jamaicans visiting London were invited to visit the offices of the *African Times and Orient Review* and articles from it were reprinted in the *Jamaica Times. (JT,* 10 December 1921, 28)

The October 1913 issue of the *African Times and Orient Review* carried an article by Garvey entitled "The British West Indies in the Mirror of Civilization." This article is significant because it shows Garvey's development of an anti-colonial perspective with regard to Jamaica. "The piratical and buccaneering heroes or rogues" of Jamaica's history are identified as Hawkins and Drake, whereas he describes Gordon and Bogle in 1865 as having "sounded the call of unmolested liberty." He continued:

> ". . . . but owing to the suppression of telegraphic communication, they were handicapped and suppressed, otherwise Jamaica would be as free today as Haiti, which threw off the French yoke under the leadership of the famous Negro General, Toussaint L'Ouverture." *(in* Clarke b, 80).

Garvey concluded his article by stating:

> "As one who knows the people well, I make no apology for prophesying that there will soon be a turning point in the history of the West Indies; and that the people who inhabit that portion of the Western Hemisphere will be the instruments of uniting a scattered race who, before the close of many centuries, will found an Empire on which the sun shall shine as ceaselessly as it shines on the Empire of the North today." (ibid., 82)

These predictions really indicate the thrust of Garvey's thinking which reflected a process of awakening of the colonial peoples. The article also carries an assumption about the liberating role of West Indian Blacks, which ignores the role that Africans and the African people were playing and continue to play in the struggle against colonialism and imperialism. At the same time, there is no denying that within a decade Garvey's work was to provide a powerful impetus to the awakening of African peoples in Africa and the diaspora.

Founding of the U.N.I.A.

After having some difficulty in raising the boat fare back to Jamaica, Garvey left England on June 8, 1914 and landed in Jamaica on July 18. By this time, he had arrived at certain conclusions as a result of his extensive travels and considerable political exposure:

> "Becoming naturally restless for the opportunity of doing something for the advancement of my race, I was

determined that the black man would not continue to be kicked about by all the other races and nations of the world, as I saw it in the West Indies, South and Central America, and Europe, and as I read of it in America. My young and ambitious mind led me into flights of great imagination. I saw before me then, even as I do now, a new world of black men, not peons, serfs, dogs and slaves, but a nation of sturdy men making their impress upon civilization and causing a new light to dawn upon the human race. I could not remain in London any more. My brain was afire. There was a world of thought to conquer. I had to start ere it became too late and the work be not done. Immediately I boarded a ship at Southampton for Jamaica, where I arrived on July 15, 1914. The Universal Negro Improvement Association and African Communities (Imperial) League was founded and organized five years after my arrival, with the programme of uniting all the Negro peoples of the world into one great body to establish a country and Government absolutely their own." (Garvey h, 126)

The Garvey who wrote these words was writing with the benefit of hindsight and from the standpoint of having become the most well-known black leader of his time. But the years 1910 to 1914 in the Americas and Europe had indeed forged a new vision which he clearly sets out in this essay, which continued:

"Where did the name of the organization come from? It was while speaking to a West Indian Negro who was a passenger on the ship with me from Southampton, who was returning home to the West Indies from Basutoland with his Basuto wife, that I further learned of the horrors of native life in Africa. He related to me such horrible and pitiable tales that my heart bled within me. Returning to my cabin, all day and the following night I pondered over the subject matter of that conversation, and at midnight, lying flat on my back, the vision and thought came to me that I should name the organization the Universal Negro Improvement Association and African Communities (Imperial) League. Such a name I thought would embrace the purpose of all black humanity . . . ." (ibid., 126-127)

The UNIA at its inception, therefore, was not the consequence of the experiences of only one country. The fact is that imperialism, since the late nineteenth century, had literally been savaging non-white peoples throughout Africa, the Caribbean and Asia. Movements against this savagery were developing among the colonial peoples everywhere. The UNIA was a response to this process. Garvey came on the historical stage, as it were, at the opportune moment; the moment when Blacks were increasingly being radicalized by their participation in World War 1, by news of the Russian Revolution and its impact, and by the growth of the national liberation movement.

In July 1914 when Garvey set up the UNIA, little was he aware of the extent of the role he was destined to play in the United States, and of the historical forces that would propel him on to centre-stage.

The Universal Negro Improvement and Conservation Association and African Communities' League was launched on August 1, 1914. It is significant that it was launched on Emancipation Day which had been historically celebrated as the day marking freedom from slavery in the British Caribbean colonies. August 1, up to Independence in 1962, had always in Jamaica been a day of profound political, social and cultural significance. It held deep meaning for Bogle, for Love, for Garvey, for the fighters of 1938, and others working in the tradition of mass struggle.

Assisting Garvey in the formation of the UNIA were other public-spirited men, like Enos J. Sloly, his friend from his Government Printing Office days; Richard A. Scarlett, a shopkeeper from Port Maria, who Garvey had met during his Port Maria stay when Scarlett and Cottrell, Garvey's printer friend, shared lodgings; Dawson, an hotelier of Princess Street, Kingston; W.A. Campbell, printer/civil servant, later to become a Postmaster General, and Archdeacon Graham of Port Maria who, though never a UNIA member, was a "firm supporter and encourager." (Scarlett) These men were in the habit of holding informal meetings at 49 Princess Street, the hotel premises of one Mr. Watson, where the men had meals and those from the country overnighted.

The first UNIA office was set up at Charles Street, west of Chancery Lane. (Scarlett)[3] Garvey was President, Adrian A. Daily — Secretary, while the Corresponding Secretary was

Amy Ashwood whom Garvey had met in the July of that year and whom he was to marry in New York in December 1919. (Ashwood Garvey)

After Garvey's departure for the U.S. in 1916, the Jamaica UNIA continued to expand. The headquarters were removed from Charles Street and operated initially out of St. Mark's School, West Street, at which time Rev. S.M. Jones of the African Methodist Episcopal Church was President and Bruce Forbes, Secretary. Premises at 76 King Street were later bought and the Kingston Division moved there. (Scarlett)

Initial Perspectives of the UNIA

General Objects

To establish a Universal Confraternity among the race.

To promote the spirit of race, pride and love.

To reclaim the fallen of the race.

To administer to and assist the needy.

To assist in civilizing the backward tribes of Africa.

To strengthen the Imperialism[4] of independent African States.

To establish Commissionaries or Agencies in the principal countries of the world for the protection of all Negroes, irrespective of nationality.

To promote a conscientious Christian worship among the native tribes of Africa.

To establish Universities, Colleges and Secondary Schools for the further education and culture of the boys and girls of the race.

To conduct a worldwide commercial and industrial intercourse.

Local (Jamaica) Objects

> To establish educational and industrial colleges for the further education and culture of our boys and girls.
>
> To reclaim the fallen and degraded (especially the criminal class) and help them to a state of good citizenship.
>
> To administer to and assist the needy.
>
> To promote a better taste for commerce and industry.
>
> To promote a universal confraternity and strengthen the bonds of brotherhood and unity among the races.
>
> To help generally in the development of the country. (*in* Hill a 60)

These were modest aims which were in keeping with the limits of Garvey's ideas at the time. They were also geared towards gaining legitimacy for the organization in a colonial society, as they were, broadly speaking, aims not repugnant to reformists within the colonial system. As such, Garvey and his group sought the patronage of the Whites. Listed among the patrons for some activities were the Governor, the Colonial Secretary, the Brigadier-General, the Bishop, and the Mayor, among "other prominent dignitaries of the country." The manifesto also carried a resolution supporting British war efforts, a resolution which applauded "the great protecting and civilizing influence of the English nation and people, of whom we are subjects and their justice to all men, especially to their Negro Subjects . . . ." (Hill a, 63-64). This was Garvey in September 1914, trying to apply Booker T. Washington's policy in Jamaica.

For example, following the practice of Booker T., a UNIA Committee of twelve persons visited the Government Farm School at Hope in St. Andrew on an inspection tour. The Headmaster promised to assist the UNIA in their farming scheme as soon as they were ready. (*DG,* 14 November 1914)

The UNIA also held evening classes for adults. Washington's work was well known in Jamaica and in 1900, even the *Gleaner* had entertained the question as to why a Jamaica Tuskegee could not be developed. (*DG*, 14 November 1900) Several Jamaicans were in touch with Washington. For instance, William Theophilus West, master at St. Mark's School, 57 West Street, was apparently in touch with Washington and Major Moton, Washington's successor, visited the school in 1916 for two days and examined the boys in their work. (Scarlett) Washington also knew of conditions on the island from Jamaican students who attended Tuskegee[5] and through the *Jamaica Times* newspaper which he received. (*JT*, 8 May 1909, 2). Garvey himself started correspondence with Washington in 1914, informing him of his intended visit to the United States. On April 12, 1915, Garvey again wrote that he was "expecting to leave for America between May and June and I shall be calling on you. I intend to do most of my public speaking in the South among the people of our race." *(in* Daniel Williams). Washington replied on the 27th April, 1915, that he would do all he could to help Garvey while he was in the United States. However, Garvey's trip was delayed until March 1916, and Booker T. had in the meanwhile died in November, 1915.

And when in 1916 Jamaica was visited by W.E.B. DuBois and Major Robert Moton, Washington's successor at Tuskegee, DuBois received a letter of welcome from the UNIA, but in it Garvey objected strongly to DuBois' statement that the race problem was at an end in the island.[6] Furthermore, J.J. Mills, who was then President of the Jamaica Union of Teachers, recalled that Garvey, "whose name had by this gone abroad as a Negro agitator . . . . had desired much to meet Major Moton," and his opportunity to have an interview with Moton came at a function being held for Moton by the J.U.T. at Mico College. (Mills, 110). Of significance in a colonial island setting was the readiness and daring to challenge 'authority' shown by young Garvey, the fledgling politician. These qualities were evident in his letter of close on two thousand words concerning the colonial situation in Jamaica, addressed to Major Moton. In it he argued that the black people who were in the majority were the most oppressed.

> "If you desire to do Jamaica a turn, you might ask those around on public platforms to explain to what propor-

tion the different people here enjoy the wealth and
resources of the country. Impress this, and let them
answer it for publication and then you will have the
whole farce in a nutshell." (Garvey to Moton, ibid.)

This letter was in the tradition of Robert Love. It certainly
gives credence to Mills' opinion that Garvey was gaining the
reputation of being a "Negro agitator", and to the vicious
campaign launched against him later in the U.S.

Garveyism in the pre-American years was not yet the
philosophy of a mass movement, but it already had the vital
element of linking everyday concerns and struggles for small
changes with broader anti-colonial questions, as seen in the
objectives of the UNIA in 1914. Garveyism developed out of the
struggles against colonial abuses by Dr. Love, the National
Club, Bedwardism and was also shaped by the influences of the
progressive tendencies in Afro-American, West African as well
as European bourgeois democratic thought. However, it was
not until after 1918 that Garveyism developed from its embry-
onic Jamaican stage. This change came in the period of
Garvey's stay in the United States when Garveyism became
rooted in the Afro-American struggle for self-determination, a
struggle to which Garvey gave an international perspective.

Amy Ashwood

Part II

UNIA — Mass Political Emergence

Chapter Four

Garvey's Radicalization

It was Garvey's visit to the United States in 1916 that was to be the decisive factor in his political career. Had he decided to go anywhere else at that time, he may have become one of the anti-colonial figures in Jamaican history but not an international leader.

In 1916, Garvey had intended to travel to the United States for the purpose of seeking aid to build a 'Jamaica Tuskegee'. This was to have been part of a "lecturing tour through the West Indies, North, South, and Central America, in connection with the movement," that is, the UNIA. (Garvey *in* Clarke a, 87). In the event, he was to remain in the United States until his deportation from there in 1927. Indeed, soon after his arrival in New York, his programme changed from a reformist one to one of militant Black Nationalism. He attributed this departure to the influence of West Indians he had met within a few weeks of his arrival in the United States. (*DG,* 24 March 1921, 11)

W.A. Domingo, a friend and political associate of Garvey in Jamaica, described Garvey's arrival in New York in the following way:

> "One day in 1916, while I was sitting at home, I heard a Jamaican asking, "Is there someone named Dolfus Domingo living here?" The maid had answered the door and she brought in Garvey. He showed me the letter he had received from Booker T. Washington and told me of his plan for a Tuskegee in Jamaica. I told him I didn't think Jamaica needed one, that Jamaica shouldn't have education with restrictions like Tuskegee." (Domingo)

The situation in the United States had made Domingo himself move towards socialist positions and away from liberalism. The encounter with Domingo was one of several with other politically active Blacks. For example, Garvey also met with the radical Afro-American journalist John Bruce, who later became a columnist for the *Negro World.* Of their first encounter, Bruce wrote:

> "I was among the first American Negroes on whom he called. He was a little sawed-off hammered down black man, with determination written all over his face, and an engaging smile that caught you and compelled you to listen to his story.... Mr. Garvey is a rapid-fire speaker (and when he delivers a speech) two stenographers are necessary to keep up with him." (*in* Vincent a, 99)

Bruce was in sympathy with Garvey's ideas and provided him with a list of "our leading men in New York and other cities who I felt would encourage and assist him." (ibid., 100)

Another important contact made by Garvey was with the Afro-American scholar, William Ferris, who was the Associate Editor of the Chicago-based *Champion Magazine.* Bruce and Ferris had both been contributors to the *African Times and Orient Review,* so it was not surprising that Garvey made contact with them. Ferris was the author of a two-volume study entitled *The African Abroad or his Evolution in Western Civilization — Tracing His Development Under Caucasian Milieu* (1913), and he fully supported Garvey's steps towards the creation of an international organization for Blacks. Ferris and Bruce both became editors of the *Negro World.* In Harlem, Garvey met Hubert Harrison, who in June 1917 introduced him at a mass rally inaugurating the Anti-War Afro-American Liberty League. Harrison was a well-known radical who had been associated with the Marxist journalist, John Reed, and with Max Eastman, in the editing of *The Masses,* a left-wing journal. A British document of 1919 which discussed radical Afro-American groups and agitators noted that:

> "Mr. Harrison's lectures might well be considered as a preparatory school for radical thought in that they prepare the minds of conservative negroes to receive and accept the more extreme doctrine of socialism." (Elkins b, 78)

Hubert Harrison was also said to have possessed a "wealth of knowledge of African history and culture" which was a great asset to the work of the Garvey press.

Such contacts helped to develop Garvey's ideas in keeping with the national aspirations of his people. In addition, he travelled through thirty-eight of the forty-eight American states. This gave him an intimate feel for all that he had merely heard about, and on returning tb New York he set about building up the UNIA. He had really intended to return to Jamaica to build up the Jamaica organization, but having "enrolled about eight hundred to one thousand members in the Harlem district and elected the officers," he preferred to stay and oversee the burgeoning movement, direct it along the lines he envisaged, and to take advantage of the wider scope a base in a black metropolis allowed.

Garvey became so fully immersed in the New York UNIA that by 1917, the Kingston headquarters had already become an outpost. Meanwhile, with the energy, enthusiasm and optimism of a man on the eve of his thirtieth year, he went about enlarging the movement in the United States. But these early months were not easy ones. He lived with a Jamaican family in Harlem and worked as a printer. What little money he could save was used for travelling and establishing contacts. Furthermore, he had to contend not only with white racism but with prejudice and jaundiced views among Blacks. Afro-Americans, who had "been in America a long time" and had no intention of "goin' nowhere", were ambivalent in their attitudes to Caribbean people who flooded into New York and who, with an immigrant mentality, became "go-getters, always up and doin', into politics and into education." The Antilleans, with smug self-satisfaction referred to Afro-Americans as "tar-heels" (Samad) while, on the other hand, most Afro-Americans:

> "knew practically nothing of the countries beyond their shores, and nothing of the history of their African ancestors; they regarded Africans as 'naked savages' and West Indians as 'monkey-chasers' .... on the other hand, coloured Americans could not understand why that 'foolish foreigner' would go hungry and stand up talking about Africa until he brought tears to the eyes of some of his sidewalk hearers, when he could use that 'silver tongue' to live well and wear good clothes. Twice

> Garvey got dizzy and fell off soapboxes because he was
> hungry.... He caught many colds because his shoe soles
> had holes in them." (Jacques Garvey a, 14)

In March, 1918, he had to be hospitalized with pneumonia.

However, the call which he had made on the eve of his departure from Jamaica fell on favourable ground here — the call for Blacks to lend themselves "to the worldwide movement of doing something to promote the intellectual, social, commercial, industrial, and national interest of the downtrodden race of which you are a member." *(in* Clarke b. 83)

As he had wished, sections of the black intelligentsia were prepared to link up and provide "true and conscientious leadership" to "the masses of the people who are still ignorant and backward." (idem.) He considered himself and others who answered such a call as fulfilling a historical role in the battle against racism. Their black ethnic identity was to be seen

> "in the light of the Pharoahs of Egypt, Simons of
> Cyrene, Hannibals of Carthage, L'Ouvertures and Des-
> salines of Haiti, Blydens, Barclays and Johnsons of
> Liberia, Lewises of Sierra Leone, and Douglass's and
> DuBois's of America, who have made and are making
> history for the race, though depreciated, and in many
> cases, unwritten." (ibid., 85)

With such an appeal, he welded together in the UNIA and the African Communities League a force that has left a mark on the history of the struggles of Black people in this century. For another decade, the movement was in its ascendancy. Recent scholarship indicates that between 1925-27 in the USA, there were between seven hundred and nineteen and seven hundred and twenty-five divisions, while scattered throughout forty-one other countries, there were about two hundred and seventy-one branches. (Martin a, 15-16) So that, all told, Garvey could rely on the support and sympathy of several million Blacks throughout the world.

United States: Conditions in the 1910's

The 1910's witnessed a new era of Afro-American consciousness which was connected with the movement of Blacks from
the South to the North, and the urbanization of a population
which in 1890 had been eighty per cent (80%) rural. (Wilson, 70)
Between 1914-17, "cotton production was severely hampered
by boll-weevil infestation and by a series of.... floods." (66) On
the other hand, "World War 1 immigration restrictions reduced
the annual average migration from Europe (particularly the
unskilled immigrants from southern and eastern Europe) from
over a million (1910 - 1914) to roughly one hundred thousand
(1915 - 1920), and when the demands of the war economy
increased the gross national product and expanded the need for
manufacturing employment, employers literally begged Negroes to work in the steel mills, the railroads, the automobile
factories, and the cotton industries." (67) So "in the decade of
the 1920's, the net black migration from the South to the North
was eight hundred and seventy-two thousand." (68) Between
1910 and 1920, "the black population in Chicago increased by
148.2% .... Pittsburgh by 117.1% .... New York by 66.3% ....
Philadelphia 58.9% and St. Louis by 58.9%" (67) This urbanization meant greater spending power for Blacks, with the result
that more than two hundred and fifty million dollars worth of
bonds and stamps were purchased in the UNIA's five major
Liberty Loan drives. (Cronon a, 28)

The war itself meant that approximately three hundred and
seventy thousand Blacks served in the U.S. Armed Forces. (Hill
d I, 292, fn. 1). These soldiers were fighting for 'democracy' and
many were dying. In Europe, the 'colour bar' existed but it was
not as entrenched and institutionalized as in the United States.
Moreover, Black soldiers were dying alongside White soldiers
and these conditions gave rise to some amount of camaraderie
between the races on the battlefields. The entire division of the
all-Black ninety-second Division was "cited for bravery and
awarded the Croix de Guerre by the French High Command.
Forty-three enlisted men and fourteen Negro officers were
awarded the Distinguished Service Cross for bravery in
action." (Cronon a, 29)

But on their return to the United States, the lives of these
soldiers were worth nothing. They faced lynching, discrimina-

tion of every type, and were treated like dirt. Garvey summed up the mood of the Black masses after World War 1 when he wrote:

> "During the world-war, nations were vying with each other in proclaiming lofty concepts of humanity. 'Make the world safe for democracy, self-determination for smaller peoples' reverberated in the capitals of warring nations opposed to Germany. Now that the war is over, we find these same nations making every effort by word and deed to convince us that their blatant professions were mere meaningless platitudes never intended to apply to earth's darker millions. We find the minor part of humanity — the white people — constituting themselves lords of the universe and arrogating to themselves the power to control the destiny of the larger part of humanity . . . . In Africa, it takes the form of suppression of the right of the African to enjoy the fruits of his ancestral lands. In America, it takes the form of lynching, disenfranchisement, burnings, and the thousand and one petty insults born of arrogance and prejudice. So now comes the Negro through the medium of the UNIA demanding the right and taking unto himself the power to control his own destiny." *(DG,* 15 April 1921, 18)

Garvey took full advantage of this new situation. He could do so because Blacks were not adopting passive positions but were fighting back. In the years 1917 - 1919, there were several serious riots against racism. In 1919, from June to the end of the year, there were twenty-six riots against racism in the United States. These riots were partly in response to the Ku Klux Klan which was showing its racist head and had stepped up the lynchings of Blacks. Thirty-six Blacks were lynched in 1917, sixty in 1918, seventy-six in 1919, and the numbers remained in the fifties between 1920 - 1922. (Hill d I, 212, fn. 9) The KKK had strong connections with the state, especially the police and the courts. Efforts were made to respond legally to the repression but cases got nowhere because the system of law itself in the various states was racist.

Thus, in capitalist America, Garvey became conscious that the Tuskegee concept was inadequate in the face of lynchings, jimcrowism, and disenfranchisement. All classes and strata of the black population, at one time or the other, were victims of racism. Garvey's appeal, based as it was on racial mobilization, took this into account. Garveyism appealed to uprooted black farmers and peasants, petty traders, small businessmen, the black intelligentsia — teachers, journalists, clergymen — and even some wealthy Blacks, such as Isaiah Morter of Belize. And unlike the situation in Jamaica where shade gradations dominated colour consciousness, in the U.S., a drop of African blood sufficed to categorize an individual as 'Negro'. A number of mulattoes and near-whites joined the UNIA. (Samad)

Elaboration of UNIA Aims

Socialized in an overseas British colony where privilege was graded according to property, skin-shade and phenotype minutiae, and exposed in England to the deceptive tolerance of practised burden-bearers of empire, Garvey was jolted away from political reformism by the overt institutionalization of the colour bar in the U.S., and by the ferment of left-wing ideas to which he was now exposed. Most importantly, by 1920, the UNIA was an international organization capable of holding its first Convention and collectively discussing and adopting a major Declaration which became the programme of the movement.

The Declaration of the Rights of the Negro Peoples of the World was a more elaborate document than the UNIA's initial Aims and Objectives of 1914. It was also more aggressive because it detailed abuses experienced by Africans, particularly in the United States, to a lesser extent in the West Indies, and less so in Africa itself. But while some of its clauses related to local abuses, others were generally applicable to the global colonial condition in which Africans found themselves. In this light, the document condemned the worldwide discrimination and deprivation of "common rights due to human beings" which were "with few exceptions" denied to black men "for no other reason than their race and colour." (Garvey h, 135) It further protested the organized inculcation in black children, through the education system, of the idea that white colonizing peoples were "superior to the Negro race" and "the publication of scandalous and inflammatory articles by an alien press tending to create racial strife and the exhibition of picture films showing the Negro as a cannibal." (137) Segregation in industry, in travel, residence, discrimination in law courts, in franchise, in taxation, in penal codes, and in examinations were all denounced.

The Declaration further endorsed the view in Resolution sixteen that,

> "all men should live in peace one with the other, but when races and nations provoke the ire of the other races and nations by attempting to infringe upon their rights, war becomes inevitable, and the attempt in any way to free one's self or protect one's rights or heritage becomes justifiable." (138)

The colonial rape of Africa was specifically treated. So whereas in the Preamble it is deplored

> "that European nations have parcelled out among themselves and taken possession of nearly all of the continent of Africa, and the natives are compelled to surrender their lands to aliens and are treated in most instances like slaves," (135)

Resolution fourteen reads:

> "We believe in the inherent right of the Negro to possess himself of Africa, and that his possession of same shall not be regarded as an infringement on any claim or purchase made by any race or nation." (138)

And Resolution twenty-seven:

> "We believe in the self-determination of all peoples." (139)

To this end, the UNIA's political objective was focused on state power on the African continent.

> "The culmination of all efforts of the UNIA must end in a Negro independent nation on the continent of Africa. This is to say, everything must be contributed toward the final objective of having a powerful nation for the

Negro race. Negro nationalism is necessary. It is political power and control . . . ." (UNIA a)

It was in the context of the reclamation of Africa that the top
honorary positions in the UNIA organizational structure were
held by Africans: Supreme Potentate — Major Gabriel Johnson
of Liberia, and Deputy Supreme Potentate — George O.
Marke of Sierra Leone.

At the same time, the politically conscious Garvey did not
reject all of Booker T. Washington's teachings. Rather he
superceded them. Garvey's subsequent carefully-worded
assessment of Washington reflected his own modification of
that precedent:

> "The world satisfied itself to believe that succeeding
> Negro leaders would follow absolutely the teachings of
> Washington. Unfortunately the world is having a rude
> awakening in that we are evolving a new ideal. The new
> ideal includes the program of Booker T. Washington
> and has gone much further.
>
> Things have changed wonderfully since Washington
> came on the scene. His vision was industrial oppor-
> tunity for the Negro, but the Sage of Tuskegee has
> passed off the stage of life and left behind a new
> problem — a problem that must be solved, not by the
> industrial leader only, but by the political and military
> leaders as well.
>
> If Washington had lived he would have had to change
> his programme. No leader can successfully lead this
> race of ours without giving an interpretation of the
> awakened spirit of the New Negro, who does not seek
> industrial opportunity alone, but a political voice. The
> world is amazed at the desire of the New Negro, for with
> his strong voice, he is demanding a place in the affairs of
> men." (Garvey h, 56)

That Garveyism incorporated Washington's ideas is seen in
the commercial enterprises of the UNIA but it was broader and
politically aggressive.

No. 5871

Shares 5

INCORPORATED UNDER THE LAWS OF THE STATE OF DELAWARE

BLACK STAR LINE, INC.

CAPITAL STOCK $500,000

SHARES $5. EACH

This Certifies that Mrs Ada Bastiani is the owner of five Shares of the Capital Stock of

BLACK STAR LINE, INC. full paid and non-assessable

transferable only on the books of this Corporation in person or by Attorney upon surrender of this Certificate properly endorsed.

IN WITNESS WHEREOF, the said Corporation has caused this Certificate to be signed by its duly authorized officers and its Corporate Seal to be hereunto affixed this 11 the day of Nov A.D. 19

Geo. T. Plus
Secretary-Treasurer

Marcus Garvey
President

J. HEYER, 302 B'WAY, N.Y.

Chapter Five

Organizational Activities

Membership Life

The relationship between the international and local aspects of the movement was reflected in the practice of the locals which maintained a relatively wide autonomy from the New York parent body. (Tolbert) And whether in the U.S., Central America, the Caribbean or in Africa, the locals all had a great deal of flexibility within which to interpret the general aims of the organization as far as their local situation was concerned.

And because the UNIA was in a significant way decentralized the International Conventions of the 1920's and 1930's were not mere show-pieces but attempts by the organization to carve, out of experiences in rather varied conditions, practical programmes for the advancement of the organization and the repossession of Africa by Africans.

The locals were to be financially independent, collecting their own dues, paying out sickness and death benefit funds, sending in a small percentage of their income to the UNIA's central fund. Like several of the American divisions, some UNIA divisions in Panama supplemented their finances by commercial projects. The UNIA Headquarters had responsibility for the Black Star Shipping Line, the Liberia Scheme and other commercial ventures. Both these schemes were eagerly supported by the worldwide Garvey membership, pledges of money and deposit instalments being among the means by which the capital for these projects were raised. (Clarisse Arthur) Public lectures by Garvey and other executive members also raised funds for the central organization.

There were regional headquarters, and both headquarters and local activities were centred around a Liberty Hall property which the division either rented or bought. The Liberty Hall was the organizational hub of a division and was in some cases maintained by a caretaker. However, small divisions either rented premises on an ad hoc basis or used a member's home for meetings.

When a division was formed, it notified the Headquarters and received a charter of incorporation into the UNIA.

The divisions held meetings on Sunday evenings. In Kingston, for example, there were business meetings during which the divisions's secretary reported on activities of the organization during the week. (Scarlett) Activities included debates, talks by sailors, merchants, professionals, students; street meetings, recruitment drives, sewing classes, concerts, dances. In Panama, Sunday evening meetings began on a religious note and then moved on to secular activities such as speeches, elocution contests, etc. (Clarisse Arthur) Juveniles were attracted into the organization through boy scout and girl guide groups established by senior UNIA members as an auxiliary of the UNIA itself. Another uniformed auxiliary was the Motor Corps (in New York and other large cities) for females, both adult and teenage. These women met once a week to practise military drill as well as to learn to drive. In the event of liberation wars in Africa, the Motor Corps would handle cars, taxis, ambulances as support services. Male adults could join the African Legion which went in for military drill and rudimentary military training (in the U.S. with guns). They also formed a bodyguard for UNIA officials on ceremonial occasions, wearing black uniforms with red and green stripes down the leg. They also constituted para-military forces in various locales to counter the Ku Klux Klan and racist aggression against UNIA meetings and black communities. (Samad) Another auxiliary was the Black Cross Nurses who once a week learnt first aid and medicare under the tutelage of a registered nurse who was a UNIA member. The Black Cross nurses received UNIA certification. Their services, too, were being groomed for liberation wars in Africa, though they served as temporary help in local hospitals (Samad) and sometimes specialized in geriatric care. (Ashdown)

The UNIA, therefore, when it functioned at its maximum, provided a self-sustaining social, educational, and religious life.

Many couples who met through UNIA activities (as happened with Garvey in his second marriage) married with the 'blessing' of the organization, their children were called 'UNIA children' or 'Garvey children' and in New York, UNIA birth certificates were issued. These supplemented state registration. The UNIA also organized pre-school play groups (Samad), and in language-differentiated migrant conditions like Panama, primary and techical and secondary schools in addition. (Clarisse Arthur) There was also Sunday school on Sunday mornings. (Samad)

'Garvey children' were taught about Marcus Garvey, George Washington Carver, and about heroic black women like Harriet Tubman and Sojourner Truth. They had to learn one Garvey poem a week, read Harriet Beecher Stowe's *Uncle Tom's Cabin*, and rehearse the UNIA's doctrine of African Fundamentalism. They were shown pictures and carvings of black angels and were given black dolls. Garvey himself was held up to children as a symbol of all the positive values to which the race aspired. So that Garvey became "guiding angel, guardian" and even "bogie man" when parents invoked his name in discipling or correcting children — "Mr. Garvey won't like that." The goal was upliftment in conduct and mental achievement, which carried with it an awareness of the civic example which the Garvey adherent should set. (Samad)

Indeed, the idea behind all these UNIA local activities was that Black people, like all other humans, were endowed with abilities which could be realized if proper opportunities were made available to them. The Garvey movement served to provide a nucleus for that opportunity and the realization of those skills. (Clarisse Arthur)

Industrial Projects

The UNIA launched a number of business enterprises, which were badly managed, and by no means least, subject to discrimination and harassment. The most ill-fated and poorly executed of these was the Black Star Line. It was in 1919 that Garvey mooted the idea of an "all-Negro steamship company that would link the coloured peoples of the world in commercial and industrial intercourse." (*in* Cronon a, 50)

In 1919, Garvey not only established the Black Star Line, but also the Negro Factories Corporation. The NFC developed a number of businesses. Among them were a chain of cooperative grocery stores, a restaurant, a steam laundry, a tailoring and dressmaking shop, a millinery store and publishing house. The corporation was capitalized at one million dollars under a charter from the state of Delaware. The corporation offered "200,000 shares of common stock to the Negro race at par value of $5 per share." (Cronon a, 60). The object was

> "to build and operate factories in the big industrial centres of the United States, Central America, the West Indies, and Africa to manufacture every marketable commodity." (ibid.)

This aspect of his plan was precisely to impress "millions of Negroes with the reasonableness of African Nationalism and Negro independence." (Garvey h, 353) Conceived on a grand scale, Garvey's enterprises had a political motive which corresponded to the struggle of colonial peoples for self-determination. So while, on the one hand, it may be easy to dismiss these efforts at self-reliance as reactionary from a dogmatic ideological perspective, that would be like branding as a reversion to patriarchialism, Mahatma Gandhi's economic projects in respect of cloth making by the spinning-wheel and salt production from the sea. The UNIA businesses were not Garvey's personal enterprises. He personally derived no gain from them. Rather, they reflected the continuing impact of Booker T. Washington's ideas in Garveyism; their social basis was a nascent Afro-American bourgeoisie. Garvey's business ventures were not far-fetched. They did correspond to bourgeois social interests among the black population whose development had been hindered by colonialism and imperialism. In any case, the example of the wealthy Black Belizean capitalist, Isaiah Morter, who bequeathed one hundred thousand dollars to the UNIA, illustrated the possibilities of gaining political support among black businessmen who themselves, subject to many forms of racial prejudice and commercial discrimination, were ardent supporters of the Garvey movement. (Garvey h, 90-92)

As for capitalism itself, Garvey argued that there "should be a limit to the individual or corporate use" of capitalistic practice.

> "No individual should be allowed the possession, use or the privilege to invest on his own account, more than a million, and no corporation should be allowed to control more than five millions. Beyond this, all control, use and

investment of money, should be the prerogative of the
state with the concurrent authority of the people." (72)

This approach was similar to current European social-
democratic and Fabian socialist ideologies which subsequently
gave rise to the capitalist Welfare State. Garvey also fully
recognized the capitalist basis of modern wars and of imperialistic aggression against non-European peoples:

> "Modern wars are generally the outgrowth of dissatis-
> fied capitalistic interests either among foreign or
> strange peoples or nations . . . . Men like Morgan,
> Rockefeller, Firestone, Doheny, Sinclair and Gary
> should not be allowed to entangle the nation in foreign
> disputes, leading to war, for the sake of satisfying their
> personal, individual or corporate selfishness and greed
> for more wealth at the expense of the innocent masses of
> both countries. Oil 'concessions' in Mexico, or Persia;
> rubber 'concessions' in Liberia, West Africa; sugar or
> coffee 'concessions' in Haiti, West Indies, to be exploit-
> ed for the selfish enrichment of individuals, sooner or
> later, end in disaster . . . ." (idem.)

The Liberian Scheme

The most important and costly step made by the UNIA in Africa
occurred in Liberia. There still exists some amount of confusion
regarding the political conception behind the Liberian programme which came to be known in the international press as
the 'Back to Africa Movement'. (Garvey h, 351-412) An
editorial in the *Negro World* expressed the conception in this
way:

> "It does not mean that all Negroes must leave America
> and the West Indies and go to Africa to build up a
> government. It did not take all the white people of
> Europe to come over to America to lay the foundation of
> the great republic; therefore, those who write dis-
> paragingly of the grand programme of Africa are doing
> so without paying attention to history . . . . we say to all
> Negroes in America, the West Indies and elsewhere,
> seize all opportunities that come to you, but remember
> our success educationally, industrially and politically is

based upon the protection of a nation founded by
ourselves. And that nation can be nowhere else but in
Africa." (*NW*, 6 February 1926, 4)

This was an explicit disavowal of mass repatriation utopian-
ism which Garvey's opponents consistently attributed to the
UNIA's plans for African 'Colonization' and which came to
dominate later assessment of his work. For instance, in 1960,
historians could write:

> "The 'Back to Africa' slogan was particularly disturb-
> ing. In essence, it was a form of escapism. There was no
> possibility of transporting millions of Negroes across
> the Atlantic to a strange and inhospitable environment,
> guarded by a half-dozen European powers." (Eisenberg
> and Miller, 193-194)

Instead, self-determination was the essential consideration
behind the Liberian programme. Garveyites had even contemplated the removal of the UNIA headquarters from New
York to Monrovia, the Liberian capital, and the establishment
of an independent settlement there. (Garvey h, 363)

In 1920, 1923, and 1924, UNIA delegations conducted
negotiations with the Liberian Government. (Cronon a, 124-
132) President King personally appointed a local Liberian
committee to co-ordinate activities with the UNIA in New
York and also offered a trial land concession of five hundred
acres. (Langley a, 163)

In 1920, Garvey had launched a drive for a three million
dollar construction loan to rehabilitate Liberia." At the 1920
Convention Gabriel Johnson, the Mayor of Monrovia, Liberia,
had been named Supreme Potentate of the UNIA. In turn, in
January 1921, Johnson "obtained a charter of incorporation
for a local Universal Negro Improvement Association from the
Liberian Legislature." (Cronon a, 125)

The overly-ambitious Liberian project foundered on two
rocks. First, the Liberian government was pressurred by U.S.
interests as well as by the French and British colonial authorities who were hostile to Garveyite nationalism. Secondly, the
Americo-Liberian ruling elite itself wanted Afro-American
capital, but without Garveyite anti-colonial nationalism.

The confidential Report sent by Elie Garcia to Marcus Garvey had realistically characterized the political prospects of the UNIA in Liberia as negative, because the ruling Americo-Liberians, in Garcia's harsh language,

> "constituted the most despicable element in Liberia. Because of their very education, they are self-conceited and believe that the only honourable way for them to make a living is by having a 'government job'. The men of this class having been most of them educated in England or other European places, are used to life, which the salaries paid by the government do not suffice to maintain. Therefore, dishonesty is prevalent. To any man who can write and read there is but one goal, a Government office, where he can graft." (Garvey h, 399)

Garcia also warned that Liberia was the "object of a close contest between America, England and France." (401). He stressed the investment potential of Liberia but discouraged the promotion of Garveyite politics, and advanced that "with diplomacy, and also modesty and discretion on the part of those who will represent the UNIA in Liberia, our work is bound to be successful along all lines." (404-405)

Political problems were not long in coming. In June 1921, a team of UNIA technicians, which included mining, civil, and mechanical engineers, was deported on arrival in Monrovia and fifty thousand dollars worth of equipment was seized. (Garvey 151; Cronon a, 129). In effecting a complete reversal of the previous arrangements, the Liberian Consul-General in Baltimore, United States, declared that no Garveyite would be allowed to land in Liberia. *(DG,* 25 August 1924, 14). Moreover, in order to get a visa, an applicant had to get an affidavit declaring that he or she was not connected with the Garvey movement. (Garvey h, 394) The Liberian government in fact issued a statement saying it was:

> "Irrevocably opposed both in principle and fact to the incendiary policy of the Universal Negro Improvement Association headed by Marcus Garvey . . . ." (389)

It is naive to conclude, as Langley does, that the Liberian Programme failed "principally because of Garvey's intemperate attacks on the Liberian government and his tactless criticisms of the colonial powers." (Langley a, 163) Granted, as was suggested by Elie Garcia, that Garvey could have exercised greater diplomacy, the fact remained that the UNIA was not an economic organization but a political one. Economic enterprises were an adjunct to a political body that was anticolonialist. Therefore, contradictions between the Americo-Liberians and the Garveyites could not have been handled purely on the basis of diplomacy. The report of the local Liberian Committee had indicated that, like the Lagos elite, the Liberian ruling group was generally sympathetic to the industrial aspects of the programme and was wary of Garvey's politics. (Olusanya)

As a result, no matter how temperate Garvey was, the political substance of his speeches, of the *Negro World,* and of main documents such as "The Declaration of Rights of the Negro People of the World" meant that conflict was inevitable. The fact is that Garvey had no political force in Liberia which could defend his programme and in a sense, there were strong political odds against the Liberian project. On the other hand, Liberia offered the best conditions in Africa for some groundwork to be done. But against that potential was the fact that colonialism was the dominant force in Africa in the 1920's and to the Europeans, as well as to some Africans, it seemed as if colonial rule would last for centuries more. And although Liberia was a legally sovereign state, it was a neo-colonial country. The British and French were old rivals who coveted the country and, given the extent to which they were informed about UNIA activities in West Africa, they could not help but pressure the Liberians into rescinding their arrangements with the Garveyites. As the *Negro World* of October 17, 1925 pointed out, quoting an article from the European press, England and France had notified the Liberian Government that admission of UNIA experts would be considered an act of aggression.

The American government was primarily concerned with the prospective investment of Firestone in Liberia. Firestone had successfully secured a ninety-nine year land lease that had previously been given to the UNIA. On learning of this, Garvey pleaded with the Liberians:

"Whilst it is not in our province to interfere with your legislation, we beg to point out to you the motives generally underlying white capitalists when they seek entry into the countries of the weaker peoples. It is our firm belief that the Firestone concessions in Liberia will lead them ultimately to seek the usurpation of the government, even as has been done with the black republic of Haiti after similar white companies entered there under the pretense of developing the country." (Garvey h, 392; also Padmore a)

Needless to say, Garvey's warning failed to impress the Liberian politicians who, in pulling off a 'big deal' with Firestone, were further enslaved by U.S. capital. From Atlanta prison Garvey warned that the Firestone investment was only the beginning of United States monopoly control of African resources. *(NW,* 31 October 1925, 1)

UNIA Delegation to Liberia, 1921 (Bottom row, left to right): G. O. Marke, Cyril A. Crichlow; (Top row, left to right): Israel McLeod, A. N. Henry, F. P. Lawrence, and Rupert Jemmott

Chapter Six

The Art of the Word

Oratory

One of Garvey's major assets was his oratorical skill, which attracted followers. The elocution and debating experience of his early years were to stand him in good stead in public life.

His reputation as a speaker has been amply documented, confirmed by friends and critics alike. A journalist of the *Panama-American* observed:

> "He would probably pass unnoticed in a crowd — until he speaks. He has the most precious of all bounties, the gift of eloquence; and as he speaks his small, dark brown eyes seem to grow, his even white teeth flash through black lips. His speech is smooth and unctuous without any touch of the American twang despite his long residence in the United States. His English is that of an Oxford scholar and when he speaks, his hearers listen."
> *(in* Martin a, 101)

No doubt to American ears, West Indian British-influenced Standard English sounded like an Oxonian accent!

J. Edgar Hoover, who later became head of the U.S. Federal Bureau of Investigation, wrote in 1919; "He is an exceptionally fine orator." (Hoover) And Robert Minor, the American communist journalist, wrote in 1924, whilst reporting on the 1924 UNIA Convention:

> "I heard Garvey speak last night. He is one of the most

powerful personalities that I have ever seen on the
platform. He is of the rare type that history finds rising
in every unsettled period to express new currents
among the masses of men." *(in* Jacques Garvey a, 138)

Another reporter corroborated:

"Marcus Garvey speaks with singular eloquence. It can
be said he masters the art of the word and that he exerts
a strange fascination on his audience. He can make
them laugh, shout and affect them emotionally as he
wishes." *(Heraldo,* 4 March 1921, 3)

And one of Garvey's schoolmates who in later years attended
one of his church services at Edelweiss park in Kingston
testified:

"Garvey was one of the greatest preachers I ever hear.
Rev. J.T. Dillon could preach, but he could not preach
like Marcus. Dillon was a Baptist minister here in St.
Ann's Bay who went to St. Andrew and died there. He
was a great preacher, but Marcus preach better than
him." (Rose, 6)

Garvey's speeches were often reported verbatim in his
publications, having been copied by adept short-hand writers
whose skill formed the contemporary method of recording data
before the widespread use of sound recording technology. In
this way, his oratory has not been lost and substantial numbers
of his speeches have been documented in his newspapers and in
pamphlets of the day.

A typical Garvey speech roused his audience by its phrasal
reiterations, its parallel syntactic structures, and his empathy
with the experience of his listeners which was signalled by
rhetorical questions, direct challenge, and first-person references. For instance, in a speech made in Montego Bay in
1921, Garvey intimated:

"I have come to you in Jamaica to give new thoughts to
the eight hundred thousand black people in this island . .
. . Montego Bay being only a part of Jamaica I knew you
had no thoughts save that given to you as sycophants
looking to the white man as superior and master. I am

not here with any sympathy for the old spirit of Jamaica,
I am here to give you if I can a new spirit of manhood.
Not the spirit to bow and cringe, to apologize, but the
spirit to strike forward for the rights of the Negro people
of the world . . . . I, like the majority of you, was born in
this country thirty-three years ago, circumvented by the
conditions of the country — the environment of this
country, an environment that sits on black men — that
he must be merely a hewer of wood and carrier of water
— a servant looking up to the white man as superior and
master — who was born to believe himself inferior to
other races — born not to have hope for himself. Under
this environment I was born myself. You all know of
this. But I did not confine myself to this environment
which keeps a black man at the foot of the ladder. I was
entitled to climb as any other man, be they white, yellow
or black." (Garvey i, 93-94)

Many of Garvey's speeches contain this psychological encouragement, this exhortation to cast aside passivity and
negation and to take one's destiny actively into one's own
hands. This theme was crucial because the heritage of slavery
and colonialism was so burdensome that many felt that their
condition was a cross they had to bear or a penance they had to
pay. They would console themselves into acceptance of this role
by scriptural justification. Therefore, the psychological appeal
of Garvey's speeches should never be underestimated, as
without this struggle against the psycho-cultural basis of
colonialism, organizational and political work would not have
been possible.

Also stressed in his speeches is the fact that Africans were
part of a larger universe of people like themselves and,
therefore, if they were mobilized and organized they could end
this oppression and take their own place in the sun, could "walk
tall before the creative forces." (Samad) Added to this is the
fact that Garvey consistently identified with the struggles of
other colonial peoples — from those in Europe such as the Irish,
to those in Asia, such as the Indians.

Garvey also addressed the issue of the shade hierarchy
among people of African descent.

"I have to disabuse the mind of some of you who came
here as black-white and brown-white men, who are

everything else except what they are." (Garvey i, 94)

These elements not only thought themselves better than Blacks because a white skin was an ideal, but because in fact many of them were materially better off than the black majority or had better prospects, socially and politically. Some of these people were Garvey's bitterest enemies in Jamaica, since his ideas constituted a big threat to their psychological assumptions and material prospects. Not only had they come to accept their favourable position in the colonial social hierarchy, but they were in fact confirmed in this overlordship by the acquiesence of many Blacks. Jamaicans, for instance, like many ex-slave New World peoples, had been socialized into niggling distinctions between "black", "sambo" (very dark complexioned), "brown" (covering a wide spectrum of brown complexion casts, essentially 'compensated for' by European-type hair and facial features), and "red" (light-complexioned, 'negatively' offset by kinky red/brown/yellow hair). Being "brown" and less so "red" entitled one to fulfill leadership roles in society, and the black masses looked up to such leaders as "people's men". On the other hand, a "black" person who managed to attain such a leadership role and/or who became culturally an 'assimilated' European, was termed a "first black"! (Patterson) These differentiations were perpetuated because of the people's social aspirations which were allowed to the extent and in the form permitted by a white colonial superstructure. Natural ambition was, therefore, diverted along a distorted channel whereby non-white people "tried to lift themselves out of themselves." On the contrary, Garvey uncomfortably assailed these divisive and self-deprecating racist preoccupations and simplified the social/racial spectrum into black and white. ". . . . it was so difficult . . . ." for people to accept, but such success as his message enjoyed was achieved because "he was so powerful." (idem.)

The Garvey Press

For a movement to be built it required organization and a press. Garvey's training as a printer and his experience as a journalist put him in an advantageous position to develop newspapers wherever he went. He published *The Watchman* in Jamaica while still employed at Benjamin & Co.; *La Nación* in Limón, Costa Rica; *La Prensa* in Colón, Panama; and was also involved with *The Bluefields Messenger* in Costa Rica. (Martin a, 91)

But, the most important Garvey publication was the *Negro World* which was published in Harlem from 1918 to 1933. This paper played a seminal mobilizing role in promoting nationalist agitation against imperialism and colonialism in many countries and was a cultural instrument of the Harlem Renaissance. Its scope was broadened when French and Spanish sections were included. Among its editors were T. Thomas Fortune, John E. Bruce, and William Ferris. Caribbean writers like Eric Walrond and Claude McKay, and the Jamaican socialist, W.A. Domingo also worked on this paper. For several years, Amy Jacques Garvey edited the Women's Page and also wrote feature articles on international subjects.

The circulation of the *Negro World* varied over the years with the fortunes of the movement and the political situation. Estimates of its circulation depend on the point in time at which this estimate was made and sometimes seem to include guess work. Starting with a few thousand copies, it rose dramatically by 1920, the year of the First Convention. Its edition of August 2, 1920 "claimed a guaranteed circulation of fifty thousand" (Cronon a, 95). At its highpoint, some estimates put its circulation at two hundred thousand. However, one *Negro World* newspaper was likely to be read by several persons so that its dissemination would naturally exceed its circulation.

The *Negro World* itself usually carried ten to sixteen pages. It featured on the front page a statement by Garvey addressed to the "Fellowmen of the Negro Race" and signed "Your obedient servant, Marcus Garvey, President General." Garvey covered many topics, from historical themes, to contemporary politics and organizational questions. Its masthead bore the organization's motto "One Aim, One God, One Destiny," and the statement that it set out to be "A Newspaper Devoted Solely to the Interests of the Negro Race."

The repression meted out to the *Negro World* provides ample evidence of its political potency in stimulating anti-colonial sentiment and germinating the seeds of nationalist organization. The *Negro World* was deemed seditious in the French colonial territory of Dahomey where the penalty for possessing a copy was death, and in other French colonies — five years imprisonment. It was in fact proscribed at some time in all the French, Italian, Portuguese, Belgian and some British colonies in Africa. (Thompson, 45) It was prohibited in the British West Indian colonies of Trinidad and Tobago, British Guiana, Barbados, Bermuda, St. Lucia, St. Vincent, British Honduras and Grenada during 1919-1920. (Elkins e)

W.F. Elkins points out that the ordinances dealing with seditious publications were aimed at the *Negro World* and had been instigated by the Colonial Secretary in London, who in September of 1919, had assured the West Indian governors that because of the unrest among Blacks, he would be prepared to approve legislation which would allow stricter control of the press. However, in several cases where the bill encountered militant opposition, for instance, in British Honduras and British Guiana, the legislation was put aside and in Trinidad extra-legal measures were used to prevent the *Negro World* from being circulated.

Garvey also published the *Daily Negro Times* in Harlem from 1922-1924. In Jamaica, he published the *Blackman* newspaper from the end of March 1929 after having purchased a printery from D.T. Wint, a local politician, in late 1928. *(JT,* 1 December 1928, 15) Publication of the paper ceased in 1931. But from 1932-1933, he ran the *New Jamaican,* and subsequently founded in Kingston the *Black Man* magazine in December 1933, which he continued in England until 1939. Garvey, of course, contributed articles to other periodicals but his role in founding newspapers and journals was of important political and cultural significance.

The daily *Blackman* newspaper served not only as the organ of the local UNIA, so complementing the New York based *Negro World,* but was also a forum for the political agitation of the People's Political Party which Garvey founded.

In the first issue of that paper, Garvey had indicated that this was the beginning of a chain of newspapers which were to be published within the following ten years in the major American and European cities, South and West Africa and every important West Indian island under the control of the UNIA. The *Blackman's* policy encompassed a very wide area of journalistic activity. The policy statement read in part:

"As the independent tribune of an oppressed people,
the Blackman records conditions affecting the Negro
masses throughout the world. Its functions embrace the
exposé and remedy of the terrorism and injustice to
which the Negro is subjected. Its scope is international.
From the remote corners of Seni Gambia, Senegal and
the Congo, it catches the cry of benighted tribesmen
suffering by the hand of ruthless despoilers; and carries
it to the scattered millions of black men and women in
Europe, the United States and the West Indies . . . ." *(B,*
21 June 1930, 9)

The small and committed staff of the newspaper supervised
by Alexander Aikman, the literary editor, assumed their political task with great vigour. Aikman was fifty years old and had
combined school-teaching with journalism. *(DG,* 19 February
1930, 8). He was assisted by A. Leo Rankin, the news editor,
and A. Wesley Atherton, a talented journalist, was the chief
reporter. J. Coleman Beecher, who had compiled and published
a history of cricket in Jamaica, contributed articles on sports
and was the business manager. Garvey, the editor-in-chief,
wrote a daily column — "The World As It Is" — and a weekly
Saturday article which was sometimes published in the *Negro
World.* The *Blackman* achieved a very creditable circulation
figure of fifteen thousand copies *(B,* April 2 and 15, 1929).
However, this was not achieved without surmounting obstacles
from the police who interfered with vendors.[1] In his column of
April 18, 1929, Garvey charged that

"Several of the post-mistresses, who are agents for the
'Daily Gleaner' have been trying to hold-up the immediate delivery of 'The Blackman' at their Post Offices, so
as to hamper its immediate circulation on the arrival of
the post. Three times within five days the matter has
been brought to our attention from different points."

On another occasion it was reported that a Jewish St. Andrew
resident had dismissed her household help for having a copy of
the *Blackman. (B,* May 14, 1929). Then, there were other cases
for libel which threatened the very existence of the paper.
    The paper started out as a daily in March 1929, became a
weekly after a year and ceased publication in February 1931.

Garvey was then in debt and even said that he would pay all that he owed and leave Jamaica for good *(B,* 14 February 1931, 1). But by July 1932, Garvey started publishing a daily evening paper, the *New Jamaican,* which ceased publication in September 1933 under the following circumstances:

> "The sudden suspension is caused through the unfortunate circumstance of my owing the landlord, Mr. S.M. Jacobsen, at the place where the paper was published, the amount of one hundred and eighty pounds — the result of my assuming the liability of previous occupants who had the use of my Printing Plant, which was an investment of four thousand pounds, and a tenant for five years paying a rent of twenty-one pounds per month. Unfortunately, through a sudden, but temporary financial reverse, I was immediately unable to pay the amount of one hundred and eighty pounds for which a levy was made and a sale ordered, in which I lost the most valuable bits of machinery necessary for the publication of the paper, including my two linotypes which are very expensive machines, and two of my printing presses. The loss to me amounts to more than one thousand five hundred pounds, in that the said machine could not be replaced in the same condition for less than the amount mentioned, and if I were to purchase new ones, at a cost of over two thousand five hundred pounds (Circular from Marcus Garvey to *NJ* subscribers, September 15, 1933).

But, yet again, the closure of the *New Jamaican* was not the end of Garvey's journalistic projects. By December 1933, he managed to out out the first number of the *Black Man* magazine which he continued to publish in London until 1939. Continuing in the tradition of the defunct international weekly, the *Negro World,* the *Black Man* magazine was circulated in North America, the West Indies, Central America, East, West and South Africa.

Garvey's papers were international in character in that they saw local issues, whether it was lynching in the United States, repression against banana carriers in Jamaica, or restricted credit to black business — not as purely local issues but as they related to a wider system of colonial rule and exploitation. They provided an important vehicle for the education of the masses. And while Garvey's projects were often over-ambitious, he tried to organize propaganda on a scale so that Blacks would be able to independently respond to the vile propaganda of the colonial masters. It is this effort to circulate black newspapers in different parts of the world that motivated him to set up these publications as an example of what could be done. It was a statement of confidence in his own people that they could do it too.

Conventions

UNIA Conventions were held in New York in August 1920, 1921, 1922, 1924 and 1926; in Kingston, Jamaica in 1929 and 1934; and in Toronto, Canada in 1938. Conventions allowed delegates to meet in a collective international forum, allowed for the exchange of experience, and the development of organizational initiatives around political, economic, and social themes. Convention resolutions and directives, in turn, functioned to mobilize the masses. Those who could not attend had access to the minutes and detailed reports of the debates which were subsequently published in the UNIA's *Negro World.* These issues were discussed at UNIA Liberty Halls in different parts of the globe.

The first Convention opened on the eve of Garvey's thirty-third birthday. It began with "three religious services and a silent march of all members and delegates through the streets of Harlem." (Cronon a, 63) This was followed by a parade of UNIA mass units through the streets. Marching to the musical strains of the UNIA band were the African Legion with ceremonial swords, the two hundred-strong Black Cross Nurses, accompanied by UNIA choristers and children who constituted the juvenile auxiliary. (63-64) This pageantry drew thousands of onlookers and constituted a bold symbolic demonstration that African people had to stand up and stake their own claim for dignity and self-determination.

To later generations, the ceremonial paraphernalia worn by Garvey, by top UNIA dignitaries, and by the mass groups may appear somewhat ridiculous — the swords, the plumed hats, the ceremonial suits and badges, the gloves. But in the context of the 1920's and the exclusive dominance of colonial/metropolitan examples of dress, and given the objective of radiating an impression of solemnity, order, and self-pride, such forms have to be understood more positively than negatively.

The delegates met at Madison Square Gardens to hear Garvey's opening address in which he declared:

> "We Negroes are prepared to suffer no longer . . . . For democracy the nations of the world wasted Europe in blood for four years. They called upon the Negroes of the world to fight. After the war we were deprived of all of the democracy we fought for. In many instances in the Southern States, coloured soldiers in uniforms, returning from the battlefields of Europe, were beaten and a few lynched; before they were demobilized they were mobbed in this land of the brave. But we shall not give up. We shall raise the banner of democracy in Africa, or four hundred million of us will report to God the reason why . . . . We pledge our blood to the battlefields of Africa, where we will fight for true liberty, democracy and the brotherhood of man." (Jacques Garvey a, 53)

Further unfurling the banner of African nationalism, he said:

> ". . . . we are coming four hundred million strong, and we mean to retake every square inch of the twelve million square miles of African territory . . . . we are out to get what has belonged to us politically, socially, economically and in every way." (*in,* Cronon a, 66)

The two thousand delegates from twenty-five countries and four continents constituted the most representative gathering of Blacks ever. The convention had taken months of planning and was a testimony to the viability of the organization Garvey had founded and to the efficacy of the historical moment.

The most important document to come out of the convention was the Declaration of Rights of the Negro Peoples of the World. It set out in twelve sections the conditions faced by Blacks throughout the globe and closed with fifty-four demands which constituted a broad programme of Black Nationalism. Garveyism should be assessed in relation to its adherence to this democratically determined document.

An initiative of the 1924 Convention resulted in the inauguration of a "Negro Political Union to raise money for and
otherwise support black political candidates." (Vincent a, 125)
This idea of developing a national black political party was
never seriously pursued in the United States. But Garvey
founded the People's Political Party in Jamaica which was
active in 1929-1930 and was part of a broader plan by him to
launch national parties in the colonial Caribbean countries.

It was also during this Convention that left-wing delegates
attempted to get Garvey to denounce the Ku Klux Klan in
strong terms that would have amounted to a declaration of war.
According to Amy Jacques Garvey:

> "The majority of delegates were in jitters: What would
> happen to them and their homes, when they went back
> South, if such a resolution was carried? Since the
> government would not suppress what was accepted as a
> legitimate organization, Garvey and his followers would
> be committing suicide to declare war on them. Yet the
> Communists expected him to take their bait and order
> his members to don black hoods and go into action.
> Tactfully he was able to put through a motion that was
> mild yet not compromising, condemning the alleged
> atrocities committed in the name of the Klan." (Jacques
> Garvey a, 145)

The fact is that the possibilities open to the Garveyites in the
1920's were few. Their actions have to be seen in the light of the
strength of racism in the U.S. which notwithstanding the gains
of the 1960's onwards, remain very strong and endemic to that
social system.

In August 1929, the Sixth International Convention was held
in Kingston. This was the first convention held outside the
United States. The ceremonial opening was attended by the
Hon. A.E. DaCosta, Custos for Kingston, Seymour Seymour,
the Mayor, and W. Landale, Acting Custos for St. Andrew. It
began with an assembly of fifteen thousand people at Edelweiss
Park that had been preceded by "a mammoth procession . . . .
the like of which has never been seen before." (DG, 2 August
1929). Similarly, the closing procession was said to have had
seventy cars, which was quite a large number for those times.
(DG, 5 September 1929, 18, 19)

For the inaugural parade, the authorities took no chances. Encouraged by alarmist correspondence, they had extra detachments of police and soldiers in readiness for any disturbance during the march through Kingston. (B, 5 August 1929, 1). This proved unnecessary as no violence occurred.

Delegates had been invited from "all Negro institutions, organizations, churches, societies, lodges, and peaceful law-abiding, legitimate and constitutional movements." (Jacques Garvey a, 202-203) Representatives came from Detroit, Louisiana, Mississippi, Texas, Baltimore, St. Louis, New York, Miami, Chicago, Kansas, New Haven, Cleveland, and Washington in the United States, as well as from Panama, Cuba, Costa Rica, Nassau, and someone spoke on behalf of Nigeria. But at least one foreign group was prevented from attending the Convention. The Guatemalan delegate reported that he was in contact with the Caribs International Association of Central America — with a membership of ten to twelve thousand — whose representatives had been prevented from coming by the authorities in Guatemala. (DG, 17 August 1929, 6)

This Convention was largely concerned with re-organization. Proposals were made for the revival of the steamship service under a new body called the African Steamship Navigation Company and the resuscitation of the political arm of the American UNIA — the Universal Negro Political Union, whose first aim was to secure the enfranchisement of the black American population. (DG, 23 August 1929, 21). Certain delegates urged that the UNIA engage in large-scale agricultural production in the West Indies, the United States, and Africa. (DG, 22 August 1929, 18). Also taking part in the discussions was Otto Huiswood, the communist and representative of the American Negro Labour Congress, who spoke "on methods that should be adopted for alleviating the conditions of Negro Workers." (DG, 10 August 1929, 9)

The Convention also considered the establishment of daily newspapers in several European capitals, in West Africa, Cape Town and the important West Indian islands in order "to shape sentiment in favour of the entire Negro race." (DG, 17 August 1929, 6) Such newspapers would supplement the *Negro World* and the *Blackman.* Other items discussed related to the establishment of UNIA consuls in black-populated areas to protect their rights (Cronon a, 152); the founding of "three

Negro Universities with Technical Colleges attached, in America, the West Indies and West Africa" (Jacques Garvey a, 203); and fund-raising. A new UNIA Department of Health and Public Education was created which was to address itself to certain social questions. (Cronon a, 152) A target of six hundred million dollars was the astronomical figure set for the new UNIA programme. This was clearly unrealistic even in the heyday of the UNIA, much less in the years of its decline.

In August 1934, the Seventh International Convention coincided with the centenary of West Indian Slave Abolition. Garvey in his opening address spoke of the British abolitionists and suggested the possibility of alliance with liberal anti-colonial Whites. *(DG,* 6 August 1934, 19)

The Convention adopted a Five Year Plan which would allow for the "development of the shipping, manufacturing, mining, agricultural and other industries which are to affect the Negroes in the United States, the West Indies, Central and South America and Africa." (Cronon, a 160) Garvey's birthday, August 17th, was declared an international Black holiday, birth control was condemned, and the delegates urged that a standard African language be adopted. (idem.)

Of significance was the censuring of religious cults in Harlem and the West Indies, namely the Father Divine Movement, Holy Rollers, Pocomania, and the Bedwardites. Garvey was also reported to have been critical of the Rastafari movement. *(JT,* 25 August 1934, 19) But this was only briefly mentioned in the press without detailed reportage of the arguments he had used. A relevant resolution on religious matters, however, deserves quoting in full for it represents the extent to which the UNIA probably felt its membership being eroded by these non-conformist religions, and also the extent to which the UNIA had departed from the radicalism of the twenties as far as its relationship with the most oppressed sectors of the population was concerned. The resolution stated:

> ". . . . this Seventh International Convention of the Negro Peoples of the World recommend that all responsible and recognized and trustworthy leaders, preachers, teachers and all responsible persons of each and every country seek the sympathy and co-operation of Government and the Police Department . . . . to assist

in putting down and discouraging the existence in the
respective communities of all immoral, vicious, criminal
and unreasonable forms of cult worship and the practice
of religious fury calculated to injure the morals, culture,
mind and general physical health of the simple-minded
and ignorant Negroes who may be influenced to join
such cults or frenzied organisation." *(DG,* 18 August
1934, 27)

Such a resolution sounded like a Colonial Office memorandum rather than a UNIA statement, and indicated the
ascendancy in the organization of colonial-minded Blacks. It
also reflected Garvey's own ambivalence. He and the *Gleaner*
were now on the same side on this issue against the masses, for a
Gleaner editorial during the Convention asked in regard to the
growing influence of Ras Tafarians:

"What is to be done to curb an evil that is gathering
strength around Kingston, St. Thomas and elsewhere in
the island?" *(DG,* 17 August 1934, 12)

Indeed, one commentator has advanced this opinion on the
relationship between Garveyism and Ras Tafarianism:

"The cult of Ras Tafari in its most fundamental form
was not accepted . . . . by the majority of Jamaican
Garveyites. The better-off black and the lower-status
born elements, the artisans, shopkeepers and clerks
who formed the backbone of the UNIA looked to the
Emperor with interest and hope, but not worship. It was
to the poorest and most exploited, the squatters and
labourers of eastern St. Thomas and the inhabitants of
West Kingston that Howell[4] and others most appealed." (Post a, 195)

But this presentation too sharply draws a differentiation
between the social forces represented in the Garvey movement
and those in the early Ras Tafarian movement. It tends to
ignore the connections in ideology, as well as personnel in the
social support characterizing both Garveyism and Ras Tafarianism. (See Hill c) So that while there was and continues to be
friction between middle-strata Blacks and the Rastafarians,

one should not forget the Garveyism also appealed to the "poorest and most exploited," to people who never occupied executive positions in the movement and could not read the publications for themselves, but who were nevertheless staunch followers. It is, however, significant that the resolution was supported by Garvey, and at a time too when he was campaigning for the election to the Legislative Council of Lewis Ashenheim, a Jewish businessman and lawyer.

The Eighth International Convention held in Toronto in 1938, was attended by 110 delegates and there were representatives from associate organizations such as the Peace Movement of Ethiopia and the New York-based Pan-African Communities League. (UNIA b, 3-5)

This convention suppported the white racist Mississippi Senator, Theodore G. Bilbo's Black Repatriation Bill, as well as discussed the attempts being made to secure Garvey's return to the United States. (32, 42-43) The delegates also decided to send a resolution to the British Government on the centenary of West Indian slave emancipation protesting that "the majority of Negroes are still under the most primitive form of civilization and economic conditions, bordering much on the slavery from which they were emancipated." (48)

UNIA conventions, then, were the most important gatherings of Blacks in the 1920's and 30's. They allowed our people to speak with a mightier voice against racism and colonialism. But more importantly, they provided an organizational structure through which particular local and national programmes could be developed.

Solidarity Actions

The UNIA Conventions were noted for their solidarity with other liberation struggles. At the second convention in 1921, resolutions were passed in solidarity with the Indian anti-colonial movement and cables were sent to Mahatma Gandhi. Again, in March 1922, Garvey pledged the support of "four hundred million Negroes" to Gandhi's struggle at a mass meeting of solidarity with the Indian nationalists held at the New York Liberty Hall headquarters. (Weisbord, 422) The fact that Gandhi was aware of Garvey's views in *Philosophy & Opinions* also gave a spirit of political camaraderie to what was

more of an attachment through solidarity. (Jacques Garvey b)
Of the acknowledgements received by Amy Jacques Garvey for
Vol. II of *Philosophy and Opinions,* the one she cherished most
was from "M.K. Gandhi, the Mahatma of India", dated May 12,
1926, and sent from the "Ashram, Sabarmati, India". (Jacques
Garvey a, 168)

In those years, the Indian nationalist movement offered the
most advanced point of resistance to British colonial rule and
involved millions of people. As such, no other nationalist leader
received the solidarity and journalistic attention from Garvey
that Gandhi did. His writings and speeches during his Jamaica
years after his deportation from the United States further
illuminate the emphasis he placed on supporting the struggles
of other colonial peoples. Time and again he pointed to the
necessity of understanding that all anti-colonial struggles
impinged on and affected the other. As such, what was
happening in India, in Ireland, in Africa was of great importance
to West Indians.

This insistence in his journalism, as well as in his Sunday
night addresses at Edelweiss Park in Kingston was an attempt
to combat ignorance and narrow-mindedness among the masses, who before Garvey's time had no idea of the importance of
anti-colonial solidarity. On the other hand, the local ruling-class
reprinted in their press articles from British newspapers which
were hostile to the national liberation struggles against any
colonial power. Colonialism, from their standpoint, was the
norm by which everything was judged. And the world was
divided between the civilizing European powers and the
barbarians. From this perspective, Garvey's attack on British
colonialism and particularly his support for the movement in
India was seen as subversive, for India was the 'jewel in the
crown' of the British Empire. India was the 20th century heart
of British imperial rule.

In reply to a *Gleaner* editorial censuring Gandhi for his salt
campaign and refusal to pay taxes, Garvey wrote:

>"Our daily contemporary in commenting on the release
>of Mahatma Gandhi, referred to him in one of its issues,
>as 'Saint and Fool'. We most vehemently resent the
>insult to the greatest living Indian.
>
>There is no one in Jamaica, as an employed editorial
>writer, who can intelligently interpret to the Jamaican

public the character of Gandhi, because our journalists
here are intellectual lilliputians, and narrow-guaged
individuals who can see no good for humanity except
through pence, shillings and pounds . . . . We want the
Indian people to know that there are intelligent Negro
people in Jamaica who appraise Mr. Gandhi . . . . and, in
doing so, we see in him nothing less than 'Saint and
Leader'." (B, 31 January 1931, 4. Cf. also Editorial DG,
January 29, 1931)

During mid-1930, the *Blackman* had a regular section called
"The Truth About the Indian Situation." (B, 7 June 1930, 11 et
seq.) That page consisted mainly of reports from the international and Indian nationalist press on the Congress movement, and included statements by Gandhi and Vithavali Patel.
(B, 12 June 1930, 6; 14 June 1930, 9). And when Garvey
visited England in 1931, he was the guest of honour at the
Indian Club in London where he was very impressed with the
"radical speeches of the Indian students who were preparing
themselves to lead in the cause of New India." (NJ, 23 July
1932, 2)

So, here was an important and novel development which the
Garvey movement fostered among Black people, that is, the
need for solidarity among oppressed people in the struggle
against the oppressor. For although Garvey perceived the world
through racial eyes, he recognized the solidarity necessary
among peoples of different races who found themselves in the
same position and faced the same enemy. In fact, Garvey once
said that the red in the UNIA flag expressed its sympathy for
"Reds of the World," the green expressed a similar sympathy
for the Irish in their struggle against the British and the black
stood for people of the African race. (*See* Martin 1, 44)

This internationalism was also expressed in the watchword of
the Garveyite pro-Indian agitation, which was "After India,
Africa." (B, 14 June 1930, 4). As Garvey wrote:

"There is a boiling sentiment of nationalism that will
shortly burst out as it is bursting out in India at the
present time . . . . We, who are Africans at home and
abroad, have hopes of the future, and so we watch, with
a friendly eye, the activities in India, because after India
may come Africa." (B, 28 June 1930, 9)

In a similar vein, he telegraphed Lloyd George, the British Prime Minister:

> "We are for the freedom of India and the complete liberation of African colonies, including the Nigerias, Sierra Leone, Gold Coast and Southwest and East Africa. We wish your nation all that is good, but not at the expense of the darker and weaker peoples of the earth." *(in* Weisbord, 122)

Garvey's newspapers gave extensive coverage to liberation struggles in all parts of Africa. These writings were polemical, as well as informative. The *Gold Coast Spectator, the Abantho Batho,* a publication of the ANC and *Umsebenzi,* a South African communist journal, were familiar to readers of the *Blackman* (*B,* 30 August 1930, 1, 9; *NJ,* 29 September 1932, 2) It could also boast of receiving "exclusive dispatches" from South Africa B, 28 June 1930, 1). The *Blackman* also published reports on the Belgian Congo, French Equatorial Africa and Portuguese West Africa. Garvey supported the fourth National Congress of British West Africa held in Lagos in 1929, and in four issues of the newspaper published J.B. Danquah's lecture on "Modern Tendencies Towards Nationality in the Gold Coast." (*B,* 10-14 March 1930)

In February 1930, the *Blackman* pointed to the inevitable opposition to British rule that would come from West Africa and simultaneously contested the Western view of Africa:

> "Sierra Leone, the Nigerias and the Gold Coast form the backbone of Britain's colonial power on the West Coast, and what these countries have gained in experience from British occupation will eventually make the African want to govern himself, and that without the interference of outsiders. To most of us in the Western world, Africa is nothing more than a dark continent. Visions of slaves, gold, heat, fever, jungles and deserts; shiploads of missionaries leaving Christian(?) Europe and America to convert Heathen(?) Africa. No reference to the commercial exploitation under the guise of philanthropic institutions is made, however." (*B,* 20 February 1930)

Garvey was equally committed to the Irish struggle. Of Eamon DeValera, he wrote:

> "We have watched his career for several years both in Ireland and the U.S.A., where he carried on a relentless propaganda in the interest of Irish Republicanism."
> (NJ, 13 July 1932, 2)

Already in 1921, the UNIA Convention had expressed solidarity with the struggle for Irish independence in a cable sent to DeValera. And during his 1931 European visit, Garvey had planned to meet DeValera at Geneva, but was unable to do so. (NJ 12 September 1932, 2) In any case, the Blackman published material from the Irish World (B, 12 July 1930, 9)

And, in the context of British imperial rule, Garvey not only sought the support of British liberals but also of the working class. To achieve these aims, he appointed Richard Tobitt UNIA representative to England in 1924. This was a time when the labour movement in England was growing in strength and was becoming more influential, as the 1926 general strike indicated. Garvey felt,

> "if you can convince the English working class that he has no cause for complaint against the Negro it would be impossible for any government in Great Britain to do anything that would affect the interests of Negroes."
> (Martin a, 48)

However, while making this assessment of Garvey's internationalism, it is possible to find statements made in particular circumstances which conflict with this general posture. For example, he was certainly less disposed to solidarity with the American working class and its poor Whites, largely because of the racism and chauvinism that they exhibited. It was more this experience rather than racial dogma which led him to be pessimistic about linking the problems of White workers to those of Black people struggling for civil and political rights.

Diplomatic Activity

The UNIA made concerted attempts at official international projection and representation. In the Declaration of Rights of the Negro Peoples of the World (1920), paragraph 43 stated:

"We call upon the various governments of the world to
accept and acknowledge Negro representatives who
shall be sent to the said governments to represent the
general welfare of the Negro peoples of the world."
(Garvey h, 141)

Paragraph 52 said:

"We demand that our duly accredited representatives
be given proper recognition in all leagues, conferences,
conventions or courts of international arbitration
wherever human rights are discussed." (142)

Garvey, therefore, paid a lot of attention to this area of
endeavour, recognizing the significance of diplomatic work in
the broader political spectrum. The visits of UNIA delegations
to Africa, Europe and the Caribbean, the petitions to the
League of Nations, and resolutions on international questions
bear testimony to this.

Although the 1920 Convention had dismissed the League of
Nations as "null and void as far as the Negro is concerned," by
September 1922, a delegation was sent to the League headed
by George O. Marke of Sierra Leone, Deputy Potentate of the
UNIA, and including William LeVan Sherrill, the American
UNIA leader, James O'Meally, West Indies UNIA leader, and
Jean-Joseph Adam of Haiti, secretary and interpreter. The
UNIA delegation went to Geneva to plead its case for the UNIA
to take over the "colonization" of the former German African
colonies, today, Tanzania and Namibia. The Persian dele-
gation, as a member of the League, presented the petition since

"the only other sympathetic sovereign countries were
Haiti, Liberia and Ethiopia. Of these, Liberia was a
foundation member of the League, but ineffective, and
Ethiopia became a member in September 1923 only.
Haiti would certainly have been willing, but with the
economy and foreign affairs controlled by the Americans since 1916, it could not dare such a step that would
antagonize the Americans." (Huggins, 159)

And in fact, the Persian Consul General in the United States
represented Abyssinia too and had himself read a personal

message from the King and Queen of Abyssinia to the Third UNIA Convention in August 1922.

In 1923, another UNIA delegation returned to Geneva to press the appeal "but the big colonial powers side-stepped the issue by adopting a new rule that nationals can only submit their grievances and petitions through their own governments." (Jacques Garvey a, 106)

In 1928, Garvey issued a renewed petition which essentially protested the continuing re-division of Africa by the colonial powers as established at the Versailles Peace Conference. This petition, presented to the League through the Secretary General, Sir Eric Drummond, suggested that

> "entire regions of West Africa could be brought to-
> gether as one United Commonwealth of Black Nations,
> and placed under the government of black men as a
> solution of the Negro problem, both in Africa and the
> Western world." (Garvey i, 219-220)

The petition was a comprehensive survey of the condition of Blacks throughout the world and retains its significance several decades after as a historical document independent of the particular demands that were being made at the time. A very concrete section is devoted to the growth of repression in South Africa with the extension of Pass Laws and Curfew Regulations. The Firestone Company's domination of Liberia and the U.S. Occupation of Haiti are condemned. The petition charged that "the black Republics of Haiti and Liberia have not been given a fair chance to develop." (219) In relation to the West Indies, parts of Central and South America, and the Southern United States, the UNIA contended that "most of the black people of these parts are kept in the lowest state of pauperism while other people . . . . are allowed to prosper and live decently . . . ." (216) Garvey also referred to lynchings of Blacks in the United States and was critical of "such gigantic trusts in Central America, as the United Fruit Company." (217) The document outlines in some detail the plight of West Indian migrant workers in Cuba and Central America, thousands of whom were destitute. The document also contained protests against anti-Garvey legislation in the colonies which resulted in the banning of 'Negro newspapers' and the prevention of travel to Africa and within the Caribbean.

So, utilizing all available channels, addressing heads of states, colonial offices, and international organizations, Garvey sought to project on to the political agenda, the issue of the right to self-determination of Africans.

In September 1931, Garvey again travelled to Europe where he spent two months. While there, he attended sessions of the League of Nations in Geneva, interviewed the Secretary General, and the Chairman of the Mandates Commission, Mr. Peter Anker. *(DG,* 18 November 1931, 19). These discussions were based on the UNIA petitions of the League by a 'national delegate' whom Garvey did not name. He was apparently very satisfied with the results of this 1931 interview, though by 1935, these issues were effectively clouded by the Italo-Ethiopian War and Garvey was then no longer optimistic about the League of Nations after its vacillation over the clear-cut aggression of Mussolini.

While in London during the 1931 General Election when the national government was formed under Ramsey MacDonald, Garvey addressed large audiences at Hyde Park "on behalf of some of his friends in the Labour Party." He challenged Britain to reorganize its relationship with the West Indian, West African and Indian colonies along lines which would have amounted to the present-day Commonwealth status. (idem.) At this time, Britain was experiencing the effects of the world capitalist crisis and there had been large demonstrations of the working class and unemployed, the like of which Garvey said he had never witnessed before. This experience encouraged him in his own efforts.

Chapter Seven

The UNIA in Cuba and Central America

Outside the United States, the UNIA was most effectively organized in Central America and the Caribbean. Data for UNIA organizations in 1926, showed that there were fifty-two branches in Cuba; forty-seven in Panama; thirty in Trinidad; twenty-three in Costa Rica; Jamaica seven; Spanish Honduras eight; British Guyana seven; Dominican Republic five; Guatemala five; Nicaragua five; Barbados four; British Honduras four; Mexico four. Single branches were spread throughout other territories. (Martin a, 16) The data show that the UNIA was most widespread and active in Cuba and Panama. In both these places, as in Costa Rica and Honduras, the movement was largely confined to immigrants from the English-speaking Caribbean islands who flocked to Latin America in search of employment and at best, better wages than those available in the islands. Given its relatively larger population than other English-speaking colonial islands, its unemployment and land hunger, Jamaica provided a large number of migrants.

Cuba

In 1919 alone, the migration from Jamaica to Cuba reached its peak with 21,573 labourers being recorded as having left for Cuba. To this number needs to be added the many unrecorded emigrants. (Cf. Proudfoot, 15). And the "average annual exodus from Jamaica, largely to Cuba, was 10,000 for the half-century before 1935." (Eric Williams, 438)

"By the 1920's, capitalism had developed strong roots throughout the island. The countryside had gone through a process of proletarianization as agriculture was concentrated in the hands of large corporations." (Valdés, 220). The intensive development of the Cuban economy in this period as a major outpost of American imperialism, created a great demand for labour in the large-scale sugar cane harvest, now centred in large jointly-owned American and Spanish corporations, but increasingly in solely American-owned companies. As a parallel, steel construction projects were intensively underway, and infra-structure development such as the building of the Havana-Santiago Carretera Central or Main Road.

President Menocal, who came to power in 1913, initiated agreements with several governments to introduce day-labourers or *braceros* to meet the needs of this economic expansion. Thus, "between 1913 and 1924, Cuba received 217,000 labourers from Haiti, Jamaica and Puerto Rico; in the single year 1920, as many as 63,000 from Haiti and Jamaica . . . ." (Eric Williams, 438)

For several reasons, English-speaking West Indian immigrants were more favourably regarded by Menocal and the bourgeoisie than Haitians. One reason was that, as English-speakers, the West Indians were preferred by American contractors. Another was that the more Eurocentric cultural attitudes and strong petty-bourgeois aspirations among the strata of skilled technicians in contrast with the less educated and Afro-centric Haitian peasantry put the latter at a relative disadvantage. Not to be underestimated also, is the divide and rule tactics of the ruling class, playing off one group against the other. Yet another reason was the fact that, comparatively speaking, British consular representation on behalf of the West Indian migrants was more active than Haitian consular concern for their nationals, a reflection of the corrupt and reactionary posture of the Haitian political elite. The educational differences between various groups of immigrants appears in the following table of migrants resident in Cuba in 1919:

Spaniards	39,573	13% women	15% illiterate
Jamaicans	24,187	11% women	75% illiterate
Haitians	10,044	5% women	97% illiterate

(Primelles, 76)

And as a result of relatively higher educational levels among them, and the fact that many were already skilled artisans and clerks, West Indians were able to take advantage of promotion opportunities. Having started out as cane-cutters, several were later able to take up work in sugar factories, or as mechanics and electricians on the railroads, or as masons and construction workers. As for the West Indian women, many were hired by the Cuban bourgeoisie and middle class as domestics and nannies for their children. (Pedro, 6)

Immigrant life was, however, no bed of roses. Some spent months looking for work, in the meanwhile dependent on relatives or fellow-countrymen for shelter and daily expenses. At the time, 40c bought "a little *frijoles* (beans) and *tasajó* (dried meat)" at the shop and 4c "a cigarette and a drink of rum." (Ryan)[1] The pressure for jobs was so acute, in fact, that in 1921 it was reported that Haitians and Jamaicans were going through the countryside and the sugar mills in bad condition, creating problems of public order and trying to rob grocery shops. The consequence was that decrees of July 20 and 29, 1921 gave the government the authority to repatriate them immediately at government expense. (Primelles, 405)[2] Employment, when it came, could be seasonal task-work. Labourers worked a twelve-hour day cutting woodlands in the mountains, planting, cutting, and burning cane. Bagging sugar in the factory earned $1.50 per day in respect of third-class sugar and $1.60 per day in respect of the first-class type. Sugar could be bagged by teams of workers over a twenty-four hour period at the rate of ten thousand two hundred sacks. Individual job possibilities included selling lottery tickets, though this brought a profit of a meagre 1c per ticket. Another possibility was peddling items like soap, perfumery, cloth, and for the successful salesman, even horses. Other forms of self-employment included shoe-making. Those with past teaching experience could also supplement artisan or manual employment by teaching English. But any demand for higher wages was an invitation to being arrested by planasse (cutlass) — bearing police, seizure of one's money and belongings, imprisonment, and the further punishment of eviction from the district. (Ryan)

Severe discrimination against Haitians and a desire to take advantage of the defenceless resulted, by a twist of fate, in the massacre of some Jamaicans at Jobabo, Oriente Province, in

1912. The Jamaican sugar estate labourers would use the local shop-keeper as a banker. In order to appropriate the money, the shop-keeper told one Capt. Cardenas that he was holding money for a group of Haitians, and they colluded to effect a ruse which would allow both men to share the booty. Accordingly, Cardenas led some Rural Guard soldiers to the district and the labourers were called behind the shop premises where they were led to believe that their photographs would be taken. Instead, they were mowed down by covered machine-guns. A cover-up then followed when it was realized that the labourers were in fact Jamaicans. (Pedro b) The British government pursued the matter, and even in 1919, continued claiming indemnity for those killed. This claim was backed by the United States government. But "the Cuban government said this matter had been dealt with definitively by the military tribunals .... and there was no case to answer." (Primelles, 150) However by 1920, President Menocal asked that compensation amounting to ten thousand dollars be paid to the families of Jamaicans who had lost their lives at Jobabo. (303)

All the immigrants were the subject of concern regarding their health standards and the adverse effect this was seen to produce among the Cuban population. The *Diario de la Marina,* 3 February 1921, 1, carried an article headlined: "Haitian, Jamaican, and Chinese Immigrations Constitute a Danger." Malaria, smallpox, and skin ailments were the main infectious diseases that were experiencing a resurgence in Cuba. Health standards generally were not being assisted by the overcrowded conditions in which immigrants lived. *La Discusión,* 7 February 1921, 2, recorded in its editorial, "A Pernicious Immigration," the observations of Dr. Plazaola of the Commission of Health in Oriente: ".... in a room of some nine square metres, I counted fifteen people lying on the ground and on boxes and among these fifteen, I recognized three with smallpox . . . ." And the *Heraldo de Cuba,* 1 February 1921, 9, carried a report that telegrams had been sent the previous day by the Association of Ranchers and Tenant Farmers in Manati and Camagüey to their sister Havana organization asking its support in protesting against Haitian and Jamaican immigration. Indeed, the migrants themselves confessed to being no strangers to Cuban hospitals. (Ryan)

As an economically exploited proletariat, and further as a minority cultural community, the West Indians were greatly attracted to the Garvey movement. The moving spirit behind the introduction of the UNIA into Cuba was a Jamaican, Leonard Bryan, who was editor of the newspaper, the *Havana Post.* He worked together with a group of black Cubans who were familiar with UNIA literature. (Pedro a, 5) Even as late as 1964, a skeletal UNIA existed, with Bryan, now very old, as President, and the Cuban, Marcos Armenteros, in his thirties, as Vice-President. (Pedro b)

But in the 1920's, "the growth of the Association was seen in the meeting places that were scattered throughout our territory to carry out their propaganda. Generally there was no lack of meeting places in the English-speaking West Indian communities, as for example, in the town of Buena Vista in the municipality of Marianao...." (Pedro a, 4). There were several divisions in Havana, throughout Oriente Province, in Santiago de Cuba, in Placetas in Santa Clara Province, in the vicinity of factories such as Bartley, Preston, Central Manati, (Ryan) and at Miranda and Guantanamo in Oriente. (Pedro b)

And while Cuban Blacks were victims of similar economic, cultural and racial oppression as the West Indians, they "did not participate much in Garveyism." (Pedro b) They attended meetings, but did not join the movement. A Cuban writer claimed that ".... no other thing could happen in a country whose sons, independent of the colour of their skin, had forged the fatherland fighting for thirty years the Spanish colonial regime." (Pedro a, 5)

Indeed, many Cuban Blacks retained strong cultural links with Africa through a distinct Afro-Cuban vocabulary, cuisine, musical and religious traditions (Mitchell)[3], and with slavery and the slave trade abolished there only in 1881, Cuba constituted one of the strongest areas of African cultural expression in the New World. The message of Garveyism, therefore, clearly held some appeal for them. The spirit of Garveyism was also filtered to Cuba through the impact of Harlem Renaissance literature and the contacts between Harlem Renaissance literary figures with Cuban men of letters, as for example, between Langston Hughes and Nicolás Guillén, the first Cuban poet to portray the Blacks in Cuba with the knowledge, sympathy, and perspective of the insider.[4]

All the same, the history of the black experience in Cuba was unlike that of West Indian Blacks. The latter came from islands which were still British colonial possessions, and where the psychological responses of the populations, even among the most oppressed, were strongly biased towards dependence on and emulation of the metropolitan "motherland." For instance, West Indians in Cuba were divided over — as late as the 1960's when several of the islands became independent of Britain — the issue of replacing the picture of the British monarch in West Indian community association halls by pictures of Cuban revolutionary leaders and West Indian heads of government. (Ryan)

On the other hand, Cuban Blacks had participated in large numbers in the Ten Years War of Independence from October 1868 to December 1878. As part of Latin America, Cuba had been caught up in the revolt against Spain of the Spanish colonies in the New World between 1810-1815, which had resulted in their independence. Only Cuba and Puerto Rico remained of this vast Spanish empire. (Foner b, 9) Despite this, "after the 1820's, independence movements rose and fell in Cuba," with the struggle for liberation being retarded only by the dependence of the white planters and conservative social sectors on the military power of Spain to repulse the formidable insurrectionary potential of the black slaves upon whom the sugar industry depended. "In 1842, the official census reported a population of 1,037,624 inhabitants: 448,291 whites, 152,838 free blacks, and 436,495 black slaves." (11)

Because of this demographic configuration,, any independence war necessitated black participation and the need for Blacks to "rise to high rank in the revolutionary army if their services proved essential to the struggle . . . ." (16) "The patriot army quickly grew as the Cuban masses, white and black (free and slave), joined the movement, especially in the rural areas . . . The blacks were to form a considerable part of the Cuban army throughout the revolution; nearly all were operating without uniforms and with an amazing variety of weapons . . . . Half-armed, ragged, ill-fed, but burning with revolutionary zeal, the patriot forces defeated the Spanairds at Yara, Baire, and Jiguani" in the early days of October 1868 and "on October 15, they laid siege to Bayamo, a city of ten thousand people, and on the nineteenth, they captured it. Céspedes established the government of the Republic of Cuba in the captured city." (19-20)

Carlos Manuel de Céspedes had, on October 10, 1868, proclaimed the independence of Cuba and had that same day liberated his slaves. However, "the manifesto proclaiming independence basically represented the interests of the Cuban landowners in the eastern provinces. . . ." and included a reformist policy on abolition — "gradual emancipation with government payment of indemnities to owners." In addition, abolition processes were "to be put into operation *after* the revolution emerged victorious." (15-16)

In the event, there was to be a twelve year lapse before the abolition of slavery came into effect on the island. But the mass involvement of Blacks in the heroic saga of the independence wars helped to weld the Blacks into the fabric of the Cuban nation's history and politics.

After the wars, the betrayal felt by Blacks at the persistence of inequality in social relations was offset by this great sense of patriotism which led them to perceive their fight against racism as aimed at securing equality of rights with other ethnic groups.

But the intensification in racial discrimination against Blacks produced by the convergence of the legacy of Spanish slave /colonial racism with American racism during the years of the U.S. occupation, led to radical political action on the part of some Blacks. This saw the formation of the Independent Party of Colour in 1906, by Evaristo Estenoz and Pedro Ivonet. Both men had distinguished themselves in the independence wars and sought to agitate for the right of Blacks to participate in all aspects of Cuban national life. But their open racially-based declaration of intent attracted a reaction from other political organizations which undermined the IPC. Further to which, the party fostered an uprising which ended with a slaughter of Blacks who, together with the IPC, were crushed by the Cuban government and its American backers in 1912.

Meanwhile, the integrationist thrust of Cuban national politics was to be inscribed in an amendment to a legislative law, the amendment itself later becoming known as the Morua Law of 1929. This was a law of association which stipulated in its amendment that no political party should be based exclusively on membership by race or religion. The law in practice outlawed the IPC while disregarding the existence of political associations of white Cubans. The law also produced problems for the UNIA and the British West Indian Associations in Cuba. (Pedro b, on information from Leonard Bryan)

Morua himself was a black state senator from Matanzas Province who had started off as a trucker. From youth, he had involved himself in the labour movement, became a journalist, and joined the conservative Autonomous Party which sought more autonomy for Cuba within Spanish colonial rule. Influenced by George Washington Carver, he constantly sought the cultural and socio-economic improvement of Cuban Blacks, but was opposed to the separatist trend of the Independent Party of Colour. Ideologically, too, on the issue of Cuban independence, he was opposed to another black senator and journalist, Juan Gualberto Gomez, who was associated with the Cuban proclamation of independence and was José Marti's personal representative in Cuba during Marti's exile. Like Marti, Gomez fought against racial discrimination in Cuba and for the integration of all races into the Cuban nation. (Franco)

Another reason for the strength of Cuban nationalism was the fact that Cuban socio-political thought was in advance of that in the West Indian islands. Already in the second half of the nineteenth century, José Marti was advocating that "the battle against direct Spanish occupation was not enough. Colonial institutions and structures had survived" in independent Latin American countries and "only the elimination of all vestiges of colonialism could assure the growth and development of Latin America." (Valdés, 218) In addition, "political independence had to be guaranteed by economic independence" which he envisaged along national capitalistic lines. Furthermore, having "witnessed the transformation of the American economic system with its imperialistic tendencies," he "called for the unity of all Latin America, expressing a well-defined revolutionary internationalism." (219)

Later, by the 1920's, the student political leader, Julio Antonio Mella "not only reasserted the principles of national liberation and anti-imperialism, but built upon them in order to demonstrate the necessity of a working class revolution." He "publicly proclaimed his faith in socialism and founded the Cuban Communist Party in 1925." (221) The communist and socialist parties in Cuba were to play an important role, together with the trade union movement, in mobilizing Blacks to struggle for economic justice and against racism. Several West Indians first came into contact with Marxism during their stay in Cuba. This was the case with Hugh Clifford Buchanan,

Jamaica's first Marxist. (Lewis f). And a Montserratian migrant recalled that he was introduced to Marxism by an Antiguan migrant, Peter Philip, in 1939 in Santiago de Cuba where Philip worked as a mechanic, and was a member of the Partido Socialista Popular (the first Communist Party of Cuba). As a result of his politics, the government of General Fulgencio Batista deported him in the 1950's. (Ryan)[5]

In fact, there is evidence of West Indian involvement in trade union activity in Cuba, a development which did not pass unnoticed by the press. For instance, in 1920 the *Evening Post* named Jamaican union leaders and commented on the dissatisfaction of Jamaican cane cutters regarding their wage levels as against the compliance of their Cuban counterparts. These workers earned between $1.20 and $2.00 per one hundred *arrobas*[6] of cut cane. The Jamaican workers managed to establish a trade union, worked a three or four-day week, and participated in Cuban trade union congresses at which they denounced the inhuman conditions of labour they endured. (Pedro b)

On account of Jamaican particpation in labour agitation, in 1925, Rubén Martinez Villena, a Cuban labour leader, called on other leaders to recognize this participation and to work for the incorporation of West Indian immigrants into the national labour movement. (idem.) For during the 1920's, "as the Cuban economy became more and more integrated into the American capitalist system," superceding Spanish economic monopoly, "the trade union movement . . . . became extremely militant and clashed with capital and the state." (Valdés, 220-221). Perhaps the most famous example of the role of Cuban Blacks in national trade union development is that of Jesús Menéndez,[7] assassinated at age thirty-seven in 1948, himself the grandson and son of *Mambises,* independence fighters, member of Cuban[7] Communisty Party since 1931 and political representative. (Galló)

This depth of Black involvement and integration into Cuban national life and historical development can, therefore, be deduced from the observations of Hugh Buchanan, who, as a Jamaican migrant to Cuba, was by 1937 forcibly struck by the contrast between the prevailing colonial mentality of Jamaica and the national spirit which predominated in Cuba.

"The illiterate Cuban *guajiro* (peasant) beats his breast
with pride and declares: 'I am a Cuban'. It is one thing to
see it written, but quite another to hear it, and guage the
intensity of emotion behind those words. This pride of
even the most illiterate Cuban is due to the fact that at a
certain time in the past they rose and did something
monumental. The deeds of a Maceo, a Marti and a
thousand patriots who distinguished themselves in the
struggle are written in prose, and poetry, and in the text
books of their schools. It is the source of a never-ending
folk-lore, the vital chord to which every Cuban re-
sponds. 'La Independencia' even though reduced to a
solemn farce by the strangle-hold of Wall Street, is
nevertheless, the motive force, the ideal of a nation of
progressive people less than one hundred miles from
us." (Letter, *POp* 18 December 1937, 14)

It was against this background of a vigorous national spirit
that the UNIA was to find itself largely a migrant forum in Cuba
and, for that matter, in the other Latin American countries, a
forum through which the cultural ties of the English-speaking
Caribbean could be maintained, the economic problems of the
migrants' marginal situation could be aired, addressed, and
improved. In those forums an identity and unity of purpose and
achievement would come gradually, and not without difficulty,
to supercede narrow insular identities and petty rivalries over
island size, and to provide a psychological bulwark against
racial discrimination in the Eurocentric value-orientations of
Latin American societies.

Garvey in Cuba

Garvey visited Cuba, travelling on the Black Star Line boat
"Yarmouth" and arriving in Havana in March 3, 1921. His visit
was a big political and morale booster for the West Indian
migrants as well as a promotion of the shipping project. The
visit was also prominently featured in the local press. *El
Heraldo de Cuba* of March 4, 1921, gave Garvey's arrival front
page coverage. In an interview done the previous day, Garvey
had stated that "In Cuba there are twenty-five sections established. But I'm going to visit only those in Morón, Nuevitas and
Santiago de Cuba . . . ." He also insisted that he had not come to

interfere in domestic politics. This disclaimer was made for tactical reasons. The local authorities held the legal power to deal not only with him but also with his supporters, whose British passports had been stamped with the warning that they should comply with the laws of Cuba and refrain from interference in the country's domestic affairs.

> "I do not have the intention of interfering in the internal affairs of this country. I'm only trying to get the support of the Cuban Negroes to achieve the understanding among all the Negroes in the world and the social and economic progress of us all . . . . The problem of American Negroes and the Cuban Negroes are essentially different although both have in common, the racial problem. I believe that to solve different problems each of them must use the appropriate procedures, but the end that I'm following is common to all Negroes."

Garvey went on to promote the Black Star Line and the Negro Factories Corporation, and encouraged the Cubans to buy shares. He also made a very clear statement on the 'Back to Africa' interpretation of his movement, with which his enemies on the right and the left had characterized the UNIA.

> "It is a mistake to suppose that I want to take the Negroes to Africa. I believe that the American Negroes have helped to establish the North American civilization and, therefore, have a perfect right to live in the U.S. and to aspire to equality of opportunities and treatment. Each Negro can be a citizen of the nation in which he was born or that he has chosen. But I foresee the building of a great state in Africa which, featuring in the concert of the great nations, will make the Negro race as respectable as the others . . . . Cuban Negroes will be favoured by the building of this African state because when this state exists they will be considered and respected as descendants of this powerful country which has enough strength to protect them."

This was the perception of many of the UNIA membership. As a Grenadian immigrant to Cuba explained, one did not join the movement in order to return to Africa, but it was psychologically important to know that one *might* be able to go there, if even not personally, then that one's children or grandchildren shoud have that opportunity. After all, he continued, already in one's middle-age, and without education and skill training, one couldn't practically think of going to Africa, but it was important that the race should and could rise and could be redeemed. (Mitchell)

In this interview Garvey elaborated his perspectives on Africa:

> ".... all Africa has been shared between the European nations. But Africa is the land of our forefathers and we have an inalienable right over it. The 'New Negro' knows that when he was told not to think of Africa because that was a dark land of wild people and cannibals they wanted him not to have anything to do with his fatherland in order to facilitate the usurpation carried out by the Europeans. . . ."

It was pointedly ironic that the Eurocentricity which was the goal of New World creole culture — and from which Garvey himself was not divorced — surfaced in the speech of Dr. Miguel Angel Céspedes who gave the welcome address for Garvey at the appropriately named "Club Atenas" (Athens Club) in Havana on March 3. Céspedes

> ". . . . considered that the propaganda pursued by Marcus Garvey is, in fact plausible, when viewed from the fundamental aspect that involves a civilizing mission on the African continent which occupies a very inferior plane in world civilization....(*Heraldo*, 4 March 1921, 10)

But Eurocentricity largely apart, Céspedes made the point about Cuban nationalism:

> "The black Cuban has expended his efforts in creating a Republic in which he might be able to live in dignity and where he might exercise all the rights of a civilized and free man. As such, he conceives of no other fatherland but the Cuban fatherland and does not share the Pan-African ideal because he holds a cosmopolitan concept of the human spirit . . . . (idem.)

To this, Garvey was forced to note that Blacks who had fought brilliantly for the independence of several countries did not care about his Pan-African ideals, but that the same efforts which were made to free Cuba were necessary to build the great African nation that he foresaw. For this purpose, as he indicated in his newspaper interview,

> "Of course we'll have to kick the Europeans out of Africa. You would like to know by what means we are going to carry out this task. Allow me not to speak for I would let out a secret of this organization. Our plan includes civilizing the African tribes. This work will facilitate the path to the redemption of Africa."

To this the journalist had inquired, "Do you believe that your campaign will lead to an armed struggle?" Garvey's reply was, "Our problem is exactly similar to that of Ireland." "But, Mr. Garvey, in Ireland there is a bloody and terrible struggle." Garvey: "It is sometimes difficult to obtain the recognition of a right without fighting. The independence of Cuba is an example of this."

In later years, this militant aspect of Garveyism was to cause the Cuban authorities to have second thoughts about the organization. Part of the preparation to liberate Africa was interpreted by some UNIA divisions in Cuba as military training, though weapon drill seems to have been confined to paltry sticks and stones! The Cuban authorities perceived an immediate threat. Cuba, after all, had always had a vigorous opposition which worked to overthrow the notoriously corrupt political leadership and the American puppet governments that succeeded each other in the years following the American occupation until the Cuban Revolution in 1959.

But in 1921, the Cuban government was prepared to give Garvey and the UNIA some licence. As a result, he was not only allowed to visit and to speak in Havana, Morón, Camagüey, Nuevitas Banes, and Santiago, but he was also received in audience by President Mario Garcia Menocal. Garvey was presented to the President by a conservative member of the chamber of Deputies from Matanzas Province, who acted in concert with certain American businessmen. On the other hand, by September 30 that same year, the United States Chargé d'Affaires called for an investigation of the UNIA. *(La Discusion* 14 January 1922)

Menocal, leader of the Conservative Party, ruled Cuba from 1913-1921. Educated at Maryland and Cornell universities in the United States, he had been made Police Chief of Havana during the U.S. occupation (1899-1902). Menocal was in charge of the Cuban American Sugar Company and represented the most reactionary interests of the oligarchy, so much so that he was nicknamed "the overseer." When Garvey visited Cuba, Menocal was completing his second term of office after having used electoral fraud and other means to maintain power. Opposition to Menocal, led by José Miguel Gomez, came especially from Oriente and Camagüey Provinces, and from Las Villas, areas with substantial black populations. But the Americans supported his regime by stationing marines in Oriente and Havana. (Peréz et al., 152-153) Since Menocal himself had inaugurated the day-labourer immigration in support of the sugar industry, he signalled his favour of the large West Indian community by affording recognition to their acknowledged leader — commonly perceived as their "consul" (Pedro b) — and so hoped to forestall any labour unrest among them.

In the event, however, a subsequent Cuban government banned the *Negro World* in 1928, and in 1929 declared the UNIA illegal. *(B,* 29 October 1929, 5; *DG,* 25 October 1929, 12). This ban on the UNIA lasted for six months and two weeks, after which time Liberty Halls in Cuba were once more re-opened under strict surveillance. *(B,* 28 June 1930, 9). As elsewhere, the Garveyites were charged under the Morua Law with subversive activities. Not content with this, the dictator Machado (1925-1933) signed an expulsion decree in 1930 which banned Garvey from entering Cuba. *(DG,* 4 February 1930, 3)[8] In justifying this ban, the Secretary of the Interior, General Manuel Delgado, who was in charge of security, stated that there was no racial problem in Cuba and that "the propaganda initiated by Garvey is prejudicial to society in Cuba." (idem.) These restrictions were prompted by several factors of internal Cuban politics and economy. Firstly, the decline in the sugar and other industries as a result of the Depression. Secondly, there was a resultant labour competition between Cuban and West Indian labour. Thirdly, the moves were also intended as reprisals against West Indian labourers on account of their increased union militancy.

As the Cuban UNIA, especially the divisions in Havana, Santa Clara and Camagüey were among the strongest in the entire Caribbean, this repression weakened significantly the viability of the UNIA as a whole, both financially and politically. The movement in Cuba fizzled out in the mid 1930's — a result of local repression and increased surveillance, the UNIA's own international decline, the repatriation and harassment of migrant workers in the thirties, and the fact that the first generation Cuban-born offspring of West Indian parents were recognized as Cuban nationals with legal and political rights, so much so that special UNIA sessions had to be conducted in private, out of their hearing. (Mitchell)

Panama

Several of the West Indian migrants to Cuba had already worked or were to work in other Spanish-speaking areas of the Caribbean. One such example was Victor G. Cohen who left Jamaica as a boy in 1907 to live in Costa Rica. From there, he travelled to Bocas del Toro in Panama where he was introduced to "Garvey's teaching." From Panama to Cuba. There he worked as a cane-cutter and became further involved in Garveyite activities. He then travelled to New York in the early 1920's, where he met Garvey. He was later to become Associate Editor of the bi-monthly New York magazine, *African Opinion*. There were many like him.

Panama attracted substantial numbers of migrants, less because of the large-scale investment of American capital in the United Fruit Company's banana holdings in Chiriqui and Bocas del Toro, but moreso because of the grand labour-intensive engineering projects envisaged for the narrow waist of the Americas on which Panama was situated.[9]

The Republic of Panama itself had come into existence on November 3, 1903, as much the product of separatist sentiments in the Panama Department of the Republic of Colombia as abetted by United States determination to acquire concessions for the construction of a trans-isthmus canal. (Dario Souza et al., 39-40)

From 1846, the United States had proposed the construction of cross-isthmus transportation and between 1850-1855, a coast-to-coast railway had been built. Because of underpopulation in the Isthmus, foreign labour was recruited to clear the tropical forests and lay the tracks for this railroad which was to carry the heaviest traffic per mile in its early days. This work was so laborious and demanding at the same time that the pay was so low, that the rail company contravened the laws of Nueva Granada province to institute its own police force and forest guards. This move was intended to prevent its manual employees from deserting either to buy land and set up their own peasant holdings or to gain better salaries in road construction. (Navas, 65). These temptations were great for the majority of the imported labourers for these schemes who came from such islands as Jamaica, Barbados, St. Lucia, Martinique and Cuba. These island immigrants were characterized as a group attracted to small-property acquisition, socialized in agriculture both peasant and estate, and intent on financial accumulation in order to return to their own homelands with a stronger personal economic base. (Westerman *in* Navas, 66)

About four to five thousand Jamaicans migrated to work on this project. (Senior a, 62). But "the peak migration was between 1882-1884 when 32,958 left and 14,962 returned" to an island which by 1889, was to have a population total of 580,000. This grand exodus and substantial return of workers reflected the fortunes of the French company of Ferdinand de Lesseps which, having already built the Suez Canal, had then contracted with Colombia to construct the Panama Canal. Work began in January, 1880, but after twenty years of work, the effort had to be abandoned. The attrition of disease and the company's financial problems made their effects felt from an early date. "After 1884, the numbers returning exceeded the numbers leaving and by 1888-1889 when the crash came, only 1,861 left for Colón while 10,985 returned." (idem.)

The United States now renewed its interest in such a project, its overseas imperial and economic interests having been boosted by its conquest of the remnants of the Spanish Empire in the Philippines, Cuba, Santo Domingo and Puerto Rico. But despite the Herran-Hay Treaty with Colombia which assured the Canal's construction, the Colombia Senate, by reason of inter-regional jealousies, civil wars, and the punitive taxation on the provinces by the central administration, revoked the treaty in August 1903. By November the same year, the United States assisted the Panama separatist movement to declare itself autonomous. The United States would defend Panama against Colombian re-annexation and in return for ten million dollars, the new Republic ceded the Canal Zone, a slip of land ten miles wide and approximately fifty miles long, which would come under the government, laws, and use of the United States in perpetuity. The Canal Zone effectively divided the Republic of Panama into two sections.

American construction of the fifty-mile-long Canal began in 1904, and was completed in 1914. If the engineering was a feat of American technology and ingenuity, the Canal construction was mainly achieved by the efforts of West Indian labour. The wide dispersal of the Panamanian population throughout the Provinces of Panama and Colón and their semi-feudal bonds with the local latifundists again necessitated the influx of foreign labour. Whereas between 1904-1920, about ten thousand local workers were employed to the United States Government in excavation and the construction of locks and earth-dams, foreign labour in 1905 amounted to seventeen thousand and in 1914 to forty-four thousand three hundred and twenty-nine. Between 1906-1908, twelve thousand workers came from Spain, Italy, Greece, France and Germany, but more than twenty-seven thousand hailed from the Caribbean islands of Barbados (30-40% of its adult males!), Martinique, Guadeloupe, Trinidad, and as well as from Jamaica, Grenada, and British Guiana. (Dário Souza, 44; Navas, 118) Even after the Canal had been built, there was further work to be had in the construction of the Boyd-Roosevelt Trans-Isthmian Highway between 1920-1930, and West Indian men worked as manual labourers in construction, on the docks, on plantations, and as railway personnel.

In fact, in 1912 the Canal Company arrived at an arrangement with the United Fruit Company and other transnationals operating in Central and South America to siphon off the excess of labourers attracted to Panama by the canal construction and who were being phased out as the scheme wound to its close. Workers were, therefore, contracted to Brazil, Honduras, Guatemala and Costa Rica. Of ten thousand unemployed West Indians in 1913, half took up employment with the United Fruit Company, many finding their way to Bocas del Toro in Costa Rica. (Westerman in Navas, 126-127)

Working Conditions in Panama

Panama already had Africans in its population — a presence dating from the earlier centuries of Spanish slavery. The descendants of these Africans were Spanish-speaking and some were able to rise in the socio-political hierarchy of the country, but colour discrimination meant that by 1914 most of the fifty thousand Blacks "occupied the bottom of the socio-political scale" (Lafeber, 64), and few persons "claimed black blood if they could pass for *mestizo*," a mixture of Spanish and Amerindian nationalities. Two hundred thousand of the population were *mestizo* or mulatto (mixed African and Spanish nationalities), while indigenous Indians, Asians and Jews numbered thirty-five thousand. (63). The national bourgeoisie was largely composed of fifty-one thousand "Whites" whose leaders emerged "from several dozen, often interrelated, families that comprised the oligarchy." (62)

The flood of African English-speaking Caribbean labourers into this traditionally latifundist but now burgeoning American-dominated economy, produced predictable inequalities and stratifications.

Contracted for two to three years, the West Indians "were bossed by men who had experience with black labour, that is, whites from the Gulf States who . . . . ' were sent to the Canal Zone with instructions to make an inter-racial society work as well as it did in our Deep South' "! (Mercer Tate *in* Lafeber, 65)[10]

With such a precedent in mind, it was, therefore, not surprising that an apartheid-like socio-economic system confronted the West Indian migrants. Financially, they faced discrimination of both a quantitative and qualitative nature. They were the worst paid sector of the labour force. Europeans (Italians, Spaniards and Greeks) earned double the wages of the West Indians even though they too were included on the Silver Roll, but the "value and buying power of the highest on the 'silver' could not compare with the minimum on the Gold Roll." (Navas, 131). Furthermore, no effort was made to upgrade the technical skills of the manual workers, for obvious economic reasons. Thus, "while the Canal was being built, some 5,300 United States citizens and a few Panamanians received wages in gold coin. The remaining 31,000 labourers, including most

Panamanians and all blacks, were paid in lesser silver coin. The gold and silver payroll made the aristocracy instantly recognizable. Soon the labels — and the segregation — spread to drinking fountains, toilet facilities, and nearly every other public service. The discrimination was hardly surprising since Jim Crow laws (segregating whites and blacks on transportation, in schools etc.) were sweeping through the United States, and as many as a hundred blacks were being lynched annually in the South. But when Jim Crow laws and lynching gradually disappeared in the United States after World War II, the gold and silver distinctions remained entrenched in the Canal Zone." (idem.)

The penalty for violating the rules of public segregation was imprisonment and loss of employment. (Prescott) The workers were kept in their place by an American police-force employed by the Canal Company. These were armed with batons. Wages ranged between 10c and 20c an hour for a twelve-hour day. There was no overtime. The men lived in work camps patrolled by policemen and guards. Lodging and a meal ticket for the camp were made possible by a day's work, so if one didn't work a day, there was no shelter for the night and one ran the risk of imprisonment. "You had to live by your wits." Five dollars bought a commissary book from the chits of which one could buy clothes, meals, and food to take back to the camp and cook in an open shed. (ibid.)

This segregation and labour-camp regime constituted "a pressure you can't see . . . . you're moving like if your feet are tied." (William Arthur). But there were additional hardships which involved the risk of death. Typhoid fever raged "up and down;" the sharpest memory of the manual workers is of torrential rain. Clothes became so soaked they could not be worn the next day. The anti-malarial, quinine, was a must. Men worked in water up to their knees, and while the Whites drove steam-shovels in covered cabins, it was four Blacks on the ground who assisted the placement of the shovel. The mortality rate was high. (Prescott)

A further danger was posed by severe landslides which occurred principally along the eight-mile Culebra or Gaillard Cut through solid rock "when deep cuts were made into the weaker rock formations." The Isthmus, whose geological framework is mainly volcanic, presented "an unusually varied pattern for such a small area." (Panama Canal Information Officer)

And there were also the premature dynamite explosions which accounted for many deaths. One such accident at Frijoles was graphically recalled: "Men died that Friday evening like it was on a battlefield." But the authorities showed no interest in identifying the dead — the whole manner of labour recruitment was, in any case, haphazard, and with no union representation, the question of paying compensation to the relatives of the dead did not arise. (Prescott)

Thus, "the state of mind of the workers was such that they were ripe for the picking for any subject which could show them that they should be united for their own benefit and to overcome these inequities." (ibid.). Garveyism was the 'subject' which struck the right note with these oppressed migrant workers. Garvey first visited Panama in 1920, after his marriage to Amy Ashwood (Clarisse Arthur) and his ringing assurance that West Indian Negroes, if united, could "make themselves a potential entity wherever they were" served, as in Cuba, to weld together in the UNIA people already divided by insular loyalties and a pernicious caste system. Separated, they were in fact unable to defend themselves and became dupes for exploitation. (ibid.)

UNIA groups were formed in Colón, Almirante, Bocas del Toro, Gamboa, and Panama City, and in towns like Góngora, Coledra and Malcachin where West Indians lived and which were subsequently inundated in the formation of the 163.38 square mile artificial Gatún Lake along which ships travel for 23½ miles. There were forty-six UNIA branches in Panama and two in the Canal Zone. (Martin b, 81)

People were galvanized by the *Negro World* and eagerly awaited the arrival of copies from the United States. As Black Cross nurses, housewives and domestic workers organized first-aid services, members paid sickness and death benefit dues, teenagers and adults got involved in elocution sessions, parents inducted their children into the Garvey movement, and 1st of August celebrations were memorably grand affairs. Grocery and bakery businesses were also operated, but in the end, the groceries declined in the face of the uneconomical need to buy produce from their business competitors and in general, "we didn't know how to manage a thing that mushroomed too big." (Clarisse Arthur) Indeed, the Black Star Line scheme "brought many people into the organization," impressed as

they were when the "Frederick Douglass" docked at Port
Cristobal in early 1920. But the BSL bankruptcy also im-
poverished many who had invested their savings in it. (ibid.)

Garvey himself was, as in Cuba, regarded by West Indians as
their President or Governor. On his first visit in early 1920, he
addressed a large crowd assembled at an open lot in front of the
balconied premises of a Dr. Hamlet at the corner of 5th Street
and Central in Colón. The inhabitants of the towns that were
flooded to make Gatún Lake, had been resettled in Colón so
that the West Indian presence there was strong.

In fact, the U.S. authorities in the Canal Zone had got wind of
Garvey's expected arrival in Panama in late September 1919,
and the American governor, Harding, had dispatched a cable to
the State Department's Passport Control Division advising
their refusal of permission for Garvey to undertake this visit. He
felt that this visit "would be detrimental to the interests of our
West Indian employees." (Harding) This disquiet proceeded
from two strikes earlier that year — longshoremen had struck
on 2nd May, and deckhands on 20th September. "However, the
most serious canal labour struggles of this period would come
on 24th February, 1920, when members of the United Brotherhood of Maintenance of Way Employees and Railroad Shop
Labourers and their sympathizers struck." (Hill d II, 34 fn. 1)
This strike involved twelve thousand five hundred West Indian
workers — seventy per cent (70%) of the work force. Garvey
cabled his sympathy with the strikers and sent them financial
assistance. (Hill d II, lii). The confrontation was severe.

> "Drawn bayonets were fixed and the workers were
> practically ousted from the Panama Canal by military
> forces. They took possession of the houses and the
> workers had to rent houses from the Panama Canal
> authorities so that they were compelled to work for
> them. Women and children were ejected from their
> homes at the point of the bayonet, and many a man has
> been forced to commit suicide from the time that work
> ceased on the Panama Canal for them.
>
> 'You cannot get a boat to leave there. If you go to the
> United Fruit Company and ask for passage on one of
> (their) boats in order to leave Colón, they say, 'No, we
> have no passage for you; wait for the Black Star Line.'

That strike is the first strike in history where men
have had to go back to work for less than they were
getting. Men who had gotten seventy-five dollars a
month had to return for fifty dollars and had to accept it
because their wives and children were there. All our
belongings were dashed to pieces. In Panama and Colón
men are out of positions they formerly held, and the
offices that were formerly held by coloured men for
years — fourteen and fifteen years — are now being held
by white men and women. The man who formerly had
a vocation now has to push a truck. But the U.N.I.A. is
still doing its utmost to relieve the situation . . . ."
(Ricketts, Colón UNIA Delegate to 1920 Convention *in*
Hill d II, 512-513)

Notwithstanding these setbacks and confrontations during
the 1920's, with government acknowledgement, the UNIA ran
its own English-speaking elementary and technical schools in
places like Colón, and such teachers as James Smellie, Cyril
Thomas and Franklyn Hector-Connor stood out. These community leaders were themselves Garveyites and the calibre of
persons attracted to the aims and ideals of Garveyism is evident
in the fact that Hector-Connor was to become the first Jamaican
to receive from the Panamanian Government the Vasco Nuñez
de Balboa Award "for outstanding community services." Like
Garvey, Hector-Connor was born in St. Ann's parish, Jamaica,
and at eight, had arrived in Panama with his parents. An early
UNIA member, Garvey appointed Hector-Connor private secretary of UNIA Commissioners to Panama. In that capacity he
served three Commissioners — Henrietta Vinton Davis, Rev.
West, and Charles Henry Bryant. He later became President of
the Colón Division of the UNIA (*DG*, March 8, 1971)[11]
Such recognition of the national contribution of the West
Indian community was to come only after years of self-
imposed and externally enforced marginalization of the Caribbean people. On the one hand, language, colour, and cultural
barriers separated West Indians and Panamanians, and this
distinction was later enforced by the tenets of racial exclusive-
ness proposed in 1941 by President Arnulfo Arias. He decreed
that people of non-Latin ethnicity should not be considered
Panamanian, and citizenship was available only to those who
could pass an exam in Spanish and in the history and geography

of Panama. By this time, the legal disadvantages of non-citizenship were palpable and the descendants of West Indians were in any case becoming assimilated to Panama society. But for their elders, groupings such as the British West Indies Welfare Association and the British Service Committee served, by virtue of their ex-UNIA personnel and their functions, as outgrowths of the activities of the Garvey movement in its heyday.

Costa Rica

Garvey's second visit to Panama was made in early 1921, as a sequel to his Cuba visit. After Garvey left Santiago de Cuba for Kingston the "Antonio Maceo" developed mechanical difficulties and he had to transfer to another ship. From Kingston, he went on to Costa Rica where he was greeted with "wild jubilation" by the fifteen thousand people at the Port Limón wharves to welcome him. As it was evident that a holiday mood would pervade the port until Garvey had gone, and in order to have three waiting banana boats loaded by the many West Indian dock workers, the United Fruit Company, who owned the wharves and the hinterland plantations, played a two-faced card — conciliating their workers and buying the company goodwill, at the same time that their business did not suffer. It arranged a special train to take Garvey and his entourage to San José, the capital, with stops at major towns on the way, and also arranged for him to be received by President Acosta. The company also put on special trains to bring in Garveyites from outlying areas to Port Limón, and furthermore, provided a launch to take him to Bocas del Toro, across the river into Panamanian territory where they also had banana holdings. (Martin b, 83). The Company was, however, profoundly distrustful of Garvey and the financial support the Black Star Line scheme attracted from Garveyites, and was supplying the U.S. State Department with details of the investment deposits made by their employees to the BSL. (Cronon a, 88-89)

In fact, as the Bocas del Toro Divisional representative to the 1920 UNIA Convention revealed, many difficulties had been put in the way of the UNIA there by the UFC.

"They have done everything in this world to prevent our organizing . . . . The place is so situated that they own entire territories of land and houses . . . . The United Fruit Company has sent their diplomatic agents all along the lines to prevent us from organizing . . . . The ministers . . . . controlling the various churches, get in contact with the people and tell them they must not allow any meetings to be held in the churches owned by the United Fruit Company. They get a small salary of $75 per month from the United Fruit Company and they are allowed to ride on the train on a pass. Knowing the United Fruit Company is opposed to the movement . . . . and knowing that the United Fruit Company can take away their passes and cut off the $75 a month . . . . they have not stood by the people . . . ." (Willis, representative to the 1920 Convention in Hill d II, 516)

The Bocas del Toro Division included thirty-six miles of territory on the Costa Rica side of the Sixola River and thirty-seven miles inside Panama.

Garvey's visit in 1920 served, however, to inspire not only the twenty-three valiantly struggling Costa Rica branches but also filled native Costa Ricans with a new respect for West Indians as they now saw that "los Negros" had a leader. (Jacques Garvey a, 63)

While in Bocas del Toro Garvey was told that he would not be allowed to land in the Canal Zone, which was American territory. He went, however, to Colón, on the edge of the Canal Zone in Panamanian territory. He spoke there, as well as in Panama City.

"Where Liberty Halls could not hold the crowds, he spoke at theatres, and bullrings; even those were packed to overflowing. In all the Spanish-speaking countries, many natives attended the meetings, some out of curiosity; others, readers of the Spanish section of the *Negro World;* therefore, it was necessary to have Spanish interpreters for parts of his speeches. (idem.)

From Panama, Garvey returned to Jamaica where he spent the next two months in, eventually, successful efforts to get a visa to return to the United States. During this time he also visited Belize, the capital of British Honduras, and Puerto Barrios and Guatemala City in Guatemala. (64)

No other organization was to champion the cause of West Indian migrants in Central America as did the UNIA. Garvey's personal experience of what it meant to be a migrant worker, coupled with his bold programme of self-determination played an important part in making the UNIA a force around which migrant workers would organize themselves in a region dominated by U.S. companies, ruthless oligarchies and cheap labour.

BSL Delegation in Cuba

Chapter Eight

Communism and the Garvey Movement

A very important and controversial question concerns the relationship between the Garvey movement and the communists. Whilst in different countries there were specific problems facing local Garveyites and local communists, the broader question which must first be established is the theoretical one of the relationship between the national liberation movement and the international working class movement.

The specifically racial character of Garveyite nationalism was a reaction to centuries of slavery, colonialism and capitalist exploitation. This process involved the brutal enslavement of African peoples, their loss of territory, their arbitrary dispersal throughout the New World, the suppression of language, culture and kinship patterns and their victimization under the inhuman conditions of plantation slavery and the pernicious stigma of racial inferiority.

As is evidenced by the repeated expressions of Africa-consciousness in the New World prior to Garvey (Clarke *in* Clarke b), Garvey's 'race' nationalism responded to a deep-felt psychological, social and political need. At the same time, his exclusive equation of 'race' with 'nation' was scientifically and historically unsound, even though such an equation has historically been one of the criteria in the process of state-formation. It has been stated that:

> "The concept of race as a biological category does not coincide with the concept of ethnos (or nation) as a sociological category, yet many communities that are

racial in their origins (e.g., Negroes in the U.S.A. or the coloured people in South Africa) prove to be social categories in almost the same degree as ethnic communities . . . . the concept of language as a linguistic category does not coincide with the concept of ethnos either, yet we know how important the role played by language is in the formation and existence of ethnic communities." (Mozlov & Cheboksarov, 19)[1]

Garvey's equation was further complicated by the dispersal of African peoples throughout the globe — which is why he sought to regularize the geographical jigsaw by positing the necessity for Black political power in Africa; and yet another complication was the miscegenation of Africans with other races, particularly in the New World. (Miscegenation among Africa nationalities on the continent was not an issue which, as a New World African, he took into account).

Despite the untenability of his equation, he spoke for and agitated on behalf of peoples linked by racial affinity, and linked as well by a common experience of racial and economic oppression, only varying qualitatively in different parts of the world. Garveyism, therefore, represented a liberation movement in that it rejected colonial oppression and exploitation, actively sought to reclaim lands and economic resources, and fought against the cumulative disinheritance of millions of Africans both inside and outside the continent of Africa. Because of its geographic spread, it was a liberation movement in its time, with its own peculiarities.

However, the revolutions that have taken place in Africa, Asia and the Caribbean point to the fact that this struggle to uproot the colonial legacy requires an alliance between the national liberation movement and the international working class movement. In the early decades of this century colonialism disrupted the traditional way of life and economies of the colonial peoples and created conditions that brought into being an immensely important new factor in the world revolutionary movement: the national liberation movements in the colonies.

Contesting the conventional view prevalent in the Second Communist International that this movement was of small or secondary importance, Lenin wrote:

"But this is not so. It (the national liberation movement) has undergone great change since the beginning of the twentieth century. Millions and hundreds of millions, in fact the overwhelming majority of the population of the globe, are now coming forward as independent, active and revolutionary factors. It is perfectly clear that in the impending decisive battles in the world revolution, the movement of the population of the globe, initially directed towards national liberation, will turn against capitalism and imperialism and will perhaps play a much more revolutionary part than we expect. It is important to emphasize the fact that, for the first time in our International, we have taken up the question of preparing for this struggle." (Lenin c, 481-482)

Lenin's remarkable foresight established the

"theoretical basis for the alliance of the revolutionary working class and national liberation movements on a world scale, so notable a feature of our times. But his ideas were put forward at a time when the imperialist powers still held firm and apparently stable domination over practically the whole of Asia and Africa, and it was many years before they were fully understood or developed . . . . even for that matter in the Communist International itself." (Lerumo, 41-42)

This continues to be a point which needs emphasizing. Simultaneously, it has taken several decades for this truth to be gradually recognized by millions of people in the course of the struggle for national economic and cultural independence, which is essentially a struggle against imperialism and neo-colonialism. But more millions need to be convinced of this necessity.

The UNIA and International Communist Bodies

At the Second Comintern Congress in 1920, Lenin stressed the vital importance of the national question in his Premilinary Draft Theses on the National and Colonial Question:

"Communist parties must give direct support to the revolutionary movements among the dependent nations and those without equal rights (e.g., in Ireland, and among the American Negroes, etc.), and in the colonies." (Lenin b, 148)

Not long before his death, Lenin reiterated the importance of this issue:

> "I have already written in my works concerning the national question, that an abstract conception of nationalism is absolutely worthless. Distinction should be made between the nationalism of an oppressed nation, the nationalism of a large nation and the nationalism of a small nation.
>
> Speaking about the second type of nationalism, we, the nationals of a great nation, show ourselves almost always in historical practice guilty of untold numbers of outrages and, what is more — we do not even observe that we are perpetrating untold abuse; it should suffice for me to cite my own Volga recollections to show with what contempt we treated non-Russians; a Pole is always referred to as 'Polak', a Tartar is sarcastically counted a count, a Ukrainian — a 'Kohkol', a Georgian and other members of the Caucausian nation — a 'Capcasian man'.
>
> For this reason the internationalism of the oppressing nation, or of the so-called 'great' nation . . . . should depend not only on the formal observation of equality among nations, but also of such inequality by which the oppressing nation, or of the so-called 'great' nation . . . . would compensate for that inequality which actually exists in life." (Lenin a, 142-3)

In many colonial countries, Africans constituted an oppressed people, stigmatized by fraudulent theories of inferiority and class exploitation.

At the fourth Congress of the Comintern[2] in 1922, the intervention of the U.S. delegation, among whom were John Reed[3] and Claude McKay,[4] contributed to the following positive resolutions recognizing the legitimacy of the Black anti-colonial and anti-imperialist struggle:

(i) The fourth Congress recognizes the necessity of supporting every form of the Negro movement which undermines or weakens capitalism, or hampers its further penetration.

(ii) The Communist International will fight for the equality of the white and black races, for equal wages and equal political and social rights.

(iii) The Communist International will use every means at its disposal to force the trade unions to admit black workers, or, where this right already exists on paper, to conduct special propaganda for the entry of Negroes into the unions. If this should prove impossible, the Communist International will organize the Negroes in trade unions of their own and use united front tactics to compel their admission.

(iv) The Communist International will take steps immediately to convene a world Negro Congress or Conference. (Document, 30 November 1922 *in* Degras a, 401)

As a response both to the fact that in the 1920's, the UNIA was an important anti-colonial movement, and to Garvey's imprisonment in 1925, a declaration of solidarity for the UNIA was issued by the Moscow-based Peasant International. This body had come into existence in 1923 when the first International Peasant Conference was convened in Moscow on October 10. Attended by one hundred and fifty-eight delegates from forty countries, this conference decided that the KRES-INTERN (as it was otherwise called) was to "establish and maintain firm ties with cooperatives and economic and political organizations of the peasants of all countries" and to "co-ordinate peasant organizations and the efforts of the peasants to realize the slogan 'Workers' and 'Peasants' government." (*in* George Jackson, 71)

Their document of support was signed on behalf of the International Peasant Council by representatives from Poland, France, Czechoslovakia, Bulgaria, Germany, U.S.S.R., Norway, Sweden, the Indo-China colonies,[5] Spain, Japan, the United States and Italy. This document read in part:

"The capitalists realized that the movement led by
Garvey, the movement for Negro independence, even
under the modest slogan of 'Back to Africa' contained
the embryo of the future revolutionary movement
which, in alliance with the workers and peasants, is to
threaten the reign of capital. And the American government decided to smash Garvey's organization by killing
him politically as a leader, by drowning him in a flood of
mud-slinging calumny. The American capitalists did
not shrink from staging an outrageous judicial comedy
accusing Garvey of 'grand larceny' . . . . The whole of this
trial was an orgy of revengeful capitalism bent on
destroying the man who had ventured to raise his hand
against the robbers, and who has organized millions of
colonial slaves. The International Peasants Council
(KRESINTERN) has proposed to all Negro organizations to take up immediately a campaign for the
liberation of Marcus Garvey as the victim of political
and racial revenge. But this is not enough. We appeal
not only to the Negro masses, but also to the peasants
and to their faithful allies, the workers of all countries, to
join their voices in protest against this contemptible
outrage perpetrated upon the Negro movement, to
demand the liberation of Garvey and to put an end to
the indignities to which the Negroes are subjected." *(in
NW, 7 November 1925, 10)*

The position of this document was so supportive that the
Negro World published it as part of the international campaign
for Garvey's release from Atlanta Penitentiary.

However, the Sixth Congress of the Comintern held in
September 1928, declared war against both Garveyism as well
as Gandhism. It described Gandhism as "an ideology directed
against the revolution of the popular masses. Communism must
fight against it relentlessly." On Garveyism it stated:

"Garveyism, at one time the ideology of the American Negro petty bourgeoisie and workers, and still
with a certain influence over the Negro masses today,
impedes the movement of these masses towards a
revolutionary position. While at first advocating
complete social equality for Negroes, it turned into a

kind of 'Negro Zionism' which instead of fighting American imperialism advanced the slogan 'Back to Africa'. This dangerous ideology, without a single genuinely democratic feature, which toys with the aristocratic attributes of a non-existent 'Negro Kingdom', must be vigorously resisted, for it does not promote but hampers the struggle of the Negro masses for liberation from American imperialism." *(in Degras b, 519)*

This sectarian position was also reflected in the agitation of George Padmore, who was at that time a member of the Communist Party of the USA and a functionary of the international communist movement. He wrote:

". . . . the struggle against Garveyism represents one of the major tasks of the Negro toilers in America and the African and West Indian colonies . . . . It must be strongly resisted for it is not a help but hindrance to the mass Negro struggle for liberation against American imperialism." (Padmore b, 125)

These ideas were fundamentally wrong and sectarian and contributed to a deterioration in the relations between communists and nationalists in the anti-colonial struggle.

The background to this was the "Thesis on the revolutionary movement in colonial and semi-colonial countries" adopted by the Sixth Congress of the Comintern. While its preamble endorsed Lenin's "Thesis on the National and Colonial Question" adopted by the Second Congress, the analysis of the political role and character of the national bourgeoisie in colonial territories was also sectarian and its recommendations on strategy and tactics dogmatic and divisive.

The document, however, made a useful distinction between various trends in the national bourgeoisie in colonial countries.

"One part, more especially the commercial bourgeoisie, directly serves the interest of imperialist capital (the so-called comprador bourgeoisie). In general, they maintain, more or less consistently, an anti-national, imperialist point of view, directed against the whole

> nationalist movement, as do the feudal allies of imperialism and the more highly paid native officials. The other parts of the native bourgeoisie, especially those representing the interest of native industry, support the national movement; this tendency, vacillating and inclined to compromise, may be called national reformism. . . . *(in* Degras b, 538)

It then went on to warn:

> "An incorrect understanding of the basic character of the party of the big national bourgeoisie gives rise to the danger of an incorrect appraisal of the character and role of the petty-bourgeois parties. The development of these parties, as a general rule, follows a course from the national-revolutionary to the national-reformist position. (541)

As such it proposed that

> "The correct tactics in the struggle against such parties as the Swarajists and Wafdists[6] during this stage consist in the successful exposure of their real national-reformist character. These parties have more than once betrayed the national-liberation struggle, but they have not yet finally passed over, like the Kuomintang, to the counter-revolutionary camp. There is no doubt that they will do this later on, but at present, they are particularly dangerous precisely because their real physiognomy has not yet been exposed in the eyes of the masses . . . . It is necessary to expose the half-heartedness and vacillation of these leaders in the national struggle, their bargainings and attempts to reach a compromise with British imperialism, their previous capitulations and counter-revolutionary advances, their reactionary resistance to the class demands of the proletariat and peasantry, their empty nationalist phraseology, their dissemination of harmful illusions about the peaceful decolonization of the country and their sabotage of the application of revolutionary methods in the national struggle for liberation.
> The formation of any kind of bloc between the communist party and the national-reformist opposition

> must be rejected; this does not exclude temporary
> agreements and the co-ordination of activities in parti-
> cular anti-imperialist actions, provided that the activi-
> ties of the bourgeois opposition can be utilized to
> develop the mass movement, and that these agreements
> do not in any way restrict communist freedom of
> agitation among the masses and their organization.
> (idem.)

An Indian communist has commented:

> "Why the sixth congress made such a sharp sectarian
> turn from the earlier policies of the Comintern . . . . is a
> matter on which full light has not been thrown to this
> day . . . . The most plausible explanation seems to be the
> betrayal of the Chinese revolution by the Kuomintang
> and Chiang Kai-shek in 1926, in which tens of thou-
> sands of communists and other democrats were simply
> butchered by the onslaught of counter-revolution led by
> Chiang Kai-shek." (Sardesai, 66)

To this explanation, however, needs to be added the fact that
the working class in the colonial countries was very weak, and
the Communist Parties young. But they tended to over-
estimate their strength relative to both the petty bourgeoisie
and the national bourgeoisie who led the anti-colonial movement.

So sectarianism further alienated progressive sectors of the
anti-colonial movement at the same time that the movement
was coming under sharp attack from the centres of power. From
these leftist perspectives, some argued that Garvey had turned
conservative and he has even been branded as the father of
reactionary Black nationalism. But these interpretations are
not justified and reflect a myopic approach to Garveyism.

For this reason, the 1978 Programme of the Workers' Party of
Jamaica stated that Garveyism "recognized, even though
instinctively, the need for a national movement based on the
alliance of the proletariat and the petty bourgeoisie albeit under
petty bourgeois leadership . . . ." However, in its anti-colonial
thrust, it "failed to link up our national movement with the
international workers and communist movement, and while on
some occasions recognized the world historic significance of the

October Revolution, on other occasions fostered anti-communism." The objective and subjective reasons for this failure generally are that firstly, "objectively the social basis of the Garvey movement in the aspirations of the racially oppressed African peasants and petty bourgeoisie opened it to anti-communism." Secondly, the colonial and imperialist powers zealously sealed off territories under their control from communist ideas. The reformist sections of the ruling class preferred to promote Fabian socialist ideas such as those espoused by the British Labour Party. "What is more, they had a lively appreciation of the deep religious traditions of the people and effectively utilized the newspapers and the parsons to spread the virus of anti-communism widely and deeply" especially from the rural pulpits. On the subjective level, the specific experience of plantation slavery out of which Garveyite nationalism sprang, erected strong barriers to strengthening the national movement by an alliance with an international movement centred on the working-class, a stratum from which slavery and indentured wage labour had psychologically, though not objectively, alienated New World Blacks. A further subjective factor was that Garvey himself "had been personally alienated by the extent to which the American and British imperialists had succeeded in infecting" the national working-class with "racist and chauvinist attitudes." (WPJ, 34-36). To this analysis should be added the sectarianism instigated by the 1928 Sixth Comintern Congress.

The UNIA and the Communist Party of the U.S.A.

Garvey's main personal experience with communists came in the United States. And of this experience he was to write in 1925, while in prison,

> "Communism among Negroes in 1920-1921 was represented in New York by such Negroes as Cyril Briggs and W.A. Domingo,[7] and my contact and experience of them and their methods are enough to keep me shy of that kind of communism for the balance of my natural life . . . . The American Negro is warned to keep away from communism, as it is taught in this country . . . ."
> (Garvey h, 333-334)

However, in his early years in the United States he was in close contact with anti-war left groups, and in 1919, an intelligence report claimed that Garvey "associates with the left wing and I.W.W. elements." *(in* Elkins b, 79). The IWW — the Industrial Workers of the World, popularly known as the 'Wobblies', was a radical-syndicalist organization founded in 1905 by progressive elements in the American labour and socialist movements, headed by Eugene Debs, Daniel DeLeon and William D. Haywood. The IWW was very active in the second decade of the century and, after 1910, made special efforts to recruit Black members and to combat racism. However, the IWW adopted a simplistic approach towards the organization of Black workers, thinking that the race problem would be solved spontaneously in the course of the class struggle. Analysing this position in later years, Philip Foner declared that the IWW failed to

> "recognize the Negro question as a special question, and its lumping of the problems of Negro workers with those of all workers, was quite in keeping with the trend in radical circles of this period . . . . that you might not be able to achieve a Socialist revolution without proper and specific attention to something as vital, as central, in our country as the Negro question, was not perceived either by the Socialist Party or the Socialist Labour Party. That a simplistic approach might even hinder the efforts to organize the Negro Workers was overlooked."
> (Foner a, 49-50)

The same erroneous approach characterized leading spokesmen of the Communist Party of the USA which was formed in 1919. So that the Garvey movement in its own early years faced another fledgling movement which would make its own mistakes on this question and which would itself have to struggle against racism within its own ranks from top to bottom. And it was some time before the American communists applied a Leninist approach to the national question. That approach recognized the national question as a specific historic problem brought about by slavery which could not be brushed aside until the working class came to power.

White American communists made efforts to apply the conclusions of the Second Comintern Congress, but in practice their work among Blacks in the 1920's and the relationship with the Garvey movement reflected serious weaknesses. In addition, advocacy of a 'Black Belt' recommended by the Comintern, whereby certain southern states would be reserved for Blacks, was too much a carbon-copy of the U.S.S.R. experience of establishing states around territorially-based nationalities. This plan was to be made irrelevant by urbanization and other demographic changes in the Black population. By the late 1940's, this theory of a separate nation was to be assessed and rejected by the C.P.U.S.A. Writing in January 1957, James Jackson observed:

> "Before the Second World War, two-thirds of all American Blacks were Southern farmers and farm workers; only five per cent (5%) are today. Now almost eighty per cent (80%) of the Black people are living in Southern and Northern cities." (James Jackson c, 158)

Thus,

> "Exhuming the corpse of a variant of the old slogan of self-determination for the oppressed Black nation in America, is self-defeating. We think life has affirmed the correctness of our Party's decision to retire that slogan a decade ago." (James Jackson b, 221)

He expanded on this theme in the following theoretical formulation:

> "A special feature of the U.S. road to socialism is revealed in the fact that their requisite preparations of the forces for fundamental social change in the system necessitates the completion of the bourgeois-democratic norms of political, economic and social development for the South in general and the Black people in particular. Furthermore, a condition for accomplishing the prerequisite unity of the American working class with its class allies for advanced social struggle is to level the main rails of the colour bar. The struggle of the Black people for the democratic goals of political,

> economic and social equality feeds into the general
> stream of the historic working class cause of which the
> Black workers are a decisive component. The multi-
> racial working class is a powerful and decisive current
> which raises the torrential power of the whole cause of
> social advance." (James Jackson a)

William Foster's biographer observed that at first Foster,
who was leader of the C.P.U.S.A. in Garvey's time, was not
"ready to drop the self-determination slogan but, he clearly
recognized the population shifts, urbanization and changes in
class structure...." and in 1959, he supported Jackson's thesis.
(Zipser, 184)

As a result of these difficulties of theoretical approach within
the C.P.U.S.A. in the 1920's and even later, communists
regarded the Garvey movement as a bourgeois one without
sufficiently recognizing its anti-colonial and anti-imperialist
content. Nor did they appreciate that the UNIA was not only an
American 'national' movement, but was an international anti-
colonial current of Blacks with diverse social and class trends.

The relations between the American communists and the
Garveyites were, therefore, complex and tortured. But the basic
difficulty for the communists stemmed from a failure to realize
(a) that to some extent, American Blacks constituted an
'internal colony' within an advanced capitalist country and (b)
that their struggle for equality had to take into account the very
recent heritage of slavery and its psychological, cultural, and
perceptual legacies. For this reason, there were two issues,
linked both historically and contemporaneously. These were
the aspirations of Blacks as a national group and the class
struggle against capitalist exploitation.

In his address to the Fourth Congress of the Third Communist International in Moscow, Claude McKay echoed sentiments felt by millions of Blacks when he said:

> "My race on this occasion is honoured, not because it is
> different from the white race and the yellow race but
> (because it) is especially a race of toilers, hewers of
> wood and drawers of water, that belongs to the most
> oppressed, exploited, and suppressed section of the
> working class of the world."

He further said:

> "In associating with the comrades of America, I have
> found demonstrations of prejudice on the various
> occasions when the white and Black comrades had to
> get together: and this is the greatest difficulty that the
> Communists of America have got to overcome — the
> fact that they first have got to emancipate themselves
> from the ideas they entertain towards the Negroes
> before they can be able to reach the Negroes with any
> kind of radical propaganda." *(in* Cooper, 93)

Foster had himself pinpointed the struggle against "this
insidious white chauvinism, in the midst of the communists
themselves." (Foster, 234). So that, on the level of the experience of the Black masses with the white working class, the
monster of racism frequently reared its head. The masses did
not know of Lenin's theory and many had not heard of the
Russian Revolution and the process of liberating subject
nationalities. What they knew was their day-to-day experience
with politically backward whites who constituted the majority
of the population. The discussion of the link between Garvey
and the world communist movement, therefore, stumbled on
this problem of the relationship between American Garveyites
and American Communists. As George Padmore was to later
accede:

> "The biggest mistake that the white Communists made
> was to attack Garvey openly and try to disrupt his
> movement before they had won confidence among the
> Negroes as a party different from the old-established
> Republicans and Democrats to which the Negroes gave
> their divided loyalty . . . ." (Padmore c, 304-305)

This aggressive approach did not contribute to joint work on
common problems between the communists and the nationalist
UNIA. Furthermore, in the 1920's in the U.S. the Garveyites
constituted a major political force among a national minority,
while the communists constituted a minor force in general
terms, but a force which often acted in the early days as if the
eve of the proletarian revolution had arrived. (Foster, 173)

By 1925, relations between the two groups had healed somewhat as communists were now supporting the UNIA in its struggles against American imperialism in Liberia, and were appealing against the unjust imprisonment of Garvey by President Coolidge's Republican regime. The American Communist Party called for black and white workers to protest against the persecution of the UNIA and the "immediate and unconditional release of Marcus Garvey." They said he should not be deported and called for the guarantee of the "full and free intercourse of American Negroes with their brothers of the African continent." (Jacques Garvey a, 173). The central Executive Committee of the Communist Party based its analysis on a recognition of the concrete anti-imperialist content of the UNIA's struggle for African independence.

This level of cooperation was to decline from 1929 due to the continuation of political clashes in addition to the new Comintern directive. In the 1930's, some changes took place which reduced the extent of the conflict. There was the weakening of the UNIA itself as a political force, a growth of communist and radical forces in struggles against the effects of the Depression, collaboration in some states between Garveyites and communists, and the mid 1930's Comintern policy directive on 'united front' action to defeat the onset of fascism. The latter helped considerably in weakening sectarianism.

The UNIA in South Africa

Another part of the world where Garvey's nationalist ideas had some impact was South Africa. Here the UNIA encountered a situation in which the African National Congress had already been founded in 1912 and the record of communists and nationalists working within the national liberation movement was being developed.

European settlement of the Cape, at the southernmost tip of the continent, commenced in the seventeenth century when it was used as a refreshing-post for ships of the Dutch East India Company. The company gradually expanded its territory. The Dutch, applying their Calvinist categorizations of "the chosen" and "the damned," over time elaborated their struggle to appropriate settlement, grazing lands and cattle from the Africans into a contest between good (themselves) and evil (the Africans).

"In 1806, as a consequence of the Napoleonic wars, the Cape Colony was taken over by Great Britain . . . . British colonialism . . . . with its organized battalions of full-time professional soldiers, and its practice of regular warfare to conquer, annex and dominate overseas colonies . . . ." continued the Dutch pattern of expelling Africans from the land and distributing it among "settlers from the Cape Colony and from Britain itself" (Lerumo, 7), in the process annexing Dutch-held territory as well. By the mid-nineteenth century, British 'native policy' "included the herding of Africans into 'locations' and the use of traditional tribal authorities as instruments of colonial policy. . . " (12)

The imperialist stage of colonialism was reached when, in 1870, vast diamond reserves were discovered, followed in 1886, by extensive gold deposits. British concern to exploit the wealth of these mineral resources, the racist dogma and land-hunger of the Dutch colonial regime, allied with the experience by both European groups of the stubborn and humiliating military resistance of the African peoples particularly during the eighteenth and nineteenth centuries, created conditions of repression and labour exploitation for the Africans rivalled only by the conditions of trans-Atlantic slavery.

In these circumstances, an internal colony with race and economic antagonisms was forged. Not only was a pool of landless Africans created in order to force Africans into slave labour and later into indentured wage labour, but European labour from England was recruited to provide the skills needed in industry. "The white Trade Union movement in South Africa dates from the end of the Anglo-Boer war of 1899-1902, although such trades as the Typos., Engineers, and Building Workers were organized previous to that." (Jones, 45). African mine workers, though not yet unionized, struck for the first time in 1882. (Lerumo, 22) Unionization of labour as well as Marxist ideas were, therefore, introduced into South Africa during the late nineteenth century, earlier than in any other part of Africa.

By 1910, with the consent of the British, the Union of South Africa was proclaimed by the Dutch. It united the "old Boer Republics of the Transvaal and the Orange Free State," and "the old British colonies of Natal and Cape of Good Hope." (Jones, 41) "The Gold Industry of the Transvaal, with its Witwatersrand gold reef sixty miles long . . . . with the town of

Johannesburg as its centre, provides the economic stimulus for the whole country." In addition, there was diamond mining at Kimberley and Pretoria, coalfields in the Transvaal and Natal, and in Natal too, extensive sugar estates, for the development of which "a considerable Indian population" had been "originally indentured." (42) Before the end of the twenties, there were already iron and steel manufacture, commercial cattle-ranching, commercial farming of cotton in addition to sugar, an extensive railway system and developed ports. As a result, in 1921, the working class was distributed as follows:

| Colour Identification | Population Totals | *Totals* Employed | Workers |
		Industry & Transport	Agriculture
Blacks & Coloureds	5,5000,000	420,000	435,000
Whites	1,500,000	145,,000	50,000

(From "Resolution on 'The South African Question' adopted by the Executive Committee of the Communist International, 1928," *in* SACP 91-92)

The glaring pay differentials on the mines during that same year were:

Identification	No. Employed	Annual Wage
Whites	21,455	£10,640,521
Africans	179,987	£5,964,528
(in Lerumo, 44)[8]		

The proletarianization of Africans, Europeans, Coloureds and Indians in South Africa had, therefore, begun before the penetration of Garvey's ideas among sections of the African intelligentsia, workers, and peasants. Indeed, it was in anticipation of the bill formalizing the expropriation of African land in 1913 which impelled the formation in 1912 of the African National Congress. (ANC, 6). Garveyism, proclaiming the universal brotherhood of black people, was therefore to encounter in the ANC an organization which sought to unite Africans of various ethnic groups against the common indignities, injustices and exploitation they all suffered. The Com-

munist Party reinforced this development by its class appeal:
"Unite as workers! Forget the things that divide you. Let there
be no longer talk of Basuto, Zulu, or Shangaan. You are all
labourers." (1918 leaflet circulated in Sesuto and Zulu *in*
SACP., 34)

In 1924, a United Non-European Congress, "inaugurated for
the purpose of protecting and furthering the educational,
commercial, political and industrial interests of the non-
European people of South Africa," was formed by an alliance of
the African People's Organization (later Coloured People's
Congress), the Cape British Indian Council, the ANC, the
UNIA, the South African Inter-Racial Association, and the
Industrial and Commercial Workers' Union. (1924 Document
32 *in* SACP , 76)

Another such example was that "Communist Party members
like J. La Guma and E.J. Khaile .... played a big part in building
up the ICU, and by 1926, four Communists were on the ICU
executive . . . ." (SACP, 84). Top ICU executives such as
Stanley Silwana, John Gomas and Brandsby Ndobi were
simultaneously members of the ANC and the South African
Communist Party. (ANC, 30, 87)

Garvey's inspiration was itself fundamental to the formation
of the Industrial and Commercial Workers Union, the ICU, "the
biggest African mass movement ever seen in South Africa."
(SACP, 84)

It was founded in 1919 after Clements Kadalie, "a mission-
trained teacher from Malawi" (Lerumo, 47), came into contact
with West Indian stevedores during the Cape Town dock strike.
Not long after the strike, some of them, including James G.
Gumbs, who was also a member of the Universal Negro
Improvement Association in Cape Town . . . . became vice-
president and later became president, a position he held until
his death in 1929. Other West Indians who came into the ICU in
its early years were James King, who became its second
chairman, a man called Roberts and another, George Deshon."
(Neame-Jahn, 1). However, by 1925, especially when the ICU
headquarters shifted from Cape Town to the "economic ful-
crum" of the country, the Rand, the greater intensity of the
ICU's involvement in union struggles, coincided with a closer
collaboration between the ICU and the Communist Party, (25) a
development which was reversed in the explusion of com-

munists from the ICU in 1926. "Kadalie himself . . . . attempted
to lay the main responsibility for the anti-Communist move at
the door of those Garveyites who were members of the ICU. . . .
But as it so happened, actual members of . . . . the UNIA were
not involved at all in the original move." (22) Indeed, Garveyite
influence was by now largely peripheral to the ICU, though
exclusive race nationalism and entrepreneurial interests tended to characterize the Garveyites within the ICU (idem.) But
the ICU eventually disintegrated by 1928 not only for reasons
of conservatism within their ranks by UNIA members and
others. Among the complex reasons for its demise was

> "its formless and all-embracing structure . . . .; the
> weakness of Kadalie and other leaders, particularly the
> tendency to substitute revolutionary platform oratory
> for mass mobilization and action; the intrigues of white
> liberals and the (International Federation of Trade
> Unions); Kadalie's fatal rift with the Communist Party
> and his misguided attempts to transform the organi-
> zation from a revolutionary organ of the masses into the
> sort of respectable and bureaucratic machine which had
> developed among the white workers and in Britain
> . . . . lengthy court proceedings following the arrest of its
> officials . . . . intimidation and violence from police and
> armed white hooligans acting in concert . . . . penetration
> by informers and provocateurs." (Lerumo, 55-56)

Meanwhile, in an environment of institutionalized racial
discrimination and segregation, as in the United States, several
of the early white socialists in South Africa had difficulty
overcoming racist concepts. In 1916, at a meeting of a precursor
organization of the Communist Party of South Africa — the
International Socialist League — one member "adduced bio-
logical evidence on the intellectual development of the native as
compared with the white," a position which was defeated,
objectively, by maintenance of the position that "there was no
native problem, only a worker's problem." In that context, the
ISL strove "to encourage the organization of the workers on
industrial or class lines, irrespective of race, colour or creed, as
the most effective means of providing the necessary force for
the emancipation of workers." Another resolution, in part,
affirmed "that the emancipation of the working class requires

the abolition of all forms of native indenture, compound and passport systems . . . ." (SACP, 26)

Attention to these issues brought about a dramatic increase in African and Coloured membership from two hundred in 1927 to one thousand six hundred in 1928. (80, 93). The Communist Party itself had been formed in 1921 through an amalgamation of six white organizations. (65) Despite its growing appeal to Africans, however, the ideological weighting of the national question and practical measures around this issue remained problems in need of resolution. By 1928, the Resolution on 'The South African Question' adopted by the Executive Committee of the Communist International following the Sixth Comintern Congress upbraided opposition to the slogan 'full and equal rights for all races', and advised that

> "the white toiling masses must realize that in South Africa they constitute national minorities, and it is their task to support and fight jointly with the native masses against the white bourgeoisie and the British imperialists . . . .

On the other hand,

> The Communist Party cannot confine itself to the general slogan of 'Let there be no whites and no blacks'. The Communist Party must understand the revolutionary importance of the national and agrarian questions . . . . to combat effectively the efforts of the bourgeoisie to divide the white and black workers by playing on race chauvinism, and to transform the embryonic nationalist movement into a revolutionary struggle against the white bourgeoisie and foreign imperialists." (SACP, 95)

Meanwhile, in the face of continuing disregard of the national question by party membership, Moses Kotane, later to be General Secretary of the South African Communist Party, was in 1934 to point out that,

> "national oppression, discrimination and exploitation confuses the class war and the majority of the African working population are more national conscious than class conscious."

For this reason, the ANC was "deeply entrenched" and its leaders extremely popular." (Kotane, 121). As such, despite intervals of weak and ineffective leadership in the twenties and thirties, the ANC was rejuvenated in 1944 by the formation of a Youth League headed by Anton Lembede, Walter Sisulu, Oliver Tambo, Nelson Mandela and others. Despite their opposition to Communism, "which they denounced as a 'foreign ideology" they were eventually to find "common ground with Communists in demanding in more positive and revolutionary ANC leadership and a turn from stereotyped and ineffective methods of struggle to radical mass action." (Lerumo, 74)

Thus, at the famous Rivonia Trial in June 1964, Nelson Mandela was to declare:

> "It is perhaps difficult for White South Africans, with an ingrained prejudice against Communism, to understand why experienced African politicians so readily accept Communists as their friends. But to us the reason is obvious. Theoretical differences amongst those fighting against oppression is a luxury we cannot afford at this stage. What is more, for many decades Communists were the only political group in South Africa who were prepared to treat Africans as human beings and their equals; who were prepared to eat with us, talk with us, live with us and work with us. They were the only political group which was prepared to work with the Africans for the attainment of political rights and a stake in society. Because of this, there are many Africans who, today, tend to equate freedom with Communism. They are supported in this belief by a legislature which brands all exponents of democratic government and African freedom as Communists and bans many of them under the Suppression of Communism Act." (Epigraph *in* Lerumo)

Garvey's Opinions on the Communist Movement

In spite of the differences between the communist and nationalist forces within the UNIA, Garvey did not ignore the valuable political contribution of communists to the worldwide anti-colonial struggle. In response to the Manifesto of the "Communist International to the Proletariat of the Entire World" put

out by the founding Congress of the Third Communist International in 1919, Garvey wrote to readers of the *Negro World*,
29 March 1919:

> "Since my last message to you, the revolutionary world
> has taken on new activities. The Russian people have
> issued a proclamation of sympathy and good will
> towards the labouring peoples of the World.
>
> Hungary has declared for a new form of government
> in alliance with Russia. All this means revolution among
> the whites. They have not yet stopped killing out
> themselves because the masses are not yet free.
>
> We are not very much concerned as partakers in these
> revolutions, but we are concerned in the destruction
> that will come out of the bloody conflict between capital
> and labour, which will give us a breathing space to then
> declare for our freedom from the tyrannical rule of
> oppressive over-lords . . . . Bolshevism, it would appear,
> is a thing of the white man's making, and whatever it
> means is apparent, it is going to spread until it finds a
> haven in the breasts of all oppressed peoples, and then
> there shall be a universal rule of the masses." *(in* Hill, d
> I, 391)[9]

There has been a tendency to argue that Garvey's early years
in the U.S. were his most radical, after which he became a
conservative. But after his deportation from the U.S. to
Jamaica, he held similar views and had exchanges with Communists. In fact, his attitude towards the Comintern could best
be described as pragmatic. For example, he allowed Otto
Huiswood, a Black field organizer of the International Negro
Congress of Labour, to advance his views on "international
labourer co-operation between white and black labour" at the
1929 UNIA Convention in Jamaica. This came in a debate
between Huiswood and Garvey during which Huiswood advanced the view of the 'Negro problem' as fundamentally a class
rather than racial issue. (*DG,* 15 August 1929, 10). He therefore
criticized Garvey for not taking sufficient account of the class
nature of society. Huiswood had put forward this view earlier on
during the Convention when he spoke "on the methods that
should be adopted for alleviating the conditions of the black
workers." (*DG,* 10 August 1929, 9) However, Garvey main-

tained that the fundamental issue of life was one of racial emancipation, and contended that Blacks should build up their own capital resources for this purpose. (DG, 15 August 1929, 10) Huiswood was correct in pointing out Garvey's weakness on the class issue, but was wrong in downplaying the racial question.

Of importance is not merely this theoretical difference, but the fact that a known communist spoke in and participated in the UNIA forum and that his views were heard by a large audience. Furthermore, Garvey's anti-colonial positions were strengthened by his political struggles in Jamaica, not only against British colonialism but against U.S. multinationals such as the United Fruit Company. In her essay on Jamaica, Nancy Cunard, rebel daughter of the shipping magnate, pointed to the exploitation of the peasantry by the United Fruit Company and observed that Garvey was "one figure that British rule had not been able to keep out of sight in the background of the Black peasantry." (Cunard, 447)[10]

It was in this anti-imperialist context that Garvey editorialized in "Russia the Hope of the Oppressed World":

> "Russia, for the last ten years, has been most active in stirring world discord among oppressed, weaker and the darker peoples. Call the Russian communists, bolsheviks or what not, the fact remains that they have been steadily carrying on their propaganda work for world disturbance in every section of the world. They have stirred India and are now stirring Africa. Year by year their propaganda grows and their dissatisfied army of oppressed people in different parts of the world.... We, as a race, have no desire to initiate war in any part of the world, we are for peace and goodwill. Nevertheless, because of our condition we shall be glad to welcome any world change that will place us in a different position to the one we now ignominiously occupy. If Russia is to bring hope, let it come. We are not parties to the Russian methods, but surely we shall be parties to the cause of relief when it is in sight." (B, 3 January 1930, 4)

The most important phrase in this excerpt is "because of our condition" — a condition of colonial domination, racism and class exploitation. Garvey's preparedness to ally himself with communism was for pragmatic considerations of effectiveness in struggle rather than theoretical agreement or disagreement with Marxist theory. A further consideration was the actual experience as to which state powers could be identified as colonial and which not. In 1930, it was not possible for him to write about the United States, or Britain, or France as the "hope of the oppressed world" because of the fact that those countries were the colonial powers and exploiters of non-Europeans races and labour power.

In September 1930, Garvey took an even more positive stand when he wrote:

> "If Russia can do any good for Africa, the Negroes of the world, when the good is done, will be thankful and grateful — so while modern writers and statesmen become nervous and agitated about possibilities of Communism under Soviet Russia, the Negro should keep his calm and equilibrium and watch for eventualities that may be to his benefit." *(B,* 27 September 1930, 4)

This tactic of exploiting to the advantage of the black race the weakening of imperialism had been consistently advocated by the UNIA. For instance, in connection with the launching in December 1919 of "a new Negro journal devoted to commerce, politics, news, industry and economics" — the *Weekly Review* — a British intelligence report had noted that, of its eight contributing editors, seven were "connected with Garvey's movement." The report had then gone on to quote from an article, 'England's Economic Position', by Arthur King in the first issue of the paper on December 13:

> ". . . . within the British Empire we must do our best to arrest production or keep it at a minimum, because we must make it unprofitable for England to hold her colonies. At the same time we must embarrass her by political agitation and propaganda in foreign countries . . . The fall of imperial England is necessary to our future." (Britain: Report)

This political line was also evidenced in the fact that Garvey published a serialized article by the Afro-American, J.W. Ford, who was the American Communist Party candidate for Vice-President. This article, "The Workers on the Offensive Against Capitalist and Imperialist Exploitation," replaced Garvey's own customary front page column in two issues of the *Blackman*, February 17 and 20, 1930. It had been excerpted from the *Negro Worker* which was edited by the then communist, George Padmore. (Hooker, 19)

For this reason, Garveyites and communists were both enemies in the eyes of the American ruling class. Indeed, some Garveyites did see themselves as part of the worldwide revolutionary movement initiated in Russia by the successful Bolshevik struggle. And on the occasion of Lenin's death, Garvey referred to him "as probably the world's greatest man between 1917 and 1924." Continuing his tribute in the *Negro World*, 2 February 1924, Garvey wrote:

"Lenin stands out greater than all because he was the representative of a larger number of people. Not only the peasantry of Russia mourn for Lenin at this hour, but the peasantry of all of Europe, the peasantry of the whole world mourn for Lenin, because he was their leader. And we also, as Negroes, mourn for Lenin. Not one but the four hundred millions of us should mourn over the death of this great man, because Russia promised great hope not only to Negroes but to the weaker peoples of the world. Russia through her social democratic system, promised a revolution to the world that would truly and indeed emancipate the souls of men everywhere. Negroes have not yet gotten to realize the effect of certain world changes. We of the Universal Negro Improvement Association who lead have studied carefully and keenly the activities of Lenin and Trotsky. ... The governments of the capitalist, the governments of the privileged class have refused to recognize Russia as a government. They are still seeking and hoping that another revolution will be enacted in Russia that will take the power and control of government out of the peasantry and pass it back into the hands of the privileged class. At that hour, all the other governments not yet recognizing Russia, will recognize her government. But we of the Universal Negro Improvement Association, as I said, had our own opinion and our own idea in the matter of the new government of Russia. And it is without any hesitancy, without any reserve, we could not but favour the existence of a social democratic government in Russia and naturally our sympathy should be with the people who feel with us, who suffer with us." *(in* Martin a, 252-253)

The importance of this speech, which through the *Negro World* reached several hundred thousand people, lies in the conscious, not instinctive, recognition by one contingent of the burgeoning national liberation movement that the Russian Revolution was on its side. The full significance of the Russian Revolution was more immediate to China and other Asian countries, geographically close to Russia. But it also served as a catalyst to anti-colonial and anti-imperialist movements in North, South and West Africa, and in Latin America.

The imperialist ruling class responded to this impetus and alliance with repression. As early as October 1919, J. Edgar Hoover, as part of his campaign for Garvey's deportation, filed a memorandum on his activities to the Department of Justice, in which he wrote: "In his paper the 'Negro World' the Soviet Russian Rule is upheld and there is open advocation of Bolshevism." (Hoover) A Jamaican landowner voiced a similar opinion, that Garvey represented a Bolshevik threat. (*JT,* 4 September 1920, 15). And from time to time in the Jamaican press similar accusations were made. (*DG,* 26 February 1925; 1 February 1927, 10)

Not surprisingly, Garvey and his supporters came under harassment, imprisonment, and in the United States, lynching as well. Nor is it a coincidence that the communists also came under harsh reprisals. Foster, in his *History of the CPUSA,* records that on November 8, 1919 "Seven hundred police invaded mass meetings celebrating the anniversary of the Russian Revolution, seizing several hundred workers." And on the night of January 2, 1920, they "struck nationally in seventy cities" at workers and communists. Ten thousand were arrested as well as leaders of the two communist parties. These raids were "carried out by Attorney General A. Mitchell Palmer and his hatchet man, J. Edgar Hoover." (Foster, 174, 175)

All the same, racism was rife and it infected the working-class movement as well. This, therefore, fuelled Garvey's own tendency to racial separatism. In a statement, Garvey warned the "Negro workingman and labourer"

> ". . . . against the present brand of Communism or Workers' Partisanship as taught in America, and to be careful of the traps and pitfalls of white trade unionism, in affiliation with the American Federation of white workers or labourers . . . . The danger of Communism to the Negro, in the countries where he forms the minority of the population, is seen in the selfish and vicious attempts of that party or group to use the Negro's vote and physical numbers in helping to smash and overthrow, by revolution, a system that is injurious to them as the white under dogs, the success of which would put their majority group or race still in power, not only as communists but as whitemen . . . . Fundamentally what racial difference is there between a white Communist, Republican or Democrat? . . . ." (Garvey h, 69-71)

When the overt and institutionalized racism of the U.S. society is taken into account, together with the scurrilous attacks on Garvey from some Black socialists in the United States like Cyril Briggs, W.A. Domingo, and Chandler Owen, and furthermore, in the context of political competition over support, Garvey's separatist position becomes understandable. It would therefore be mistaken to accept this editorial as a definitive statement of his attitude towards communism. This would be to fly in the face of the ample evidence that a basis did exist for cooperation between nationalists and communists in the fight against imperialism.

Marcus Garvey addressing a crowd in Port Limón

Chapter Nine

Contribution to African Liberation Struggles

Continental Africans were part of the millions Garvey awakened to anti-colonial political consciousness in the 1920's. So much so that Garvey had told a mass rally in Kingston in 1921 that, for him, the African question "was the highest political question in the world today and only Negroes did not know it." (*DG*, 11 May 1921, 13) Indeed, as has been pointed out, the UNIA was structured in such a way that the top offices of Potentate and Deputy Potentate had to be filled by Africans. Among the other Africans who held executive posts in the UNIA were Prince Alfred McConnely, a Ghanaian, Dr. D.D. Lewis from Nigeria, Prince Kojo Tovalou Houenou from Dahomey, and two other Liberians, Emily Kinch and Justice Dossen. (Jacques Garvey b) And as the activities of African Garveyites had very often to be conducted secretly, some organizations and individuals did not declare their identity but assumed covers such as Friendly Society Associations or even religious groups. Nevertheless, Garveyism was influential in West and South Africa where there were a number of strong divisions. In addition, Garvey had personal connections with many African students and seamen.

West Africa

"In English-speaking West Africa branches of the UNIA were established in all territories save The Gambia." (Hughes, 117) Apart from the dissemination of Garveyism in certain Nigerian towns, there were two divisions in Freetown, Sierra Leone, and another two in the Gold Coast (later Ghana), one centre being at Accra, the capital. (Cf. 129, fn. 2). Official French sources also took note of UNIA activities in Portuguese-run Guinea Bissau in 1921, while by 1923, they noted the presence of Garvey's ideas in Cameroun. (130, fn. 16). As such, the various European administrations along the West African coast had already seen the necessity of inter-colonial liaison to combat the virus. For instance, in 1922, the British Consul General in Senegal had sent a report to George Curzon, Principal Secretary of State for Foreign Affairs of Great Britain, which suggested that the stern measures taken by the French authorities against Garveyites should also be adopted by the British in their West African colonies, and that this position should be put before the Governors of Gambia, Sierra Leone, Gold Coast and Nigeria. (See Elkins a, 322-323; Hughes). The occasion for this report was the deportation from Senegal, then the centre of the French colonial administration in West Africa, of four Sierra Leonean Garveyites, among them Francis Webster, Farmer Dougherty, and H.W. Wilson. The Sierra Leoneans had been holding meetings at the UNIA branches they had established in Dakar, Senegal's capital, Rufisque and Thiès. Both these coastal towns had been important slaving ports in previous centuries and as such had been long settled by the French and were bastions of their assimilationist policy. The report also commented on a fifth person fro the United States. He was John Kamara, the UNIA's travelling Commissioner, who had previously left Dakar for the Gambia on a tour of the West African divisions.

The British Consul General, R.C.F. Maugham, noted:

> "In this person's honour meetings were held in the various established centres which were addressed by him in violent language exhorting his hearers by all means to spread the revolutionary movement which would, in the end, cast the white man out of Africa."
> (Elkins a, 322)

On the whole, though, it is thought that in British and French West Africa between 1920 and 1923, Garveyism was strongest in Lagos, capital of Nigeria. While this may be true, it may also be a notion fostered by the fact that the movement there operated comparatively openly and that there is more documentary evidence about this division than others.

In Nigeria there were Garveyite groups at widely separated British administrative centres such as Ibadan, Minna, Kano, Ilorin, Calabar, and Lagos.[1] But "there was no organized membership . . . . outside Lagos." However, "there were individuals throughout the length and breadth of the country who became either members or sympathizers. . . . although such membership was limited to West Indians, educated Southern Nigerians and other Africans of this class resident in the North." (Olusanya, 142) For at that time Africans in Northern Nigeria were "still greatly sheltered from the inroads of Western forces, and thereby to some extent, free from the frustrations of a subject people in a colonial situation." (ibid.)

The Lagos UNIA attracted professionals, both Nigerian and West Indian. Among the three hundred members listed in 1921 were lawyers, journalists, clergymen, teachers, missionaries, civil servants, technicians, merchants. This UNIA appears to have been a male preserve, reflecting the conservative, traditionalist-cum-petty bourgeois club-like character of its membership. It essentially, therefore, represented a forum for the grievances and racial self-confidence of men whose career prospects and entrepreneurial drives were thwarted by British colonial rule and racial discrimination.

The interest of West Indians in the UNIA is significant in that they constituted colonial-oriented individuals who, for the most part, had been recruited to assist the missionary and technical needs of British colonial rule in Africa, while at the same time, they harboured subjective anti-colonial sentiments because of the humiliations they suffered at the hands of their supervisors. They were provided housing accommodation usually inadequate to their family needs — cramped quarters at obvious variance from accommodation provided Europeans; their quarters were segregated from the European 'station', and they were hospitalized differently from Europeans as well as from the 'natives'. Furthermore, despite manifest ability in many cases, it was impermissible for a West Indian to be made missionary-in-charge of a station, added to which in some cases, training prepared the West Indians to serve in the subsidiary capacities of deacon and catechist rather than as fully ordained parsons. In any case, there were salary and benefit differentiations for Europeans and West Indians at the same level. Moreover, although several West Indians did much of the work in translating the Bible into African languages, credit was not publicly accorded to them. West Indian missionaries are known to have been stationed at Kano and Calabar, while several were employed as skilled technicians during the years of the expansion of the Nigerian Railway.[2]

The Lagos UNIA was, however, initiated by Nigerians, S.M. Abiodun and W.B. Euba, both clergymen, in 1920. (Olusanya, 138) Its headquarters was at Tinubu Square in the centre of Lagos Island; its president was Wynter Shackleford,[3] a Jamaican employed to an English commercial firm, and its Secretary, Ernest Ikoli, ex-teacher at King's College, Lagos who later became editor and manager of *The African Messenger*. Because of objections to the political aims of the UNIA, Ikoli subsequently resigned from the organization and was replaced as Secretary in 1922 by Reverend Ajayi of the Church Missionary Society. (ibid.) And by 1925, with the failure of the Black Star Line, the lynch-pin of the division's objectives, and the preference by the Nigerian elite for a locally-directed path to political independence, the Lagos UNIA fizzled out.

This division had in fact developed at the same time that West African nationalists led by J. Casely-Hayford organized the first National Congress of British West Africa. (Langley a, 159) These congresses, which were held in different West African capitals in 1920, 1923, 1925 and 1927, were hailed by American Garveyites as marking a forward step for African Nationalism. (Thompson, 318; Jacques Garvey b) In fact, at one of their meetings, progressive sections of the British West African Congress "recommended support for the constitutional attempt by Garvey's UNIA to get a foothold on their own mother continent by his appeal to the League of Nations." (La Guerre, 34)

It is interesting to note that both Casely-Hayford and Garvey found in Blyden a political predecessor worthy of emulation and in fact, Casely-Hayford's book *Ethiopia Unbound* (1911) owed much to Blyden's pioneering work. (Thompson, 318). At the 1922 Convention the UNIA honoured J. Casely-Hayford by making him "Knight Commander, Order of the Nile." *(DG,* 19 August 1922, 3)

Garvey's Pan-Africanist ideas which were discussed at the First National Congress of British West Africa were partially accepted by the delegates. The conclusion arrived at was that

"Garvey's politics should be ignored and the Black Star Line patronized." (Langley a, 159) This preference for the commercial aspects of the UNIA programme was also shared by the *Times of Nigeria.* (idem.) For, like certain members of the Jamaica League, the native elite of Nigeria was avowedly pro-British and they rejected what they considered Garvey's anti-colonial outbursts. The Nigerian, J. Babington Adebayo, himself critiqued that the elite "clung closely to 'the best traditions of British rule', forgetting that sometimes these 'best traditions' were not always in their own interests . . . ." (Langley a, 72). These social attitudes were reflected in the press. While the *Times of Nigeria* was, at the outset, partially sympathetic, the pro-British *Nigerian Pioneer* remained hostile to Garveyism. The latter paper was of the view that:

> "To speak, as Marcus Garvey speaks in flamboyant language, of a 'United Africa' driving out the alien usurpers of Africa, is to add fuel to the fire of racial hostility . . . ." *(in,* Langley a 161)

For this reason, the paper advised the police "to keep an eye on the Garveyites in Nigeria." (160). The colonial influence was not, however, exclusive: the *Lagos Weekly Record,* while refusing to "endorse the political programme of Marcus Garvey with its aggressive and militaristic tendencies," (idem.) went on to say:

> ". . . . we entertain no doubts whatever in the soundness of his doctrine of worldwide cooperation among Negroes for their economic and industrial upliftment." (Thompson, 37)

The Lagos elite who sympathized with Garveyism did so primarily because of the economic programme. Even the radical Ghanaian lawyer and writer, Kobina Sekyi, who sympathized with Garvey's political ideas, adopted the view of the *Times of Nigeria* when he wrote:

> ". . . . the most we can allow is to open a way for the influx of the money of the capitalists of our race in America and the West Indies in order that we may ourselves compete with the gigantic combinations that are being formed in England for the undisguisable purpose of

establishing a sort of legal or legalized monopoly of trade." (Langley a, 168)

Garvey's economic ideas fell on favourable ground "at a time when European and Lebanese competition was felt to be ruining African traders and reducing the value of produce sold by African farmers." (Hughes, 120) And this was part of the rationale underlying the UNIA's establishment of the Black Star Line and the Black Cross and Navigation Trading Company. Furthermore, African seamen and traders often came to the New York headquarters reporting "how valuable cargoes were left on wharves to rot if African owners showed any spunk in asking for better prices." (Jacques Garvey a, 34)

But, as in the Caribbean, some wealthy Africans as well as African intellectuals supported colonialism. Blaise Diagne, the Senegalese member of the French Chamber of Deputies, together with a Deputy from Guadeloupe, denounced Garveyism at the 1921 Paris meeting of the second DuBoisian Pan-African Congress. (Jacques Garvey a, 72)

Diagne's ultra-colonial attitude is indicated in a letter he wrote to Garvey on July 3, 1922:

> "We French natives wish to remain French, since France has given us every liberty and since she had unreservedly accepted us upon the same basis as her own European children. None of us aspire to see French Africa delivered exclusively to the Africans as is demanded though without authority, by the American Negroes, at the head of whom you have placed yourself." *(in,* Thompson, 103)

In Paris, Diagne's reactionary politics was the prime target assailed by the radical Dahomean, Kojo Touvalou Houenou, who had been nominated the UNIA's representative in France. (Langley a, 169) Houenou attended the 1924 Convention where he was presented to the gathering by Garvey. (Langley b, 76-77). Houenou founded a Pan-African body, the Ligue Universelle pour la Défense de la Race Noire, in that same year and became proprietor of its journal *Les Continents,* in which Garvey's speeches and accounts of UNIA meetings in the United States frequently appeared. (Langley a, 169). One of the editors of this journal was the Martiniquian-born novelist, René

Maran, who had won the coveted French Academy's Goncourt prize in 1921 for his novel, *Batouala,* the preface of which flayed the colonial system in French Equatorial Africa.[4] Much was made of Maran's literary and journalistic work in the *Negro World.* (*NW,* 15 August 1925, 4)

Through Houenou the *Negro World* reached Dahomey where the penalties for having a copy were very severe.[5] For example the 1923 Porto Novo disturbances were claimed by the French Administration to have been "influenced by revolutionary propaganda from Paris," a typical view, blaming external instigation, on the part of colonial and neo-colonial powers when faced with local uprisings and protests. The fact was that the protests in Dahomey were a response to French colonial rule, graphically retailed by Ho Chi Minh in an article published in *La Vie Ouvrière* of March 30, 1923:

> "In Dahomey, the taxes, already exorbitant for the natives, have been increased. Young people are dragged from their homes and land to become 'defenders of civilization'. The natives are forbidden to have weapons to defend themselves against wild beasts which devastate entire villages. Education and hygiene are wanting. On the other hand, no means are spared to submit the "protected" Dahomeans to the abominable status of native, which is an institution placing man on the level of beasts and dishonouring the so-called civilized world. The natives, at the end of their tether, revolt. Whereupon, there is bloody repression. Harsh measures are taken. Troops, machine-guns, mortars and warships are sent to the place and martial law is declared. People are arrested and imprisoned en masse. This is the kindness of civilization!" (Ho Chi Minh, 44)

One does not know the extent to which Garvey's propaganda contributed to the revolt but the *Negro World* certainly reached Cotonou and Porto Novo (Langley b, 73-74). In May 1931, a UNIA observer who had travelled through French West Africa wrote:

> "I have never seen a group of black people anywhere in the world during my travels that were more enthusiastic over the *Negro World,* Marcus Garvey and the Black

Star Line, than the natives of Lagoland (Togo), French
Dahomey in West Africa. If ever an uprising should start
in that part of Africa from the wholesale manifestations
of the spirit of Garveyism, I have personally observed
among the various but peculiarly united tribes, that it
would really be a fight between Garveyites and French-
men; for the noble principles of Garveyism are against
French colonial oligarchy or tyranny." (Batson)

This may, of course, have revealed more the author's enthusiasm than the actual situation, but at least it indicates that
Garveyite influence continued into the 1930's.

In 1926, the Ligue was succeeded by the Comité de Défense
de la Race Nègre of which Amy Jacques Garvey became a
honorary member. (Langley b, 73-74; Jacques Garvey b). The
Comité was itself reconstituted into the Ligue de Défense de la
Race after 1927. (Langley b, 84-85). When writing of his visit to
Paris in 1928 where he held discussions with the Ligue and
other radical groups, Garvey declared that the UNIA had
"already cemented a working plan with the French Negro by
which we hope to carry out the great ideals of the UNIA. My visit
to France is, indeed, profitable, and I do hope for great results."
(NW, 4 August 1928, 11)

South Africa

The Garveyite influence in British and French West Africa was
equally evident in South Africa where the level of political
activity was higher, what with institutionalized racism, a higher
level of industrialization than anywhere else in Africa, with the
African National Congress having been founded in 1912 and
the South African Communist Party in 1921. There were very
active UNIA divisions in Johannesburg and Cape Town which
maintained regular correspondence with the New York headquarters. (Jacques Garvey b). The UNIA had first taken root in
Cape Town, a seaport and site of the first European settlement
in the colony, and, therefore, a locale receptive to external ideas
and with a comparatively high concentration of education
Africans. Some West Indians were also based there and notable
among those in the Garvey movement were J.G. Gumbs and
Arthur McKinley.

Garvey's message was "particularly suitable in the context of growing racist oppression" and contributed to "a refusal to cowtow to the racist myths of the inferiority of black people..." As such, it appealed "to relatively cultured urbanized petiti-bourgeois strata, suffering under colonial-racist oppression" at the same time that it "found a response amongst patriarchal peasants (and strata closely connected with them) who were relatively isolated from the state machinery and from the urban classes and strata." (Neame-Jahn, 4, 5) For instance, in the Eastern Cape, Garveyism was subjected to mystic interpretation by an African non-conformist religious sect (Hughes, 112) a phenomenon not uncommon among similar churches in various parts of the continent.

The popular appeal of Garveyism is evident from the charismatic mode of a report submitted by a *Negro World* agent, J. Barnard Belman:

> "The general opinion of the black people in the Transvaal is that the Honourable Marcus Garvey is the Great King. They simply swear by him. I am sure they would go through fire and water for and with him. My sale of the paper is exceptionally good considering the fact that I have not handled them long. I am looking forward to the time when I may sell many thousands a week. There are more than one hundred and eighty-five thousand Negroes in the Transvaal alone, and our papers should have an exceptionally large sale here, considering the interest the people have in the work. *(NW,* 24 October 1925)

By this time, the mid 1920's, there were about eight UNIA divisions in South Africa and two in South West Africa (Namibia). Indeed, Garveyism exerted a formative influence on Clements Kadalie, organizer of the Industrial and Commercial Union, (Neame-Jahn,[1]) and influenced leaders of the A.N.C. such as Sol Plaatje[7] and Selope R. Thema. (Jacques Garvey a, 277-278). Garvey frequently referred to *Abanthu Batho (The People),* organ of the ANC, in his speeches, and material from it was published in the *Negro World.* Moreover, the methods of struggle adopted by the ANC prior to the 1940's — the holding of public meetings to air grievances, press publications, and the practice of making "representations for redress by means of resolutions and deputation," — were similar to those used by Garveyites. (Simons and Simons, 136) By the early 1940's, however, faced with increased repression and pressured towards radicalism by the African youth and by communists, the ANC launched a Youth League in 1944 and embarked on militant street protests.

But in the 1920's, the interconnection between the personnel of the UNIA and the ANC was marked. For example, on the occasion of the ANC acquiring a Liberty Hall in Cape Town in 1925, the *Negro World* noted that the South Africans had credited Garvey "as the pioneer and chief spokesman of all Negroes who are fighting for African redemption and repatriation." The two organizations, the *Negro World* editorialized, were "working by the same sign, and by it they cannot but succeed in arousing and unifying the Negro people." *(NW,* 19 October 1925). In fact, in May 1925, James Thaele, an ardent Garveyite and an important contributor to the *Herald,* newspaper of the Industrial and Commercial Union (but expelled from the Union around April that year), founded his own counterpart of Garvey's newspaper, calling it *The African World.* It was a weekly with the slogan "Africa for the Africans". Thaele was also involved with the ANC and had become President of the Western Cape section of the Congress in 1924. (Neame-Jahn, 30-31) The Garveyite content of the *African World* provoked "a furore among the whites" *(NW,* 19 October 1925) as is obvious from the venom of the *Sunday Times* of Johannesburg:

> A more treacherous, inflammatory, deluded and deluding publication it is difficult to imagine. In any but a British country those responsible for its publication would instantly be dealt with in swift and certain fashion.
>
> The avowed aim of the *African World* is to "free Africa from the incubus of European control" and "to instill the psychology and traits of Zaghbul Pasha in the Africa race." In its third issue, published on June 13, it had the barefaced impudence to refer to "the imperishable messsage of His Highness, Marcus Garvey — Potentate of the Universal Negro Improvement Association." Every well-informed native knows Marcus Garvey to be an unprincipled rogue and swindler who is now

serving five years in prison for cheating the Negroes of the United States out of huge sums of money. (Garvey h, 355-356)

This hostility was echoed in the *Ilanga Lase Natal,* which timidly contended that African land could not be taken back by force since the whites were far stronger and had come here to stay. The white man was "very strong, far stronger than the native, especially in his well-developed brain . . . . It will do our cause no good at all to impress upon the native that he is as good as the white man, for this cannot be demonstrated in practice." (356)

The reason for these views may be better understood in the context of the following critique by David Jones in a paper, "Communism in South Africa" presented to the Executive of the Third International in Moscow on behalf of the International Socialist League of South Africa in 1919:

> There exists a body known as the Native Congress (ANC), with sections functioning in the various Provinces and for the whole Union (South Africa). This is a loosely organized body composed of chiefs, native lawyers, native clergymen, and others who eke out a living as agents among their compatriots. This body is patronized and lectured by the Government. It has weekly newspapers in the various provinces, 'Abanthu Batho' in Johannesburg, 'Ilanga Lase Natal' in Natal, etc. These are subsidized by Government advertisements, which are often withdrawn when the Congress drops the role of respectable bourgeois which it normally tries to assume. It is satisfied with agitation for civil equality and political rights to which its members as a small coterie of educated natives feel they have a special claim. But to obtain these the mass cannot be moved without their moving in a revolutionary manner. Hence, the Government is dubious about the Congress, and the Congress draws back timidly from the mass movements of its own people. (SACP, 53)

However, this view was "disparaging" and later assessed within the Party as showing "no inkling of the enormous and revolutionary significance of these rights in a country such as

South Africa." (Lerumo, 42) But at that time, it was not surprising that *Umsebenzi* or *The South African Worker*, weekly organ of the Communist Party of South Africa and published in Cape Town, felt that Garvey's demand for a native republic was a bourgeois one. *(NW,* 8 November 1930, 4). The Communist Party proposed in 1929 an Independent Native Republic with the aim of

> Self-determination of the African peoples, i.e., their complete liberation from imperialist as well as bourgeois and feudal or semi-feudal rule and oppression, whether 'British' or 'South African', and wresting of power for a Workers' and Peasants' Soviet Republic wholly independent of the British or any other Empire, and comprising all the toiling masses, whether native or otherwise, of the Union and adjacent protectorates, etc., under the leadership of the working class, with the slogan of 'An Independent South African Native Republic as a stage towards the Workers' and Peasants' Republic, guaranteeing protection and complete equality to all national minorities (such as Europeans): leading to the reconstruction of the country and rehabilitation of its people on a non-Imperialist, Socialist basis. (SACP, 104)

For all that, however, there was a close though troubled relationship between nationalists and communists which surfaced, among other instances, in June 1930 when the South African UNIA was reported to have organized a protest meeting against the Riotous Assemblies Act at Verde which was attended by one thousand two hundred Africans. *(B,* 23 August 1930, 6). Garvey was of the opinon that "some of our boldest leaders of nationalism have appeared" in South Africa. *(B,* 6 September 1930, 4). And of the communists who had made inroads among the Blacks, Garvey wrote a sympathetic piece in September 1932:

> ". . . . in the absence of anything that will be more hopeful for the native it is preferable that they (sic.) become communists than be entirely left to the mercy of the heartless Africaaners who have no other purpose

but to deprive the people of land, of life and of liberty.
(NJ, 15 October 1932, 2)

The passage is not only important from the standpoint of "sympathy" towards communism but demonstrates how necessity drew anti-colonial nationalists and communists closer in practice particularly when the fight against oppression intensified.

That several of the UNIA divisions were still functioning in the late 1930's is evident from several obituaries in the Garvey press. In the November, 1938 issue of the *Black Man,* there was an obituary for Mrs. Edward Zibi of the Fairview Farm Division in Tsolo. In June 1939, there was another for Mr. M.C. Kehane of the Lichtenburg Division, as well as for the Jamaican Arthur McKinley, described as a well-known agent of the *Black Man* in Cape Town. And in 1938, before his departure from London for Canada, Garvey instructed his secretary to "pay special attention to all South African letters particularly those from the people to whom we have issued Charters." (Garvey e)

East Africa

Garveyism also affected East Africa and parts of Central Africa, so much so that the history of East African protest was deeply marked by Garvey's influence. (Davidson, 287-288) There is the often quoted statement made by Jomo Kenyatta to C.L.R. James, that

> "In 1921, Kenya nationalists unable to read would gather round a reader of Garvey's newspaper, the *Negro World,* and listen to an article two or three times. Then they would run various ways through the forest carefully to repeat the whole, which they had memorized, to Africans hungry for some doctrine which lifted them from the servile consciousness in which Africans lived."
> (James, 397)

Harry Thuku, the East African Nationalist and secretary of the East African Association, had corresponded with Garvey and the latter's programme was discussed by the Muganda, Daudi Basudde, in his journal *Sekanyolva.* (King, 78). When Thuku was arrested in March 1922 and twenty-five Africans protesting his detention were shot dead in 'Sharpeville fashion', Garvey organized a massive protest meeting in New York where the massacre was denounced and a protest lodged with the Colonial Office. (idem.) In a telegram to Lloyd George, Prime Minister of Britain, dated 20th March 1922, Garvey stated:

> "Four hundred million Negroes through the Universal Negro Improvement Association hereby register their protest against the brutal manner in which your government has treated the natives of Kenya, East Africa. You have shot down a defenceless people in their own native land exercising their rights as men. Such a policy will aggravate the many historic injustices heaped upon a race that will one day be placed in a position to truly defend itself not with mere sticks, clubs and stones but with modern implements of science. (*in* Hill d iv, 576)

Garvey's influence in Kenya was to intensify. By the mid 1930's, the Kikuyu people of Kenya were to form a separatist church, and in about 1935, they brought in one of Garvey's bishops to train and ordain pupils. It was from these churches and schools that the Mau Mau grew. (Jenkins, 119)[7]

Central Africa

In the Belgian Congo Afro-American missionaries distributed Garvey literature. (*NW,* 27 October 1923) One white missionary informed the *Negro World* that "Bantu workers, who were being exploited by Belgian capitalists on the railroad, had initiated a strike for higher wages and better working conditions and that they were thrilled at a chance to join the movement initiated by Marcus Garvey, the Jamaican black, who had a plan to organize the black people of the world into one big union...." (ibid.)

By 1930, the *Blackman* was still publishing reports on the Belgian Congo, French Equatorial Africa and Portuguese West Africa. And in July 1930, two African nationalists from the Belgian Congo arrived in Jamaica to see Garvey. Educated in South Africa, they were also officers of Clements Kadalie's Industrial and Commercial Workers Union of Johannesburg and were en route to Faircroft College, Birmingham, on a Trade

Union course. (B, 5, 12 July 1930). They travelled incognito and the police harassed Garvey to find out their identity and the nature of their mission. The London correspondent of the *Blackman* who interviewed them after reported that "their visit was directly connected with the scheme initiated by certain influential African chiefs and princes to induce Marcus Garvey to visit the continent." (B, 5 July 1930, 1, 9)

The Belgian imperialists had been ruthless in their exploitation of the Congo and any opposition to them resulted in severe punitive raids against the African population. After two weeks of consultation and travel in Jamaica the African emissaries issued a statement

> "imploring the sympathy of the outside world for the native sons and daughters of Africa whom white intruders . . . . have subjected to the greatest injustice while they extract super-profits from our raw material resources . . . . . Tribal chiefs, Kings and Princes throughout Africa are now propagandizing against this oppression and forcible proletarianization of the native masses who have been forced by poll tax and hut tax to abandon their pastoral life and become wage slaves for French, Belgian and British landlords . . . . Not only in Africa, but in the West Indies and elsewhere, the Negro must unite to recover his lost place in the world . . . . Subjugation of the Negro is a crime which must be stamped off the face of the earth. To this end we are working and we plead for the help of all those who share the same view." (B, 16 August 1930, 1)

The wide influence of Garveyism in Africa, therefore signals that the current data on UNIA groups there is probably underestimated, as also is popular response to the hope of salvation from colonial bondage through a black messiah.[8] So far as is known to date, in around 1920, the UNIA had eight branches in South Africa, three in Sierra Leone, two in the Gold Coast, two in Liberia, two in South West Africa, and one in Nigeria. (Martin a, 16) Even as late as 1939, three Africans out of a total of seven graduated from Garvey's School of African Philosophy: O.J. Nwanolue of Onitsha, Nigeria; H. Illitintro from Cape Province, South Africa; and D.S. Musoke of Kampala, Uganda. (BM, 1938, 1939 passim)

While some of the UNIA groups throughout the continent may have been ephemeral, it is clear that Garveyism played a vital role in the early African nationalist struggles, and this gives the lie to colonialist propaganda that African militants were non-existent and that colonized Africans, satisfied with the colonizer, had nothing to do with Garveyism. It also shows the real political connections Garvey developed in Africa.

There existed also an incipient power struggle between New World and African Pan-Africanists. Among the causes of such differences was the New World Blacks' Western "civilizing" concepts regarding Africa.

The Italo-Ethiopian War

> "The Psalmist prophesied that Princes would come out of Egypt and Ethiopia would stretch forth her hands unto God. We have no doubt that the time is now come. Ethiopia is now really stretching forth her hands. This great Kingdom of the East has been hidden for many centuries, but gradually she is rising to take a leading place in the world and it is for us of the Negro race to assist in every way to hold up the head of Emperor Ras Tafari."

This was part of the editorial in the *Blackman* of November 8, 1930 marking the coronation of Emperor Haile Selassie of Ethiopia. Garvey also forwarded a telegram on behalf of the UNIA acknowledging this signal event. The coronation climaxed a year of unrest in colonized Africa brought about by the world economic depression, and for Garveyites, the coronation pointed the way towards the future political independence of Africa, the greater part of which was subject to the rule of foreign white sovereigns.

For reasons of its Biblical associations, the mere name 'Ethiopia' excited powerful emotions in the hearts of Christian Blacks. Now, in this ancient, revered and romanticized Kingdom was added the contemporary symbol of a Black Emperor. Already in 1922, when the Persian Consul General in the United States had read to the Third UNIA Convention a message from the Ethiopian rulers inviting members to return to Africa, "wild demonstrations" were said to have taken place in the assembly.

(DG, 6 Sept. 1922, 13) The invitation was in fact taken up by individual Garveyites and the *Negro World* of April 9, 1932, continued to advocate that UNIA members should "establish bases" in independent African countries like Liberia and Ethiopia from which to spread the gospel of "a united and liberated Africa." But the growth of anti-colonial consciousness among Africans world wide was to be fuelled from another and more cataclysmic source.

The Italo-Ethiopian war broke out in 1935. But its roots went further back. Benito Mussolini, Italy's fascist dictator, was intent both on securing an overseas empire for Italy and on avenging the shame of Italy's defeat in a previous colonial adventure.

> "The Ethiopian victory at the Battle of Adowa on March 1, 1896, was total . . . . The invaders sustained a defeat so crushing that the government of Crispi, confronted by 'a wave of national grief and indignation' was compelled to resign." (Ethiopia, 8)

After his ascent to power in 1922, Mussolini continued to be haunted by the 1896 "ten thousand dead and seventy-two cannon lost." (ibid.) At Walwal in December 1934, a clash was provoked between Ethiopian frontier guards and encroaching armed Italian bands "to spring aggression against Ethiopia and to use the incident as a shield to perfect the fascist military machine that was to go into action less than a year later." (4) By the end of the war in 1941, the Italian fascists had left the country in ruins. Seven per cent of its population and its entire intelligentsia had been killed. The figures presented by the Ethiopian Government to the Paris Peace Conference in 1946 showed the following losses:

Killed in action	275,000
Patriots killed in battle	78,500
Women, children & infirm killed by bombing and poison gas	17,800
Patriots killed by court martial	24,000
Persons who died in concentration camps	35,000
Persons who died from privations following the destruction of villages	300,000

Further to this, the Black Shirts massacred thirty thousand people on February 1937, after an attempt in Eritrea Province on Marshall Graziani's life. In addition, two thousand churches and religious establishments were burnt; five hundred and twenty-five thousand homes were destroyed; five million beef cattle, seven million sheep and goats, one million horses and mules, and seven hundred thousand camels were either slaughtered or confiscated. (Ethiopia, 19-20) Ethiopia was trampled.

By 1935, Garvey had relocated himself and the UNIA headquarters in London. Soon after his arrival in London, Garvey conducted a series of public meetings in Hyde Park on the Ethiopian war and was reported to have attracted large audiences. *(BM,* July 1935, 12) And some time in October 1935, he addressed a meeting of the West Kilburn Liberal Association in London on "The Crisis in Abyssinia'. *(BM,* October 1935, 15) The organizer, Ernest J. Core, in turn presided over some of Garvey's Hyde Park meetings. (idem.) Along with C.L.R. James and George Padmore, Garvey contributed an anti-fascist statement to the *Left Review* which had published the answers of one hundred and forty-eight writers and poets of Great Britain on fascism. *(PT,* 20 August 1938, 4)

In every issue of the *Black Man,* Garvey continued his agitation on behalf of the Ethiopian resistance. In addition to writing political and historical articles on the war and Ethiopia, he also wrote poems like "Il Duce — The Brute" and "The Smell of Mussolini" which expressed his indignation at Italian fascism. The significance of Garvey's political poems can be judged by the fact that he wrote at least fifteen poems on this topic (Martin d) and that they were memorized and recited at Liberty Hall assemblies. In fact, the Liberty Halls were meeting places for front rank solidarity with the Ethiopian resistance, together with such organizations as the Peace Movement of Ethiopia, founded in Chicago in 1932 and the Ethiopian Club of Cleveland, Ohio, which grew up in the Garvey tradition. (Essien-Udom, 48-49) Both the *Blackman* in London and *Plain Talk* in Jamaica raised funds through their columns and in fact, the latter journal was commended by Dr. Bayen, Haile Selassie's personal representative in the United States. *(PT,* 7 August 1927, 7)

Indeed, throughout the West Indies, mass demonstrations of solidarity with the Ethiopian people had taken place. (Weisbord b) In Jamaica, the UNIA together with *Plain Talk* a weekly newspaper, whose proprietor, T.A. Kitchener, was a Garveyite, were also ardent protagonists of the Ethiopian resistance to Italy. *Plain Talk* reported that "a group of Jamaicans had decided to launch a series of meetings throughout the entire Island, for the purpose of getting together a Battalion of stalwart men to defend the Ethiopian frontier from the Italian invaders," and that the contingent would be assisted by a Black organization in Chicago. *(PT,* 20 July 1935) *Plain Talk* also published the text of a speech by Amy Jacques Garvey which she had delivered at a mass meeting in support of Ethiopia at the Kingston Liberty Hall on October 13, 1935. She concluded that the war would result in the "rising up of the peoples of Africa in one great effort to emancipate themselves." (*PT,* 26 October 1935, 5) At this rally, a petition signed by no fewer than one thousand four hundred persons was drafted asking the British Government to allow Jamaicans to enlist in the Ethiopian army so as "to fight to preserve the glories of our ancient and beloved Empire." (Weisbord, 35-36) This petition was sent to the Colonial Secretary through Governor Denham. However, the British Government did not accede to the suggestions of the Jamaican Garveyites, evidently seeing in their request the seeds of opposition to their own colonial rule. In fact, one British official wrote contemptuously of the "bellicose sons of Ham in Jamaica, so anxious to serve two masters." (idem.)

Demonstrations also took place among Rastafarian groups in Kingston, though these were not reported in the press, which preferred to report only those acts which gave cause for villification of the movement. (For insights into the evolution of the Rastafari movement in Jamaica, see Smith et al, 4-5; *DG,* 17 Aug. 1934, 12; and Chevannes) Of their demonstrations, Randolph Williams, who later became a prominent figure in Jamaican cultural life as an actor and broadcaster, wrote:

> "There were sections that wanted to send a petition to His Majesty the King of England praying that they be allowed to recruit men in Jamaica to be sent to Abyssinia to do service in the Ethiopian ranks, others wished to collect money to send to Ras Tafari to be used for the purchase of arms, some decided upon just praying three times per day for the triumph of Abyssinia." *(in* Weisbord, 35-36)

Likewise played down by the press was the fact that demonstrators in Kingston beat up Catholic nuns and priests and caused Catholic schools to close down. (Scarlett) In Montego Bay, two thousand persons demonstrated against Italian aggression. Similar developments occurred in Guyana, Barbados, Trinidad, St. Kitts and other West Indian territories, attesting to the solidarity with the Ethiopian resistance in the region. The Italian invasion of Ethiopia was to the English-speaking Caribbean what the Spanish Civil War was to Europe and Latin America as far as its impact on mass consciousness and activity were concerned.

But the attitude that Garvey took toward Haile Selassie after he arrived in England from Ethiopia was bitterly criticized by his opponents as well as some of his supporters. As early as October 1935 he had argued that the Italo-Ethiopian war "affords only another example of what unpreparedness means to a people." *(BM,* October 1935) Less than two years later he stated the following in his main critique of the Emperor.

> "He kept his country unprepared for modern civili-
> zation, whose policy was strictly aggressive. He resorted
> sentimentally to prayer and to feasting and fasting, not
> consistent with the policy that secures the existence of
> present-day freedom for peoples whilst other nations
> and rulers are building up armaments of the most
> destructive kind as the only means of securing peace . . . .
> and protection . . . . The results show that God had
> nothing to do with the campaign of Italy in Abyssinia, for
> on the one side we had the Pope of the Catholic Church
> blessing the Crusade, and the other, the Coptic Church
> fasting and praying with confidence of victory . . . . It is
> logical, therefore, that God did not take sides, but left
> the matter to be settled by the strongest human
> battalion." *(BM,* January 1937, 8)

Garvey's criticism was a substantial one and was to be repeated by an official Ethiopian assessment forty years later.

> "A million men were called to arms. Ill-equipped and
> virtually untrained in the arts of modern warfare, they
> were now pitted against a four hundred thousand man
> mechanized fascist army with unlimited quantitites of
> the most modern arsenals of destruction." (Ethiopia,
> 15)

Garvey's sharp attack on Ethiopia's feudal structure showed that he was not one to idealize tradition, and was in favour of modernization. He saw that Ethiopia was in dire need of rapid development, and correctly stressed the need for the Emperor to take cognizance of the advantages to be gained from a Pan-African perspective:

> "If Haile Selassie had negotiated the proper relationship with the hundreds of millions of Negroes outside of Abyssinia in Africa, in South and Central America, in the United States of America, in Canada, the West Indies and Australia, he could have had an organization of men and women ready to do service, not only in the development of Abyssinia, as a great Negro nation, but on the spur of the moment to protect it from any foe."
> *(BM,* July-August 1936, 4)

In this article Garvey also criticized the Emperor for leaning on white advisers and for refusing to receive a black delegation that had been seeking audience with him. (6) Clearly, too, Garvey saw the UNIA as the already extant international black organization with which the Emperor and the anti-fascist forces could treat, and which could mobilize widespread support for the cause. However, the UNIA of the late 1930's was a shadow of what it had been in the 1920's. Instead, in 1937, Dr. Bayen was put in charge of organizing the Ethiopian World Federation Inc., in the United States. The E.W.F. acted as a clearing house for financial and other forms of contribution to the resistance and set out among other things to promote "love and goodwill among Ethiopians at home and abroad, and thereby, to maintain the integrity and sovereignty of Ethiopia." *(in* Essien-Udom, 49) Although the creation of the E.W.F. was not a direct response to Garvey's criticisms, it was a moderate start in the direction explicitly stated in the *Black Man.*

However, to some, Garvey's criticism of Haile Selassie was tactically inopportune at a time when the major issue was the organization of the broadest possible support to defeat Italian fascism, and he lost support in the United States, the Caribbean and parts of Africa because of these criticisms.

It was rumoured that because of these critical remarks Garvey was not made a patron of the International African Service Bureau led by C.L.R. James and George Padmore.

Among the patrons chosen were Mr. D.N. Pritt, Victor Gollancz, Sylvia Pankhurst, Nancy Cunard from the British left, while membership was drawn from Ethiopia, Sudan, West and East Africa, Trinidad and Tobago, and British Guiana. Associate membership was reserved for Europeans. (*The People,* 16 October 1937, 5)

Garvey saw the Ethiopian war within the wider context of African decolonization, and because he appreciated the need for the alliances that helped to defeat fascism, in 1936 he contended that in the event of an Italo-German alliance the "Negroes of Africa and the British colonies" should support Britain because "Mussolini must be smashed with his mad idea of a new Roman Empire. Germany must be prevented from regaining the African Colonies." *(BM,* July-August 1936, 1-2) But this strategic alliance with Britain against fascism did not imply that Britain was let off the hook. That she was also an imperialist power, Garvey clearly remembered:

> "We have greater hopes for Africa, an Africa that will be free as Europe is free, an Africa that will rise out of her conquered Dominions and Colonies into a free and independent state . . . . Let Mussolini, Hitler, and the British Statesmen who think of Africa only in terms of conquest remember history shows that large numbers of men may be conquered today, but they generally become free tomorrow." *(BM,* November 1934, 2)

A by-product of Garvey's stand on the Italo-Ethiopian war is that some historians have allowed superficial comparisons between Garvey's oratorical style and those of the fascist leaders, Hitler and Mussolini, to mask his efforts to rally support for the Ethiopian cause and his clear-cut anti-fascist position. (Cronon a, 198-199) This stems from taking out of context a statement Garvey made in 1937 about Mussolini having copied the UNIA programme. Garvey had pointed out that Mussolini had "made a war on the last sovereign state in Africa for the specific purpose of economic expansion for the Italian people and their industrial development." (*BM,* December 1937, 11) He then went on to criticize Emperor Haile Selassie for keeping Ethiopia unprepared for the Italian invasion which had been in the making for some years. And he

went on to tell his audience that had he received the full support
necessary for the advancement of the UNIA programme:

> "Mussolini would have been scared to touch a black
> Kingdom because we would have had an intellectual,
> political, scientific power, that would have demanded
> respect from every man, but you lost your chance and
> Mussolini took it up and Hitler took it up. The UNIA
> was before Mussolini and Hitler were ever heard of.
> Mussolini and Hitler copied the programme of the
> UNIA — aggressive nationalism for the black man in
> Africa." (12)

The impression given that Garvey was some early fascist is
perverse when his own words indicate that he was concerned
only with the tardiness of black men in realizing what Mussolini
and Hitler were up to in Africa. It was a statement of an anti-
colonial character. Only the naive or those whose writings serve
imperialist interests can confuse Garvey's nationalism, which
was a response to the world-wide oppression of African peoples,
with the fascist ideology. (Howe)

Other Pan-African Spheres of Work in London

A number of West Indians and Africans in London were also
involved in the solidarity work with Ethiopia. Among them were
George Padmore and C.L.R. James of Trinidad. Padmore
worked with James on the International African Friends of
Ethiopia on whose executive were I.T.A. Wallace Johnson,
(Spitzer) secretary of the West African Youth League, J.B.
Danquah (Gold Coast), Jomo Kenyatta of the Kikuyu Association, Amy Ashwood Garvey (Garvey's first wife) and the
Grenadian politician and writer, T.A. Marryshow. (Nation, 6
November 1959, 2; Asante, 45) Padmore reorganized this
group into the International African Service Bureau which
became the nucleus of Pan-African struggle. James then
became editor of their paper, the International African Opinion,
which was succeeded by the journal, Pan-Africa. Garvey knew
of their activities but there does not seem to have been much
collaboration with them.

Dr. Harold Moody, a Jamaican who headed the League of Coloured People was also active in this front. (*See* Hooker, 41-42) The League was founded in 1931 and their journal *The Keys* was first published in July, 1933. This was succeeded by the *Newsletter* which seems to have had as wide a circulation as Garvey's *Black Man*. Unlike the International African Bureau which had as its primary purpose, the decolonization of Africa and was left-wing in orientation, the League was reformist, seeing decolonization in an evolutionary sense. Some of the men associated with the League were W. Arthur Lewis, (St. Lucian Nobel Prize winner for Economics) who was once editor of *The Keys,* and a member of the Executive Council, H.W. Springer, A.A. Thompson and later Learie Constantine who became President.[9] Hastings K. Banda of the Nyasaland African Congress was President of the Liverpool Branch of the League. (*Newsletter,* August 1942, 111) Jomo Kenyatta was also a member of the Executive. (*JT,* 15 Aug. 1931, 7)

Political differences between Padmore's group and Moody's emerged at a meeting on Africa of the League of Coloured Peoples in June 1937. One of the main speakers whom Moody had invited was Sir Donald Cameron, an ex-Governor of Nigeria who spoke on "Indirect Rule". (*PT,* July 24, 1937, 11) The speech was reported to have provoked heated discussion especially among the African delegates who pointed out how repressive the system was and that the "Chiefs were being used as catspaws by the white officials to facilitate the exploitation of the Africans in the interest of British Imperialism." The ex-Governor's indignant response to this criticism was resented by Padmore who moved a resolution to censure him. In his indictment, Padmore also blamed the League for inviting people "who despite their professions of sympathy and love for Africans, are fundamentally Imperialists in mentality, and obsessed with the ideology of racial superiority, which was most blatantly demonstrated by Sir Donald Cameron." This resolution was supported in speeches by Wallace-Johnson, Kenyatta, and the Guyanese, T. Makonnen. This 1937 debate reflected two political trends — one a radical-nationalist trend and the other reformist.

The antagonism between the League and the Pan-African group was repeated in the League's relationship with the West African Students' Union. The Union had been organized in the

mid 1920's by H.C. Bankole-Bright, a Sierra Leonean doctor,
J.B. Danquah (Gold Coast), Ladipo Solanke (Nigeria), and it
had co-operated with the National Congress of British West
Africa during the 1920's. (Asante, 45) Solanke himself was an
ardent West African anti-colonialist who had completed in
1927, a manuscript entitled "United West Africa (or Africa) at
the Bar of the Family of Nations". (Thompson, 30)

"WASU inherited the mantle of the National Congress and is
credited with the creation of some of the leaders of post-war
Africa." (31) Garvey had a more vital relationship with WASU
than he did with any other group in London. Solanke was in fact
a personal friend of his.[10] The first WASU hostel acquired in
1928 was said to have been donated by Garvey who also
assisted in financing their journal. (Coleman, 18; Fryer, 325)
Solanke in turn supported Garvey's efforts. He contributed an
article to the July-August 1936 issue of the *Black Man* where he
discussed "Life and Conditions in West Africa".

By the early 1930's, however, WASU had its offices in a
London hostel called 'Aggrey House', which Dr. Moody is
purported to have placed at their disposal. But the students
soon discovered that it was being financed by the Colonial
Office who wanted to keep an eye on some of the militant anti-
colonialists among them. As such, the students withdrew from
it, protesting against the British Government's surveillance of
African students and denouncing Dr. Moody in the strongest
terms as being a "tool of British Imperialism". (Thompson, 335-
338)

The League, nevertheless, presented memoranda to the
Moyne Commission, calling for self-government and adult
suffrage, with Moody himself writing several to the Colonial
Office and in 1945 assisting in the organization of the Fifth Pan-
African Conference. (Geiss, 736) And in 1939, while Garvey was
ill, the League addressed a letter to him in recognition of his
work and in their obituary of July 1940, they characterized him
as "one of the greatest men our group has so far thrown up".
(*Newsletter,* July 1940, 63-64)

A group of ladies of the African Motor Corps on parade in New York City during the convention of 1925.

Part III

Pioneer of Jamaica's
Socio-Political Advancement

Chapter Ten

Persecution and Setbacks

During his life, Garvey faced considerable odds. He built a movement which constituted one of a growing number of anti-colonial forces. This meant that he was a target of official machination and abuse.

Harassment in the United States

J. Edgar Hoover's memorandum from the U.S. Department of Justice to Special Agent Ridgely, dated October 11, 1919, is revealing as to the plans being conceived in order to deport Garvey, and the urgency with which it was considered desirable to have this done. Hoover was "transmitting herewith a communication which has come to my attention from the Panama Canal, Washington office, relative to the activities of Marcus Garvey. Garvey is a West-Indian Negro and in addition to his activities in endeavouring to establish the Black Star Line Steamship Corporation, he has also been particularly active among the radical elements in New York City in agitating the negro movement. Unfortunately, however, he has not yet violated any federal law whereby he could be proceeded against on the grounds of being an undesirable alien, from the point of view of deportation. It occurs to me, however, from the attached clipping that there might be some proceeding against him for fraud in connection with his Black Star Line propaganda. . . ." (in Hill d II 72). The U.S. authorities had therefore developed a plan to imprison Garvey and discredit him.

Indeed, in that same month and year, Garvey survived an attempt on his life in New York city. Three shots were fired by the would-be assassin, a Southern unemployed Black named Tyler. The first shot went wild; the second "passed so near his temple, that the skin was seared" and the "third bullet hit his leg". Tyler "committed suicide" a few days later under questionable circumstances, after having admitted he had been sent to do the crime and would not bear conviction alone. (Jacques Garvey a, 37-8)

It is not known in whose pay Tyler was. What is however known, from F.B.I. files and the intelligence and colonial archives of the British, French, Belgian and South African governments, is the magnitude of the efforts made to contain the spread of Garvey's anti-colonial teaching. A listing of dates will condense only the significant episodes of his harassment in the United States between 1920 and 1927.

1920 — Tried for criminal libel during the first 1920 Convention. Delegates raised the U.S. seven hundred dollars for his legal expenses. Legal harassment continued to precede Convention so as to stymie this major gathering. (Martin a, 187)

1921 — Efforts made to keep him out of the U.S. by denying him a visa.

1923 — Convicted for alleged mail fraud. Refused bail. This led to cancellation of the annual convention. Garvey spent three months in the Tombs prison. Eight prominent Black Americans, some of them members of the National Association for the Advancement of Coloured People, sent a letter to the Federal Attorney General of the U.S. urging him to hasten the trial of Garvey, deport him and exterminate the UNIA. A "Garvey Must Go" campaign was launched. Garvey's trial took place in a court charged with malicious hysteria. Garvey was indicted on the assumption that an empty envelope with a rubber-stamped return address of the Black Star Line contained either a letter or a handbill from him. No other officer of the UNIA was convicted. Garvey was sentenced to five years' imprisonment and fined one thousand dollars. Before the trial he had been released on bail put up by the UNIA to the tune of fifteen thousand dollars raised from among his supporters. (Jacques Garvey a, 124)

— Indicted for failure to make an income tax return in 1921. He had to stay out of the country for five months because of difficulty in getting a visa. The objective was to pin him on this charge if the Black Star Line charge failed to secure a conviction.

1925 — Garvey's appeal was dismissed. He was sent to the Federal prison in Atlanta.

1927 — Released from prison and immediately deported to Jamaica, never again to return to the U.S.

This sequence, of course, continued until his death. But in relation to his trials in the United States, Armin Kohn of the law firm Kohn and Nagler stated:

"In my twenty-three years of practice at the New York Bar, I have never handled a case in which the defendant has been treated with such manifest unfairness and with such a palpable attempt at persecution as this one." (Garvey h, 150)

A similar scenario was to face Garvey in Jamaica.

British Colonial Containment

Apart from restricting his travel and residence possibilities, the colonialists sought to cripple the finances of the organization. In the American tradition of public guest lectures and lecture tours made by celebrities for fee-paying audiences, Garvey raised money by his public speeches, but it was not possible to raise much in Jamaica because of the poverty of the people and the absence of such a tradition. His potential audience in the United States was estimated at twelve million Blacks, as compared to Jamaica's less than one million.

As for the people's poverty, Garvey knew this from his own experience, from observations as he travelled through the rural districts, as well as through personal correspondence. In 1928, he claimed to have received, since his return to Jamaica in December 1927, some two thousand letters in which requests were made for assistance, "such as 4/- to pay a month's room rent, 3/- to buy tools . . . . 6d. for some trifles . . . ." (*JT*, 15 December 1928).

Garvey not only had difficulties on the local level but also the task of holding together an international organization with a distinctive anti-colonial character in a very self-conscious British colony. The problems attendant on this were many. In the first place, overseas communication was poor and his organizational correspondence was tampered with by the Jamaican and American postal authorities. During early 1929, U.S. postal authorities intercepted some forty thousand letters sent out by Garvey to his supporters. (*JT*, 2 February 1929, 18). These letters requested the recipients to answer certain census-type questions in connection with the UNIA programme. One American postal official stated that the letters had been withheld until more facts were available about the Scheme for fear that Garvey would use the lists "in some plan that may be fraudulent." This harassment was another source of difficulty for a great deal of money was 'lost' in the mail, and Garvey was working very hard towards the Sixth UNIA Convention in 1929. (Jacques Garvey b).

Secondly, his international impact was considerably weaker in Kingston than Harlem, for very obvious reasons. The most important reason was that in the 1920's Harlem was, in a sense, the cultural and political capital of the Black World, while Kingston was a relatively insignificant colonial city. It was in Harlem that Garveyism became important although Kingston had been the birthplace of the UNIA. Another crucial factor is that from Harlem, contact with UNIA divisions in Africa and even in the Caribbean was easier. In Kingston, Garvey had to re-work the entire underground network he had created, the operation of which took a much longer time.

And although he telegraphed his weekly front-page articles to the *Negro World*, this could not substitute for his own presence in the United States and the cohesive effect this could have had on the organization which was in crisis due to internal splits.

UNIA Factionalism

While in the United States he had been able to hold together the contending factions among the second-tier leadership, but after his deportation, these conflicts broke out as attempts were made to take over the New York headquarters. Indeed, Garvey was to charge that even "during his imprisonment the organization had fallen into the hands of men without character and integrity who within ten months made the organization in the States bankrupt." *(DG,* 6 August 1929, 17) For example, some persons in charge of UNIA business projects in New York appropriated the equipment *(B,* 7 June 1930, 9), all of which staunched the flow of revenue into the headquarters. In July 1930, E.B. Knox, Garvey's representative in the United States, was deposed and replaced by Madame DeMena of Nicaragua after a gun-duel in New York in which Knox had attempted to take over the *Negro World* facilities. (Samad)

Indeed, the schisms and factionalism that beset the organization after Garvey's imprisonment came to a head with the existence of two UNIA organizations after 1929. Leaders of the American organization such as Henrietta Vinton Davis, William Ware, George McGuire and Lionel A. Francis wanted the headquarters to remain in New York and continued in the UNIA (incorporated) 1918, while Garvey became President General of the UNIA (unincorporated) 1929, which issued a new charter. (Cronon a, 154) But the UNIA (1918) under Lionel Francis, a Trinidad-born physician, who was elected leader in 1932, was but a pale reflection of what the U.S. organization had been under Garvey in the 1920's.

Apart from the personal anguish which these splits and defections occasioned Garvey, he was to suffer a massive financial loss as the result of the two competing UNIAs. Isaiah Morter, a very wealthy Garveyite from British Honduras, died in April 1924. He bequeathed an estate of three hundred thousand U.S. dollars to the UNIA. This was eventually awarded to the UNIA (1918) group of American Garveyites. Morter's estate included some two hundred and ten square miles of British Honduras, with an island and twenty-three residential lots in Belize. Twenty-five dollars was left for his wife (Ashdown, 50), who contested this on grounds of insanity, but her claim was "quietly disposed of" and "lengthy litigation ensued regarding both the identity and the legality of the intended beneficiary." (idem.) Garvey visited British Honduras in 1929 to consult his lawyer, Frans Dragten, over the case. But by then the UNIA in British Honduras was also weak, though the Black Cross Nurses "continued to provide a much needed service for the poor and unemployed." (ibid., 51) Eventually in 1931, the Chief Justice of British Honduras ruled in favour of the American UNIA led by Lionel Francis and not Garvey's UNIA based in Kingston. This ruling was upheld by the Judicial Committee of the Privy Council (London) in 1935. As Amy Jacques Garvey bitterly commented:

> ". . . . the court awarded judgement in favour of a UNIA Inc. of New York City, which was represented by one man, without members and with no programme for African redemption" (Jacques Garvey a, 260-1)

Furthermore, some highly placed UNIA leaders, not pre-pared to make sacrifices, had used promises of good salaries made in better times as a basis for their own self-advancement. In addition to the outstanding case of George Marke, several other UNIA officials had demanded their full salary, regardless of the state of the organization and the fact that Garvey had himself gone without pay from time to time. (Cronon a, 153-5)

In 1929, G.D. Marke, the Sierra Leonean First Deputy Potentate for the UNIA, brought a case against the organization claiming back-pay. (155) The Chief Justice of Jamaica attemp-ted to "enforce a New York judgement of . . . . US$30,000 against the Jamaica UNIA, its properties and assets. (Jacques Garvey a, 204) On reading the proceedings of the case, which was given extensive verbatim coverage in the Jamaican press (DG and B, August 1929, passim), it becomes quite clear that the real intent of the Chief Justice was the economic and political strangulation of the Jamaica UNIA which was now Garvey's headquarters. It was, indeed, significant that there were numerous other divisions, in fact one thousand branches, incorporated in America but no effort was made to recover the American judgement against any of these. (DG, 22 August 1929, 6)

Financial Losses and Strains

As a result of the Marke case, the Liberty Hall at 76, King
Street, Headquarters of the Kingston UNIA, was sold in auction
for one thousand and fifty-five pounds.[1] But after an appeal it
was restored to the UNIA. (B, 13 December 1930, 5) However,
a levy was made on the UNIA press (DG, 29 August 1929, 14,
18), and the following items seized: four typewriters, one soda
fountain, one large ice-bucket, three tables, one cask, one
ammonia cylinder, one ice chest and one cream chest, three
small glass cases, six tables, one drum, one old piece of horn,
nine musical stands, two hundred flags, one hundred and fifty
bulbs, four large flower pots, one Singer sewing machine, one
rocking chair, one organ, one arm chair, one wicker chair, one
Ford car — all kept at Edelweiss Park. Reams of paper stored at
the printery at 5-7 Peters Lane were also seized (DG, 24 August
1929, 6)

The Court proceedings had gone on during the 1929 UNIA
Convention and emphasized the political pressure brought to
bear on the organized assembly of Blacks, the first since
Garvey's release from prison in the United States. Indeed, in
the midst of the Convention, Garvey was fined twenty-five
pounds for contempt of court for allegedly instructing a clerk
not to show UNIA books. (DG, 8 August 1929, 1) As usual, the
delegates attending the Convention paid the sum. But their
tempers were high, as what was happening in Kingston was a
carbon-copy of his past New York experience. Anger was so
great that at one of the sessions of the Convention, a youth who
was accused of spying was nearly beaten and was only saved by
the intervention of Garvey himself.

By February 6, 1930, the Gleaner was reporting that Garvey
along with Lady Henrietta Vinton Davis had been charged
"with submitting to the Collector General a false return in
respect to entertainments held at Edelweiss Park during
August 1929", and on the next day reported that an Egyptian
statue worth two thousand U.S. dollars and a Moroccan mirror
worth five hundred U.S. dollars had been stolen from his
"Somali" residence on Lady Musgrave Road. The same issue of
February 7th, also carried the story that Garvey had been
banned in Cuba and all branches of the UNIA there closed.

But already in September 1929, Garvey's seat on the Kingston and St. Andrew Corporation Council had been declared vacant after he had been convicted and imprisoned for contempt of court for advocating legal reform. The *Blackman,* in its editorial written by T.A. Aikman and published the very next day following the KSAC vote, took up arms. The editorial read in part:

> "The Muncipal Council recorded yesterday, the most atrocious and unprecedented deed of evil-daring yet witnessed in the annals of the Colony. To understand the prejudice and hate .... and the vice, concentrated in this crowning act of a series of criminal efforts to injure a single individual and destroy the influence of his leadership among the people of his race is to realize the limits of human depravity .... the Council presided over by Mayor (sic) Seymour and his successor Mayor (sic) Vaz, were a group of vagabonds entirely opposed to the welfare of the country .... There exists no doubt whatever that the hands of the government are thrust deep in this hostile attempt to shed innocent blood and that they have instructed and used the Director of the Public Works and Supt. Medical Officer in furthering... this evil intent on Mr. Garvey and in aiding the evil designs of Garvey's opponents .... We have concluded also, and we feel justified in the conclusion that the Council has all along been fighting Seymour's election to the Legislative Council, against Garvey, and that the Government have joined the issue in favour of Seymour". *(B,* 14 January 1930, 2)

This lucid and scathing indictment of the government's actions and underhand measures earned for Garvey, Aikman and Beecher the charge of sedition. *(DG,* 14 February 1930, 18, 21). Garvey was sentenced to six months hard labour, Aikman to three and Beecher was acquitted. *(DG,* 22 February 1930, 1, 6) This judgement was given in spite of the fact that the editorial was written by Aikman who was in charge of the newspaper. For the judge, Aikman was "more or less the tool of Garvey." *(in* Jacques Garvey a, 217) Yet since his release from prison in December, 1929, Garvey had been on an island-wide tour and was so completely taken up with campaigning that he only wrote the Saturday front-page article. The Resident Magistrate, A.K. Agar, in sentencing Garvey, told him:

> "You have been recently convicted of contempt of court. You attempted to flout the authority of the courts of this colony. You were punished for that. It has had no effect on you. You, now through your paper have attempted to flout the authority of the government. If you are not stopped in the course, serious harm may arise among the people of this colony. A person in your position as head of an important organization, one that could be used for an immense amount of good, has used that as a channel to create trouble in the island."
>
> *(DG,* 22 February 1930, 1, 6)

Meanwhile, the Great Depression of the 1930's also had a negative effect on the Garvey movement. It resulted in the impoverishment,unemployment and starvation of thousands of Garveyites and the closure of many Liberty Halls. It succeeded in accomplishing the task of emasculation attempted by official intimidation and legislation against the UNIA.

The frustration of that period in Jamaica was aptly recorded in a dialect poem, the first stanza of which summed up the situation tersely:

> What ah sinting deh pon de lan'!
> Depression grip de bes' ah man;
> Faver lacka de wul' ah dun
> Man no hab time fe cut an' run
> *(JT.,* 16 January 1932, 25)

And in 1933, because of financial troubles, the press on which the *New Jamaican* was printed had to be sold. (Jacques Garvey a, 230). But this was only part of the financial problems that Garvey was experiencing during this period. In December 1934, "the mortgagee foreclosed on Edelweiss Park, and put it up for sale at public auction, at which a relative of his (the mortgagee) bought the place for even less than the accumulated principal, interest, taxes, etc. An agreement was made by which the UNIA remained as tenants, as the new owner had no immediate use for the property". (Jacques Garvey a, 231). In fact, it is said that the property owner, one José Benjamin of

Port Maria, had wanted to sell it to the UNIA for a nominal price, but Benjamin, having died before this transaction was effected, the property passed to Alderman Dolphie. To keep the premises, the UNIA needed to pay the market price. So eventually the UNIA moved back to King Street, where after Garvey's departure for London, S.U. Smith started a Liberty Club. (Scarlett) But when Edelweiss Park was sold off, a lot of Garvey's personal property was also auctioned. (idem.)

Attempts to resuscitate the UNIA

It was against the background of these massive financial and organizational setbacks that the November 1934 issue of the *Black Man* magazine carried a notification that

> "From November of this year the International Head-quarters of the UNIA will be located in London, England. This may come as a surprise to some people who did not think deeply enough, but outside of the USA the most important and possible place for the Headquarters of an organization like the UNIA at the present time, is London, because it is the central city of the world, not only from a European point of view, but from the point of view of Negro interests."

From the standpoint of the British control of Africa, the Caribbean, India, and other parts of Asia, this was true. But on the other hand, there were no black communities in England to sustain Garveyite forms of struggle.

One of Garvey's objectives in going to London was to reorganize the UNIA. In October 1935, the *Black Man* had listed seventy-two active UNIA divisions in Cuba, Canada, the United States, the West Indies and Central America *(BM,* October 1935, 13). This represented a great diminution of the organization's force since the 1920's.

Following Garvey's relocation, the American and Canadian divisions met in conference in Toronto in the summers of 1936 and 1937 to implement the Five Year Plan which had been drawn up at the Seventh International Convention in 1934. *(PT,* 4 September 1937, 5). Furthermore, in 1937 after the Conference, Garvey conducted in Toronto "a Regional Conference,

not only of representatives from the UNIA, but other frater-
nities." (Jacques Garvey a, 237) There he met Garveyites from
the U.S. and was introduced by the Black State Senator Diggs
of Michigan. He also met the Mayor of Toronto.

A significant move towards consolidating the UNIA was the
inauguration, after the 1937 Conference, of the School of
African Philosophy to train leaders for the UNIA. Garvey, who
was the principal, opened the School on the 1st September,
1937, with an enrolment of students from the United States and
Canada. The course which lasted until the 23rd September, was
brief but vigorous. Students had to attend classes day and
night. Classes started at 10 a.m. and finished at 10 p.m. There
were ten graduates, nine of whom became UNIA Commissioners. These graduates became official representatives of the
UNIA in North America. Preparations were also made for
degree courses lasting up to five years and an extensive
correspondence course. In discussing this educational programme the *Black Man* wrote:

> "The School of African Philosophy has come into
> existence after twenty-three years of the Association's
> life for the purpose of preparing and directing the
> leaders who are to create and maintain the great
> institution that has been founded and carried on during
> a time of intensified propaganda work. The philosophy
> of the school embodies the most exhaustive outlines of
> the manner in which the Negro should be trained to
> project a civilization of his own and to maintain it. This
> school is something positively new in the intellectual,
> cultural and general educational life of the race, and the
> UNIA from now on will use no one in connection with
> leadership who is not a graduate of the school . . . . it
> covers a wide range of over forty-two subjects touching
> vitally every phase of human life." *(BM,* December
> 1937, 4)

This was in part a response to the fragmentation of the UNIA
since the late 1920's and the emergence of other black
nationalist organizations. For whereas in the early 1920's the
UNIA had been the single most powerful black organization in
the U.S.A., in the 1930's it was one of several.

The financial target which the UNIA had set itself in 1934 was five million dollars (U.S.) to be raised in five years. However, at the Eighth Convention the financial report showed that it was very far from realizing this amount. As a result, the plans for reorganization and development faltered. Between 1934 and 1938 (June) a total of US$5,655 had been pledged and of this the total amount collected had been US$1,740.21. Garvey's salary and miscellaneous expenses from June 1935 to June 1938 amounted to one thousand U.S. dollars. (31, 16). Cash receipts from June 1935 to June 30, 1938 had been $8,914.86 and cash disbursements for the same period $7,763.-66. This left a balance of US$1,051.20. (16) A great deal of the burden of running the headquarters in London had consequently been placed on him, which even resulted in his having to pawn his wife's jewellery in order to meet pressing commitments. (Jacques Garvey a, 6). So great were the financial difficulties that Garvey was not able to send for his wife and two sons until June 1937, that is, over two years after his departure from Jamaica for England.

The UNIA Headquarters in London consisted of five employees among whom were his wife, Amy Jacques Garvey, his personal secretary, Miss Whyte, two contributing editors of the *Black Man,* the writer Eric Walrond[2] and James S. McIntyre, who was also the Chief Clerk. All were West Indians. One other employee was an English stenographer, one Miss Brooks, who was responsible for typing the correspondence courses of the School of African Philosophy and the general running of the office.

This was a far cry from the UNIA administrative apparatus of the nineteen-twenties. His personal letters indicate the nature of these difficult circumstances. Before leaving for the Eighth Convention he budgeted to the last penny for a payroll of eleven pounds per week for this staff and insisted that their work be disciplined and diligent.

> "All employees are supposed to report for work at 9.00 a.m., leave at 1.00 p.m., return at 2.00 and work each and every day up to 5.00 p.m. Any employee who is absent half an hour in any day will not be paid for the amount of time and if more than two hours in a week the same to be deducted at the end of the week. There

> should be no leave of absence during my absence and any absence from work shall not be paid for that particular time." (Garvey e)

Yet despite these severe constraints, Garvey remained as committed as ever to the anti-colonial struggle.

His strength of character was reflected in an article he wrote on the suicide of the black editor, William Monroe Trotter,[3] who had gone bankrupt.

> "We have had similar experiences like Mr. Trotter, but fortunately for us, we never contemplated suicide, but only made up our minds to fight ever harder to hold our own, not only against the opposing foes from without but the opposing foes from within." (*BM*, May-June 1934, 3)

Agitational Role of Amy Jacques Garvey

A big role in Garvey's resistance to the multiple setbacks in his political life was played by his second wife, Amy Jacques Garvey, whom he married on July 27, 1922 when she was twenty-six. (Jacques Garvey a, 189)

Her main attributes in the Garvey cause were her discipline, her sense of administrative organization, and her flair for methodical record-keeping. A Jamaican middle-class mulatto, she had been educated at Wolmers' Girls' School and had worked as a trained legal stenographer before migrating to the United States in 1918. There she put her skills to the service of the UNIA, developing at the same time into a good speaker and publicist. Single-handedly, she raised thirteen to fourteen thousand dollars in six weeks for the Black Star Line.

Energetic, determined and beyond financial corruptibility, in 1923 she edited and published Vol. 1 of *Philosophy and Opinions,* and issued a second volume in 1925. These books were intended as part of the struggle to gain public sympathy for Garvey after his conviction on trumped-up fraud charges in the United States. They did more than this. They still constitute an indispensable collection of Garvey's thoughts and ideas. The volumes were in fact commonplace in Garveyite homes and inspired many readers with nationalist zeal. Kwame Nkrumah, for instance, said,

> "I think that of all the literature I studied the book that did more than any other to fire my enthusiasm was the Philosophy of Marcus Garvey published by his wife." (*in* Jacques Garvey a, 168)

In 1925 Amy Garvey recorded her physical strain in the Garvey cause:

> "I thought I had done almost the impossible, when I was able to rush a first copy of Vol. II to him (Garvey), but he callously said, 'Now I want you to send free copies to Senators, Congressmen, and prominent men who might become interested in my case, as I want to make another application for a pardon'. When I completed this task I weighed ninety-eight pounds, had low blood pressure and one eye was badly strained. Two doctors advised complete rest." (idem.)

But she was not to have much rest as she was the central figure in the campaign for his release. She wrote many articles, gave many speeches, wrote letters, and travelled to many parts of the United States armed not ony with the ideas she shared with Garvey but also with her own self-protective Colt gun. (idem. 166).

After Garvey's death in 1940 and until hers in July 1973, Amy Jacques continued, by self-financed publications, private correspondence with UNIA members and Garvey researchers, and through political activity on behalf of the People's National Party in Jamaica, and independent organizations, to present data and to assiduously file newspaper clippings and historical documents so as to preserve the Garvey legacy — a legacy severely obscured by silence and later battered by the printed lies about Garvey. Such distortions, even among progressive people, have fulfilled colonialist plans to perpetuate the image of Garvey as a common criminal or else a nincompoop.

This ability for indefatigable dedication and self-sacrifice led Garvey to write in June 23, 1923 after being sentenced to five years of imprisonment:

> "I commend to your care and attention, my wife, who has been my helpmate and inspiration for years. She has suffered with me in the cause of service to my race, and

if I have any sorrow, it is only on her account, that I cannot be alongside of her at all times to protect her from the evil designs of the enemy, but I commend her to your care and keeping and feel that you will do for her as much as you have done for me. Her tale of woe has not been told, but in my belief that truth will triumph over wrong, I feel sure that a day will come when the whole world will know the story of her noble sacrifice for the cause that I love so much." (Garvey h, 218).

MARCUS GARVEY, D. C. L.

in robe of office as President General Universal Negro Improvement Association.

Chapter Eleven

Choice Between Local and International Politics

Return to Jamaica

Deportation from the United States in November 1927 came after two years and nine months in the Atlanta Federal Prison. Garvey had spent his fortieth birthday in prison. Still quite young, he could look back over a decade in which his labours had contributed to the emergence of a mass movement. Martin Luther King Jr. was later to say that Garvey's true place in history was due to the fact that he was "the first man, on a mass scale, to give millions of Negroes a sense of dignity and destiny."[1] This he accomplished between his thirtieth and fortieth years. Even while in prison, his writings, which included poetry (Martin d), provided leadership and inspiration to people of African descent.

His widely publicized journey from the United States and the demonstrations of support for him along the route of his return in New Orleans, Panama and finally, Kingston, coupled with his militant pronouncements added to the fears which were rampant in local colonial circles concerning the effects of his arrival. He had reaffirmed his position before leaving New Orleans:

> ".... the programme of nationalism is as important now as it ever was. My entire life will be devoted to the support of the cause." (*DG,* 14 December 1927, 4)

When he landed in Kingston on December 10, 1927, the conservative *Daily Gleaner* reported that "Mr. Garvey's arrival

... was perhaps the most historic event that has taken place in the metropolis of the island", and "no denser crowd has ever been witnessed in Kingston." *(DG,* 12 December 1927, 3; also Nembhard, 53). So historic in fact that the *Gleaner* account was reprinted by other papers including the *Trinidad Guardian* of December 22, 1927.

After Garvey descended from the "Santa Marta", "the cheering of his followers and sympathizers can better be imagined than described." (idem.) He was welcomed by C.V. Johnson, head of the Kingston UNIA, S.M. Jones, High Commissioner for Jamaica, and Henrietta Vinton-Davis, second Vice-President of the UNIA. "It was a most enthusiastic welcome . . . . The people on the pier . . . . surrounded him . . . . After inspecting the (UNIA) guard, a band of music preceded him along Port Royal Street" as he was driven in Mr. T. Wells-Elliott's car. As he turned on to Port Royal Street where there was "a surging mass . . . . deafening cheers were raised and the remarks heard on all sides in the huge crowd showed the high esteem in which he is held by the ordinary people of this country . . . . The banners and emblems of the organization were swayed. The cheering was intense . . . ." So dense was the throng that it became "a difficult proposition" to drive up King Street and instead "the triumphal march" proceeded up Church Street. "Although at various stages attempts were made to drive the car . . . . at a fast pace, it was useless. At the crossings it had to slow down, and when approaching the Coke Chapel" where a UNIA welcoming function was planned, "the number of persons formed such a huge phalanx that they closed in on the car." Given all the "harassment" of "people jumping and shaking his hands", as Rev. Isaac Higgins, chairman of the UNIA reception described it, Garvey spoke to the crowd from the Coke Chapel steps for three minutes, but decided to postpone his address to the assembly inside. Instead the audience gave Garvey and the UNIA officials three cheers and concluded by singing "Ethiopia land of our fathers", the UNIA anthem. *(DG,* 12 December 1927, 3, 6, 19; *TG,* 22 December 1927, 5)

International Prospects and Activity

With his eyes still set on the international horizon, Garvey initially planned "to reside in London" where a "bigger and broader outlook" was possible. In fact, he entertained hopes of being allowed re-entry to the United States should the Democrats win the next election. (idem.) His primary objectives were therefore to continue UNIA work and organization. He planned strengthening the local UNIA and touring the divisions in the Caribbean and Central America. He also planned to go to Europe where he would petition the League of Nations and lobby anti-colonial groups in Britain.

But his Caribbean tour did not come off as "none of the consuls for the Central American countries would vise his passport for entry." (Jacques Garvey a, 190) He was also *persona non grata* in the other West Indian islands and British Guiana. The *Jamaican Times* had to remark that:

> "The British Government seems to still fear him and had recently refused to grant a passport for himself and his wife to go to British Guiana or any of the nearby islands." (*JT,* 5 May 1928, 16)

So that a major tactic of the colonial powers was to pin him down to Jamaica where he could be watched, and not only that — he would be out of personal contact with the main divisions of his movement. T.A. Marryshow of Grenada pertinently noted:

> "We will not be surprised to find that Jamaica is meant to be his St. Helena on authority of a powerful international combination whose interest some observers say is to keep Garvey down." (*Herald,* 11 February 1928, 8)

And the *Panama Workman* commented:

> ". . . . his freedom abroad might be restricted by strong forces but his basic ideas cannot possibly be destroyed. On this score, his future operations must remain indefinite. However, that dynamic force is at present in the island from which place he can operate with good effect . . . ." (*in Herald,* 7 April 1928, 15)

Garvey apparently took the *Workman's* suggestion, for in the face of these setbacks, he concentrated during the first three months of 1928 on building up the local membership of his organization and preparing for a European tour. Moreover, he had to cope with resettling in Jamaica.

Within a month of his arrival the Kingston UNIA was said to have increased its membership by one hundred per cent (100%). *(Herald,* 21 January 1928, 16) In February he began a six-week tour of the island and by mid-March one of his organizers, I.G. Aarons, who travelled ahead of him, had already visited twenty-three centres at which Garvey was to speak and organize branches. *(JT,* 17 March 1928, 29)

In April 1928, Garvey and his wife travelled to England where they were based until September. In London, Garvey concentrated on establishing contacts with African students and seamen, the latter being important couriers for Garvey publications, messages, and ideas generally. "For the entire period of our stay," noted Amy Jacques, "he did splendid work in organizing and financing the underground movement to all parts of Africa." (Jacques Garvey a, 191). On the public level he "spoke in Hyde Park, sent circulars to members of Parliament and some church and liberal-minded secular leaders explaining his program". (idem.) This was preliminary work for the meeting at the Royal Albert Hall on June 6, 1928. But this turned out to be a very disappointing occasion. It attracted a very small audience. Garvey accused the London press of sabotaging his efforts and the single London newspaper that reported the meeting proved itself adept at unkind sarcasm by headlining its story '9800 Empty Seats', in an auditorium which seated ten thousand, noting that "each member of the audience had the choice of fifty seats." (Cronon a, 145-6) Tellingly, the London paper responsible for this report had refused to accept advertisements about the event. No doubt the Colonial Office had a hand in this.

The Royal Albert Hall programme featured not only speakers like himself and Edward Knox, but also a soprano, Miss Ethel Clarke, an organist, Edgar Pito, and a small band. This was indeed an over-ambitious programme. (Jacques Garvey a, 192) Garvey's speech, "The Case of the Negro for International Racial Adjustment, Before the English People", was directed at the British public and was similar in content to his article

"Appeal to the Soul of White America" which he had written in the United States in October 1923. (Garvey h, 1-6) He reminded his audience of the African's right to self-determination and of Britain's role in the slave and colonial system. He pointed to the fact that the

> ".... cotton mills of Lancashire, the great shipping port of Liverpool, tell the tale of what we have done as black men for the British Empire. The cotton that you consume and use in keeping your mills going has for centuries come from the Southern states of the United States; it is the product of negro labour. Upon that cotton your industry has prospered and you have been able to build the great British Empire of today."
> (Garvey f, 17)

Garvey's appeal to the conscience of the English people was but a cry in the wilderness.

> "We want to be friends of the English people; we want to be the friends of the white race the world over; because neither the black race nor the white race nor the brown race nor the yellow race can achieve anything in the world lastingly except through peaceful methods . . . . Our attitude and our acts prove conclusively that we are not inclined to disturb the peace of the world. All we want is justice; and we are appealing to the ears of you Englishmen at home and abroad to listen to the plea of bleeding Africa." (ibid., 22)

Garvey dealt at length with his experiences in the United States, particularly the political motives for his imprisonment. This was important in combatting the propaganda that he was a common criminal. Returning to his idea of a homeland for Blacks in Africa, Garvey said:

> "At Versailles when the Peace Treaty was to be signed you called everybody in and you distributed the spoils of war to everybody. You gave to the Jew, Palestine; you gave the Egyptians a larger modicum of self-government; you gave the Irish Home Rule government and Dominion status; you gave the Poles a new government of their own. But what did you give to the Negro? (A

voice: "Nothing"). What did you do to the negro? You threw his dead body on the streets of Cardiff, smashed the coffin and kicked the corpse about and made a football of it after he came back from the War. In America, 200,000 boys' had hardly taken off their uniforms when, on parading in the streets, one of them was lynched in the very uniform of the United States which they had bled (sic.) on the battlefields in France and Flanders. Is that a just reward for service so generously given? Yet we are not sore about it; we are not vexed about it; we only want you people to know the truth; because we do not believe that the hearts of all Englishmen are bad . . . ." (ibid., 17-18).

This non-racial element of Garvey's political approach has to a large extent been overshadowed by interpretations which tend to the view that Garvey wanted nothing to do with Whites. But this is the same line of thinking which says that he wanted to ship all Blacks back to Africa. Garvey was, despite many blunders, a more sophisticated politician than that and recognized the need to gain support among ordinary voters in the metropolis of the British Empire. As he once declared, he wanted to touch

"the hearts of Englishmen and women so that those who are innocent and know not what is being done in their name may understand and reach the point where they will use their influence to see that justice is done to the darker peoples of the world." (Garvey a, 24).

From London the Garvey couple travelled to Paris in August, where the reception was much better. They were met and shown around by officers of the Comité de Defense de la Race Nègre and were briefed on conditions in the French colonies. (Jacques Garvey a, 193) Garvey later on addressed French intellectuals at the Club du Faubourg on the subject "Les Noirs devant les Blancs" ("Blacks and Whites Face to Face"). (JT, 3 November 1928, 13)[2] He also visited Geneva, Belgium, Berlin and Hamburg, where he met and interviewed a number of political contacts.

The meetings he held on his return to England were more successful than the one held at the Royal Albert Hall. On 2nd

September, he delivered a speech at the Century Theatre in London which climaxed his European tour. This speech was published in several installments of the *Jamaica Times* weekly newspaper which had reported on most of the significant events of Garvey's European tour. (*JT*, 27 October 1928, 13, 20) More than once in this speech he referred to the struggles of the Indian and African peoples and did not spare the imperialists responsible for colonial exploitation and the politicians who acted in their interests. He attacked colonialism, but in addition his experience in the United States had made him particularly sensitive to American imperialism. Its aggressions in Nicaragua and Haiti were referred to and he claimed that President Hoover "has been pampered by the monopolist class; he is himself a millionaire; he can only see American politics and American power from the capitalist point of view." (Garvey a, 20) He was also sharply critical of H.G. Wells' popular excursions into world history, warning

> ". . . . a lot of things your Mr. Wells has said we Negroes treat as bunk. Mr. H.G. Wells may divert civilization for the benefit of his Anglo-Saxon group, but that does not make it the fact that the people who laid claims to the civilization he attributed to others are going to give them up easily. The black man knows his past. It is a past of which he can be nobly proud. That is why I stand before you this afternoon a proud black man. (ibid., 26)

At the end of September, Garvey travelled to Canada. As he was unable to enter the United States, he sent his wife to the American divisions to deputize for him. While in Montreal he was arrested on a charge of "illegal entry". (Jacques Garvey a, 194-5) Although he showed the police that his landing card was quite in order, he was not released until the following day after the Montreal UNIA had secured a lawyer and telegraphed the Canadian Prime Minister on his behalf. Cronon's version is that the American Consul in Montreal complained to the Canadian authorities about Garvey's political speeches against Herbert Hoover. The matter was a particularly sensitive one at this time as the Presidential election was approaching and Garvey had urged his supporters to vote against Hoover. (Cronon a, 150) After leaving Canada, he journeyed to Bermuda where the British authorities prevented him from landing. (Jacques Gar-

vey a, 195) But he visited the Bahamas. Towards the end of
November 1928, Garvey and his wife returned to Kingston
where they immediately set about preparatory work for the
Sixth UNIA Convention scheduled for August 1929.

Local Political Demands

From the day after his return to Jamaica Garvey was asked by
various sympathisers and by the press whether he intended to
enter local politics. Clearly, he was perceived to be of such a
stature that it was assumed that he would enter the local
political stage at the highest possible level, the Legislative
Council.

   Garvey's eyes had been drawn from the day after his return,
quite naturally, to the physical beauty of his island home and he
remarked ironically that "it is hard to imagine that in the midst
of such beauty there can exist so much suffering". (TG, 22
December 1927, 5) And while it was as UNIA leader primarily
that he intended to right the many wrongs of Jamaican society,
that role could very easily merge with that of the local electoral
representative. In fact, the dual national and international roles
of the UNIA had been a feature of the organization since its
inception in 1914 when its programme of general Aims and
Objectives was followed by a section that dealt with specific
Jamaican projects. This duality was also a marked feature of the
1920 Declaration of the Rights of the Negro Peoples of the
World which focussed on a number of civil rights issues in the
United States and the Caribbean, while addressing in a general
way broader issues of self-determination. Certainly, the UNIA
urged its membership to engage in politics when this furthered
the "progress of the race". Garvey had, moreover, formed in the
United States an umbrella political body called the Negro
Political Union which set a precedent to his Jamaican activities. And after having launched a political party in Jamaica, he
envisaged that if it met with success there, he would have the
party similarly organized in the French and British Caribbean
territories with the UNIA divisions as its primary units.
(Jacques Garvey a, 215)

   So that some overlap of focus was evident in Garvey's initial
pronouncements on his political future in December 1927, for
instance, in his statement to the first rally in Kingston after his

arrival. To the "thunderous applause" which greeted him as "he stepped forward to speak" at the Ward Theatre, "striking a characteristic pose with his hands in the pockets of his trousers and his coat thrown back", he challenged:

> "You shall find no coward in me. You shall find a black man ready and willing to represent the interests of the black people of this country and the black people of the world without any compromise. We have had this rot long enough and Marcus Garvey is here as a British subject to constitutionally see that Negroes living under the British flag receive their constitutional rights." (*DG,* 12 December 1927, 10, 19)

"Stepping up and down across the stage, Mr. Garvey in impassioned tones continued:

> "But I do not only represent the interests of British Negroes. By virtue of my office as President-General of the Universal Negro Improvement Association of the world, I represent the interests of the black peoples of the world . . . ." (idem.)

Tactfully declaring his intention to "respect all constituted authority," he continued:

> "I shall not allow the scoundrel under the guise of constitutional authority, whoever he may be, to rob and infringe upon the rights of my people. As a citizen, it is my bounden duty to uphold the constitution and the law, but why should I make any clique within the citizenry under the guise of patriotism, that subtle guise, that so many rascals hide under to rob and oppress the people . . . . to shatter the rights of other citizens . . . .?" (idem.)

The inference was clear and the irony of the contradiction between the 'British citizen' and the 'black colonial', both said to be British subjects, yet so unequally treated, was very well put. And in fact these assurances spoke pointedly to the Jamaican context rather than to the international.

Yet he considered his main task to be that of solving "the great world problem of the Negro." He therefore "had no

aspiration to enter domestic politics. As an international figure
it would be imprudent for him to mix up with local politics. The
Negro race whom he represented might differ in political views.
To take sides would probably have the effect of splitting them
up. It was for them . . . . to elect the best man who would serve
them faithfully and well". (idem.). He clearly preferred the
supra-national arena of political activity to the confines of a
national political lobby. But a number of factors were to impel
him to pay more attention to the immediate conditions and
needs of his native environment.

One was the manifest need for a man of his stature, abilities,
and experience to represent the masses. He himself advocated
that the labouring masses should identify able people from their
own race to represent their interests. He himself fell into that
category, and clearly public pressure to declare himself available for the limited sufferage manifested itself as early as March
1928 when in Montego Bay, he hinted that he would be
contesting the 1930 General elections. At this UNIA meeting he
proceeded to deal at length with the inequity of the land tenure
system which oppressed the peasantry. (NN, 17 March 1928,
4).

Another factor was likely to have been the difficulties he
faced on arrival in England in the spring of 1928. He and his wife
experienced a great deal of trouble in securing lodgings.
(Jacques Garvey a, 191) Added to this was the disheartening
experience of the Royal Albert Hall and the fact that in those
days England, unlike the United States, lacked a sizeable black
population.

And while on one hand there was a political vacuum waiting to
be filled by a man of Garvey's political acumen, the machina-
tions of his opponents in Jamaica appear to have goaded him
into making a stand. On December 13, 1928, a public meeting
took place at the Ward Theatre "to expose the *Daily Gleaner*".
It was announced that the proceedings were being held under
the aegis of the People's Political Party. The meeting had been
called at short notice to protest articles appearing on December
10th and 11th. The Ward Theatre was said to have been
crammed. Associated with Garvey on the platform were veteran
politicians H.A.L. Simpson, OBE, Rev. S.M. Jones, S.M.
DeLeon, L.P. Waison, and Mr. Charles D. Johnson. In his
introductory speech, Garvey identified himself as the "prime
mover" of the PPP. (Garvey b, 1) He declared:

> "I want everybody in Jamaica to understand that we are
> going to have decency in the political life of this country.
> The *Gleaner* has had its day. The people are going to
> have their day (applause). We are not going to have any
> more government by the *Gleaner*, we are going to have
> government by the people". (ibid. 2)

The *Gleaner* articles had been directed at Garvey and arose
out of the beating up of a city businessman, John Soulette,
which it was claimed had been politically motivated. Garvey
replied:

> "a most sinister, false and dangerous effort has been
> made through a publication of the *Gleaner* to stir up
> public sentiment so as to suggest that the people of this
> community are vulgar, disloyal and contentious and
> everything that is bad". (idem.)

L.P. Waison, a Garvey activist, then explained the background to the *Gleaner* propaganda.

> "Some time last week I was sitting at the office where I
> work about 7 o'clock p.m. The phone rang and when I
> went to the phone, a certain person called me and said to
> me: 'Listen, is that Waison speaking?' I said: 'Who is
> that?' They mentioned the name and the person said to
> me, 'Look here, I see you all have beaten up Soulette.' I
> said: 'I don't understand you. What you mean?' He said
> 'Your party had decided to beat J. Soulette and
> according to what I understand they are going to beat
> five men: J.A.G. Smith, John Soulette, Hill, DeLisser
> and DaCosta . . . ." I don't believe you would support
> Simpson from your heart of hearts but because Garvey
> is supporting Simpson, why you are supporting him?
> And a man with your intellect should not allow yourself
> to be swayed by Garvey . . . ." (ibid. 4)

Waison commented, "According to the opinions of Jamaica's
gods, only persons that are following Garvey are hooligans . . . ."
(ibid, 5)

Garvey's closing speech moved from the particular incident
to general questions. He said the articles reflected "a cul-de-sac
endeavour on the part of an artful group using the writer or the

author of the article to lay the foundation upon which they can plot securely to prevent the evolutionary rise of the people to a better condition." (ibid., 12) Continuing, he explained:

> "Understand what the *Gleaner* is. It is a private concern with a small group of men who dictate the policy of the newspaper. There is no soul or conscience in the newspaper; and the mistake we have made all the time is to believe that the paper has a conscience and a soul. It has none, so you will treat it as a simple commodity. Whether you want it or not it is printed. You will use your choice as to whether you want it or not from now on". (ibid. 13).

He added sarcastically:

> "The *Gleaner* has done enough to show that it doesn't mean anything to the poor people of this country, in that up to now — they have been established since 1834 — men are still running around and the people are still hooligans (applause) . . . ." (idem.)

Referring to political figures with whom he had been associated as a young man in the National Club, Garvey said:

> "I saw what they did with Sandy Cox, Dixon and the other people who tried to open their mouths. Dixon went bankrupt, Cox couldn't pay his grocer's bill. Dixon died of a broken heart, Cox had to run away. I took all that in and I laid my foundation so well that nobody will be able to starve me in Jamaica." (ibid., 15-16)

It may have been to escape this fate that he felt impelled to leave Jamaica in 1935. He did not starve, but it was with great effort that he kept himself from doing so given the legal ravages made on his sources of income and his organizational infrastructure.

Chapter Twelve

Garvey's Jamaican Commitment

The Policies of the People's Political Party

1929 was a year of intensive political activity. Priority had to be given to organizing the Sixth UNIA Convention which was held in Kingston in August. And by September, Garvey was ready to launch the People's Political Party.

On September 9th — a Monday night — Garvey held a public meeting in Cross Roads where he spelt out the PPP's political programme. At the end of the month, some five thousand people were reported to have attended a party convention at Edelweiss Park. (*BM*, 1 October 1929, 1). But it was the public meeting that became historically important. It was the first time that a political party defending the interests of the masses, though loosely organized, had been launched in the island. Moreso, it was one which carried a broad anti-imperialist programme. Not surprisingly, Garvey's speech and his programme (*BM*, 11 September 1929, 2, 7) provided the colonial rulers with another opportunity to use the courts against him.

The fourteen-plank platform read as follows:

1. Representation in the Imperial Parliament for a larger modicum of self-government for Jamaica.

2. Protection of native labour.

3. A minimum wage for the labouring and working classes of the island.

4. The expansion and improvement of city, town or urban areas.

5. Land reform.

6. The compulsory improvement of urban areas from which large profits are made by Trusts, Corporations, Combines or Companies.

7. A Law to encourage the promotion of native industries.

8. A Jamaica University and Polytechnic.

9. A National Opera House.

10. A law to impeach and imprison such judges who in defiance of British justice and constitutional rights will illicitly enter into agreements and arrangements with lawyers and other persons of influence to deprive other subjects in the realm of their rights in such courts of Law, over which they may preside, forcing the innocent parties to incur the additional costs of appeals, and other legal expenses which would not have been but for the injustice occasioned by the illicit arrangements of such judges with their friends.

11. The creation by law of a Legal Aid Department to render advice and protection to such persons who may not be able to have themselves properly represented and protected in courts of law.

12. A law for the imprisonment of any person who by duress, or undue influence, would force another person to vote in any public election against his will.

13. The granting of the townships of Montego Bay and Port Antonio the Corporate rights of cities.

14. The beautifying and creating of the Kingston Race Course into a National Park similar to Hyde Park in London.

This manifesto was expanded to twenty-six planks and modifications were made after plank ten resulted in Garvey being sentenced to three months imprisonment and a fine of one hundred pounds. This plank was so detailed as to clearly have been a response to the Marke case, but more generally it reflected Garvey's condemnation of the use of courts as instruments of ruling class repression and he had good reason for these sentiments. However, there is no doubt that the formulation of this point played into the hands of his enemies clothed in the very same garb of the courts. They were out to destroy him. So they read his speeches and articles carefully to see in what way they could catch him in their legal rat-trap. Garvey's Cross Roads speech with its direct attack on the courts provided them with yet another reason to bag the tiger and stop him prowling the districts of Jamaica.

Garvey therefore had to modify the wording of his programme on this and other points. Plank sixteen of the revised twenty-six plank programme spoke simply of "legal and judicial reform". Plank one in the version sent to the Colonial Office spoke of "Representation in the Imperial Parliament or a larger modicum of self-government for Jamaica". Point four was reworded and became Plank six. Plank six now called for "The expansion and improvement of city, town or urban areas without the incumbrance or restraint of private ownership". In addition to a National Opera House, the revised manifesto called for "a National Opera House with an Academy of Music and Art". To Point twelve, which called for a law against bribery of voters was added the clause "because of obligation of employment or otherwise".

In her book *Garvey and Garveyism,* Amy Jacques Garvey uses this subsequent version, with certain further modifications. For example, Plank five on land reform is expanded to include an "All-Island Water Board, to secure domestic irrigation and industrial supplies"; and Plank ten reads: "A law to impeach and imprison Judges who, with disregard for British justice and Constitutional rights, dealt unfairly". Other changes were minor.

Twelve of the clauses that made up the full programme show Garvey's concern for the workers, his continued struggle for reforms in the legal system as well as economic and social changes. The relevant planks are numbered below in the order in which they appeared in the twenty-six—plank manifesto:

4. A Law to protect the labouring and working classes of the island.

5. A Law to compel the employment of not less than sixty per cent of native labour in all industrial, agricultural and commercial activities engaged in, in this island.

7. An eight hour working day throughout Jamaica.

12. The establishing of a Government High School in the capital town of each parish for the supply of free secondary education. Attached to the said High School to be a night continuation school to facilitate those desiring to study at night for the advance of their education.

13. A public library in the capital town of each parish.

15. Prison Reform.

17. The appointing of official court stenographers to take the official notes of all court proceedings in the Supreme Court, Resident Magistrate Courts and Petty Session Courts of the island.

21. A Law to empower the Government to secure a loan of three million or more pounds from the Imperial Government or otherwise to be used by the Government under the management of a department of the Director of Agriculture in developing the crown lands of the island, agriculturally and otherwise with the object of supplying employment for our surplus unemployed population and to find employment for stranded Jamaicans abroad, and that the Government purchase such ships as are necessary from time to time to facilitate the marketing of the produce gathered from those crown lands and at the same time conveniently offering an opportunity to other producers to ship and market their produce.

23. The establishing by the government of an electrical system to supply cheap electricity to such growing and prospering centres as are necessary.

24. A Law to establish clinical centres from which trained

nurses are to be sent out to visit the homes in rural districts and to teach and demonstrate sanitary and better health methods in the care of home and family.

25. A Law to empower the parochial board of each Parish to undertake under the direction of the central government the building of model sanitary homes for the peasantry by the system of easy payment to cover a period of from ten to twenty years.

26. A Law to prevent criminal profiteering in the sale of lands in urban and suburban areas to the detriment of the expansion of healthy home life for citizens of moderate means — profiteering such as indulged in, in lower St. Andrew by heartless land sharks. (Garvey c)

This manifesto was the first of its kind in the island's electoral history. It represented a break with traditional practice where individual merchants, planters and penkeepers were returned to the Legislature not on the basis of a programme but on their ability to hand out patronage to the voters and on the support of their class. In some cases it was common for certain seats to go uncontested because of the social and economic sway some of the candidates held in their areas. So, recognizing the momentous nature of this manifesto, the *Gleaner* cautioned:

> ". . . . perhaps we are too conservative, even too reactionary, but we think that the average man free to use his intelligence and his conscience in the Council, will do more good for the country and for specific organization than those subscribing blindly to a party. . . . Parties do not thrive in Jamaica." (*DG*, 23 September, 1929, 12)

This editorial, written with characteristic hypocrisy, was penned at the time when the newspaper was enjoined in battle against the PPP with its programme that challenged the island's vested interests.

This party programme is also of historic significance because it was not only used in the 1930 legislative election and abandoned after Garvey's electoral defeat, but it formed the basis for his work in the City Council, for his speeches at mass meetings, his journalism and his letters and petitions to the Colonial Office.

Garvey's elaboration of his platform on September 9 enables us to understand his orientation on a number of questions. With regard to the question of self-government, Garvey put forward his position in this way:

> "There is absolutely no reason why Jamaica, a part of the British Empire, should not have a part in the Imperial Parliament that rules Jamaica . . . . France allows her colonies equal rights of representation in the mother parliament as she allows her colonial possessions such as Morocco and other French colonies in Africa . . . ." *(B,* 11 September 1929, 2, 7)

He argued that "Englishmen at home are not competent to rule these people who are outside England." He was therefore prepared to advocate the French colonial model, but this was not done as an end in itself but as a means of furthering the struggle for self-determination. It was a criticism of the British colonial administration and one around which a political campaign could be geared. He also said:

> "We think it is right for England to give us representations in the Mother Parliament, or give us Dominion status as they have given to Canada." (idem.)

From a constitutional point of view, the status enjoyed by Canada and Australia was similar to the status achieved in the 1960s and 70s in the English-speaking Caribbean.

An editorial in the *Blackman* of September 7, 1929 stated:

> "It is to arouse the peasant to the consciousness of his power that the People's Political Party has come into being."

Garvey sought in his campaign to arouse the masses. He spoke out against Indian indentured labour which was supported by the big landowners to get cheaper labour. He talked about the need "to break down the power of the plantocracy' *(B,* 11 September 1929, 2, 7), and the need to have legislators who would represent the interests of the "labouring classes" along the lines set out in the programme. Garvey lashed the plantocracy:

"Everybody in Jamaica knows that the land of this country is really in the hands of a few large landed proprietors. We have a population of nearly one million people, and out of that number, not five per cent can find land to settle on. The bulk of the land is in the hands of about one per cent of the population — absentee proprietors and resident property owners who have no other interest in Jamaica and its people than to bleed the country of what they want and the rest can go to hell! We have in Hanover, Trelawny, Westmoreland, St. James, St. Thomas and St. Mary, thousands of waste acreages. In certain settlements.... we have thousands of people who have no land on which to work their farms, whilst thousands of acres of land lie idle — one man having fifteen thousand acres of land and twenty thousand people have no place to build on and no farm to work.". . . . (idem).

Garvey also wanted to end other abuses committed by landlords against the peasants. He was sharply critical of the banana multi-national, United Fruit Company:

"If you go to towns like Sav'-la-Mar and Lucea, you will find them in a most dilapidated condition while on their very steps companies like the United Fruit Company have made millions from such seaport towns as Annotto Bay, Port Maria, St. Ann's Bay and Lucea. The United Fruit Company, from the time of Captain Baker, have made millions, and they have not even made a decent dock on the North side. They have not even put up a hospital in return for the kindness they have received in Jamaica." (idem.)

He also spoke out against the total repatriation of profits by foreign companies arguing for their reinvestment. He defended the development of "native industries" pointing to the fact that in recent years, powerful foreign interests had contributed to killing "the soap factory, the match factory and the tannery." He told his audience that his policy, if elected along with the other candidates, would be to "so tax waste lands in Jamaica as to compel owners of land to sell or to cut it up so that people can get back to the farm."

The 1929 Municipal Elections

The political direction of Garvey's programme was clear and he had to be stopped. The police were put on the alert. Point ten in the original PPP Manifesto gave the authorities an excuse for bringing him before the very law courts whose abuses the manifesto sought to curb. The *Gleaner,* in an editorial entitled "The Garvey Case" in its issue of September 28, 1929, outlined how, on one charge or another, Garvey had fallen foul of the law:

> ". . . . anything that tends to unsettle profoundly the belief of a population in the integrity of the government and the Courts, and might induce them to adopt dangerous methods, is regarded by law as seditious. Consequently, if Mr. Garvey could not have been proceeded against for contempt of court he might still have been prosecuted for sedition . . . . The uprising in 1865 in St. Thomas was partly motivated by the well-founded distrust of the people in the tribunals which heard their cases, and a sweeping and necessary reform was effected after that uprising. But although the Courts of these days may make mistakes . . . . we do not believe that any large body of well-thinking people feel that they are not to be trusted."

But there had been no sweeping and necessary reform after 1865. In fact, the situation of the people worsened in every sense and this is why Jamaica was entering a decade, the end of which would witness an island-wide rebellion that was decisive in ending the old colonial political framework.

Garvey was sent to prison on the 26th September and was released on December 19th, 1929. Yet prison for Garvey was another place from which to conduct his political campaign. He continued writing articles for the *Blackman* and sending notes of advice to his colleagues. The same issue of the *Blackman* that reported he had gone to prison also announced that he was standing in a municipal bye-election for the No. 3 Urban Ward of the Corporate Area of Kingston and St. Andrew. (*B*, 27 September 1929). Meanwhile, there was a lot of work to be done: a petition for Garvey's release made to the Governor, campaign meetings to be organized, and the necessary propaganda battle engaged.

For instance, on October 29th the *Gleaner's* final advice to the voters in the bye-election was:

> "We hope that the voters of the district will show their disapprobation of hooligan conduct by going to the polls on Wednesday and by voting for Mr. Bailey . . . ."

But Garvey won the election with three hundred and twenty-one votes to one hundred and two for W.F. Bailey, a retired school teacher who had been a president of the Jamaica Union of Teachers. *(B,* 31 October 1929, 1) And J. Coleman Beecher was elected to the KSAC in another bye-election.

But no sooner had Garvey been elected to the KSAC than his opponents took steps to unseat him. These efforts formed part of a general plan by the local merchant and planter class to kill him politically. The major anti-Garvey spokesman on the Council was the Jewish capitalist, G. Seymour Seymour.

Garvey's first letter to the Council from the St. Catherine District Prison requested ten weeks leave of absence and a promise that "immediately I shall have regained my freedom, I shall make and subscribe to the oath set forth in the third schedule of the Corporation Law." (KSAC Minutes, 4 November 1929) The Council at its meeting on November 4, 1929 referred the matter to its solicitor, H.H. Dunn, who later advised, "It is within the power of the Council to grant the leave, should it see fit so to do, the question of leave being entirely in the discretion of the Council." (ibid., 18 November 1929) This legal opinion gave the Council a free hand. However, when Councillor Beecher suggested at the next meeting that Garvey be granted eight weeks' leave the motion was rejected in a very close vote. (idem.) The 'ayes' were Beecher, Clough, Gordon, Hay, Simpson, McLaughlin, Penso. Among the 'noes' were Mayor D.C. Vaz, G. Seymour Seymour, and Councillor Duval, a black landowner from Gordon Town who consistently supported Seymour. (ibid., 2 December 1929)

From prison Garvey wrote a further letter in which he exposed the sinister implications of their refusal to grant him leave of absence and declared his intention to fight against their decision.

> "I understand . . . . that there are others who would prefer to see my seat vacant even though elected

thereto; in that case it may be assumed that the non-
granting of the leave of absence and my non-attendance
at three consecutive ordinary meetings would auto-
matically make my seat vacant and that such parties
may be desirous of taking advantage of this technical
assumption . . . . I may point out however, that should
under any circumstances my seat be declared vacant, I
shall immediately seek re-election which would throw
the responsibility upon the Councillors who refuse to
grant me leave of absence of practically forcing the
burgesses or taxpayers to bear the cost of another bye-
election when there was no need therefor." (idem.)

He again requested leave for only thirty days as his sentence
would soon be terminated. And Councillor Beecher once more
took up the issue on the 2nd of December when he suggested
that the Town Clerk swear in Garvey at the St. Catherine
District Prison. This motion was also narrowly defeated by a
three—two vote. (idem.) The three 'noes' were registered by
Mayor D.C. Vaz, Seymour and Duval.

So as to settle the impasse, it was agreed that N.W. Manley,
then a prominent city barrister, should be asked to give his
opinion as to whether Garvey's seat should be declared vacant
or not. (KSAC Minutes, 28 December 1929; DG, 30 December
1929, 1, 6) At a special meeting of the Council on 13th January,
1930 Manley's opinon was read. It stated unequivocally, "I
advise that it is the duty of the Council to declare the seat of Mr.
Garvey vacant." (KSAC Minutes, 13 January 1930)

But this opinion did not prevent Garvey's re-election, un-
opposed, to the Council in February 1930.

However, from the beginning of December until Manley's
opinion was given much had happened. Garvey was in fact
released from prison on December 19, 1929, several days
before the expiration of his sentence.[1] This was done in order
to prevent the demonstrations organized for the day of his
release. (DG, 20 December 1929, 1) A letter from the Governor's residence at King's House to the Colonial Office explained
that Garvey:

"was due to come out of prison on the 24th December
but we learnt that his release on Christmas Eve would
mean that he would be hailed as a 'Black Messiah' and a

> monster procession from the gaol at Spanish Town to Kingston, a distance of twelve miles, with bands and all the rest of it, was being organized. That, of course, would not have done at all, so with a secrecy which was highly applauded throughout the Island, Mr. Garvey was released about three or four days before the proper time. He was shown the door of the prison at a moment's notice and found his own way back to Kingston. I think he came back in a Police car which we sent out to assist him!"[2]

Thus circumventing the extensive preparations for a procession of one hundred cars and a big reception in Kingston!

But Garvey did not have time to relax during the traditional Christmas and New Year holidays. On December 30, he attended his first Council meeting. Seymour, in his hostility, went so far as to vote against a motion to welcome him to the Council. (KSAC Minutes, 30 December 1929) And although he had taken the oath of office, his seat was still in doubt. Garvey nevertheless continued the fight on behalf of the masses by giving notice that he would be moving resolutions in favour of a minimum wage and an eight-hour working day for all employees of the Kingston and St. Andrew Corporation. (idem.) These were the issues which capitalist interests in the Council never raised, being primarily concerned with consolidating their positions, utilizing public issues to this end, and of course, lining their own pockets with graft. In fact, correspondence with the Colonial Office from Jamaica stated that Garvey "is all for exposing the colossal graft that is believed to exist in the Corporation."[3]

The 1930 National Electoral Campaign

When Garvey confirmed his intention of standing for election to the Legislative Council as a member for the St. Andrew constituency, the *Jamaica Times* noted that if he was elected he would make a good member and would have "full scope to display his powers of oratory in the Council Chamber," but added "he will also benefit by the mental discipline which the new atmosphere will provide for him." (*JT,* 1 December 1928, 15) To some extent this could be interpreted as meaning that

Garvey would beome more pragmatic, limiting himself to reforms within the ambit of the colonial situation. Indeed, Garvey did, from time to time, make excessive statements and claims, with his oratory getting the better of him. For example, early in December he was reported to have promised that "in twenty-four months with the co-operation of all the black and coloured people of the island, I shall rid you of the economic slavery under which you now suffer." *(JT,* 8 December 1928, 7)

While Garvey was in prison, the legislative campaign had been vigorously waged for the PPP through the *Blackman* newspaper and at public meetings. In an editorial in the *Blackman,* November 19 1929, it was stated that

> "the politics of Jamaica has received a wholesome stimulus from the advent of the People's Political Party, who have already received results exceeding the expectation of many. The wholesale denunciation by which persons, blinded by prejudice and moved to the desire to hoodwink the masses, have tried to destroy their influence, was only to be expected inasmuch as nothing in all the world which has for its decisive object the benefit of the common people can possibly escape the condemnation of those who affect a superiority altogether unjustifiable, in either their antecedents, their own personal conduct or their pre-eminence in public life. The Party has no mercenary aims. Its purpose is to educate the people and by the people we mean the seven-eights proportion of the inhabitants of the country, who exist in political servitude in spite of the privileges and rights which are undisputably theirs, under the powers accorded them by the constitution of the semi-representative government which we possess.

This latter was a reference to the restricted franchise then available. As the *Blackman* pointed out, voting eligibility depended on one's ability to pay "1/- in taxes or 17/-, to be accurate 16/-8, per month rent, or earn £1 per week or £52 year. ... Women may vote on the same terms as men saving that they must pay two pounds per year in taxes." (idem.)

Meanwhile, Garvey wasted not a moment. From the day after his release from prison until the election at the end of January he had his most intense period of political activity in Jamaica and possibly in his entire career, especially given the bad conditions of the roads — the roads leading to rural districts being unpaved. On Friday, December 20, he began a tour covering St. Thomas, St. Mary, Portland and St. Ann, returning to Kingston on Tuesday, Christmas Eve. That same day, December 24, the *Blackman* announced that Garvey would be speaking on December 28th at Ocho Rios at 10 a.m., at St. Ann's Bay at 12.30 p.m. and at Brown's Town at 3 p.m. On January 2, 1930, the *Blackman* listed the following meetings in Garvey's electoral constituency of St. Andrew:

> Monday Jan. 6th — Red Hills, 7 p.m.; Half Way Tree, 9 p.m.;
> Tuesday Jan. 7th — Dallas, 7 p.m.; Bull Bay, 9 p.m.;
> Wednesday Jan. 8th — Mt. James, 7.30 p.m.;
> Thursday Jan. 9th — Parks Road, 7 p.m.; Cavaliers, 9 p.m.;
> Friday Jan. 10th — Mannings Hill, 6.30 p.m.; Stony Hill, 8 p.m.;
> Sat. Jan. 11th — Mt. Charles, 7 p.m.; Lawrence Tavern, 8.30 p.m.;
> Sunday Jan. 12th — Mavis Bank, 3 p.m.; Gordon Town, 5.30 p.m.

The PPP campaign was dominated by questions of political servitude and racial discrimination. And the class question was dealt with by Garvey in the following way:

> "Now in all parts of the world we have class legislation. Mr. Herbert George DeLisser, a very cunning man, a subtle man, has recently said in a criticism of me that he has always advocated that our legislators should not represent any one class but all classes of the community, and that he is sure that all the legislators we have had never represented any particular class; but always represented all the classes. Now the very proof that this is not true is a survey of your condition and a survey of the condition of those who have represented us in the past. (hear, hear) You will find that the people who have represented us in the past are all belonging to the class of success and of prosperity, whereas the common people who elected them are belonging to the

suffering class and poverty stricken classes. It is evident, it is plain to us, therefore, that the men who have
represented us have only used the power at their control
for the advancement of their class (voice 'Yes') .... Mr.
Farquharson's the great banana magnate, and Mr.
Horace Myer's interests must be different to yours, and
therefore they will seek legislation to protect their
interests as against yours. You have certain peculiar
interests that are not in common with other people's
and therefore if you want to advance those interests....
you must get somebody from among you to represent
you and to get that legislation so that your interests can
be protected." (B, 18 January 1930)

To get the masses thinking along these lines was indeed a
formidable task, given the slave legacy and the colonial system.
Many people despised themselves and always looked up to
those with lighter complexions, straight or curly hair, better
social positions, and prosperity. Those lacking these attributes
were perceived as being born to that situation. These self-
indicting prejudices held by Black people were skilfully manipulated by the authorities.

But the question of land distribution was paramount. In one
of his campaign speeches at Papine, S.M. DeLeon, a PPP
Organizer, carried a vigorous position on this issue; he

"struck out at the Jamaica Producer's Association,
stating that it stood only for capitalists and large land
owners . . . . and that the Party intended to get laws
passed whereby large areas of land will be so taxed that
their owners will be forced to rent them to the smaller
people." (B, 9 December 1929)

Another Garvey campaigner, Charles D. Johnson, characterized Seymour Seymour as

"a big landowner... interested only in those people who
could pay him his price for his lands. They could not
afford to pay three hundred pounds an acre for land and
that was the price at which Seymour lands were going."
(idem.)

Complaints on the matter came in from ordinary citizens. A letter to the *Gleaner* of January 7, 1930 written by one B.C. Cooper pointed out that in Westmoreland there were one hundred and eighty thousand acres; twenty thousand acres were crown and swamp lands. Of the remaining one hundred and sixty thousand, twenty people owned one hundred and thirty thousand.

And in St. Ann, members of the Lime Hall and Associated Districts Citizens' Association pleaded for more school rooms, for water, and for land. Their letter was addressed to D.T. Wint, the incumbent member of the Legislative Council for St. Ann, who was again contesting that constituency:

> "Our greatest need here is land for small holdings. Hemmed in by large properties and having a comparatively large and ever growing population, our struggle for bare existence becomes every day more tense. Hope was held out to us as regards our purchasing a section of the Seville Mt. Lands but such hope was not realized. We are still waiting but we wait not in idleness. We have established here a Cooperative Loan society which furnishes the medium for cooperation not only between residents of these districts, but of districts further afield." *(DG,* 7 December 1929, 34)

Politicking with bragadoccio, defiance and humour about his personal experience of repression, Garvey, in his first speech after his release, reminisced on the role of prisons in his political life:

> "I had a happy time in prison, because I went to prison in the cause of justice; in the cause of human liberty . . . . The first time I went to prison, I was so physically upset and so near dying that I never knew it until I found out that my nerves were partially gone. So that saved my life . . . . And I never knew I was suffering from diabetes until my good friends sent me over to Spanish Town where I got better (laughter). I have escaped death several times. When I was a boy, I escaped from a shark, and had it not been for the providential appearance of my good mother who prevented me from eating a bit of avocado pear which I found in a remote corner of the

pantry, I would have probably died from rat poisoning (laughter). A man shot at me six times and I escaped. I was even able to run after him and catch him and deliver him up to the police. The next time I was about to die I had over-worked myself. I worked eleven years without rest and I was almost dying. But they sent me for five years in the penitentiary and it was after they sent me there that I found out how bad I was. And then I came to Jamaica and had this big convention with all the excitement and worry. I was just about embarking on another big job when they said: "No, Garvey, you had better take a rest" (laughter).

And now I feel strong (laughter). You cannot stop me with jail, neither can you stop me with anything else. The scaffold, the guillotine, the gallows, the electric chair — these are the things that are responsible for our civilization and Marcus Garvey is not ignorant of the way of the reformer . . . . And so the world is crazy and foolish to think that four hundred million people would so easily give it up because somebody goes to prison. The thing is laughable; and I am glad I went to prison because I have added another plank to my platform (cheers). We are going to have better prisons so that when we go to prison we will have better conditions here (laughter), since we have to pay for the upkeep of the prison we had better have a better prison anyhow." (*B*, 28 December 1929)

A master of oratory, Garvey carried his audience with him, making them laugh when he wanted to, without distracting from the political objectives of his speech.

But all did not go so smoothly. Attempts were made to break up some of his meetings. In a letter to the *Gleaner* of January 7, 1930, Garvey reported his experience in St. Ann:

"I addressed three meetings last Saturday, one at Moneague at 10.30 a.m., one at Claremont at 1 p.m., and one at Alexandria at 3 p.m. I should have addressed a meeting at Cave Valley at 4.30 p.m. but owing to being delayed at Alexandria I was unable to reach Cave Valley in time to address the meeting at daylight. When I arrived there it was dark and late in the evening. The report you published .... states that the meeting at Cave Hill was broken up. The following is really what happened .... It is stated as a fact that on Friday last, the day before my meeting in St. Ann Mr. Wint drove from place to place advertised by me to speak at and arranged with the teachers in the localities to attend the meetings and create obstruction. It was also stated that drunken men were employed to assist the teachers in creating disorder. When we started our meeting at Moneague on Saturday morning, four teachers grouped themselves together and endeavoured to harrass the chairman of the meeting. I had to make an appeal to the decency of the teachers and warned them that they were setting a bad example to the poorer and less intelligent people of the community. They continued their interruption until I took the platform when I silenced them and when the huge crowd demonstrated its displeasure against their bad behaviour."

Trouble also occurred at a meeting in Linstead in St. Catherine where Garvey was speaking on behalf of Mr. Mc-Neil's candidature.

"At this stage Mr. Garvey stopped to have a drink of water, there were derisive cries from a section of the crowd."

Mr. Garvey continuing said:

"You are enemies of your community. It is impossible to do good for people who will make so much noise over a simple thing as a man stopping to drink a glass of water. I am harrassed by people who are not even interested in themselves." (DG, 18 January 1930, 31).

In Glengoffe in St. Catherine hecklers also interrupted him on several occasions. Finally, he warned two of the most vociferous hecklers:

" 'If you interrupt again I will put you out because we get no protection from the police and Mr. McNeil has paid for the use of this market'.

The Corporal said 'Man don't talk fool'. The two men, as Mr. Garvey was about to continue, said 'In fact, away with you'. Mr. Garvey called on the police to put out the two men but the police did not act. Mr. Garvey then stepped from the platform and put out the men. The people began to scatter and became restless . . . . After a while the meeting was again called together." (*DG*, 20 January 1930, 9)

In the end, however, the electoral results were hardly a measure of Garvey's influence. One reason was that the majority of his supporters were disenfranchised.[4] (7.75%) of the population was registered to vote and only 2.74% of the total population actually cast ballots out of an estimated population of 1,014,163 in 1930." (Hill b, 10). In analyzing his own defeat Garvey reckoned:

"The thousands who attended and cheered at the Party's meetings indicate that if you, the poor people had a vote, our Party would have been sent to the Legislature. The voters have turned back the clock for another ten years but (the) Party system is well established in your minds, and it will come, it is bound to come."

Garvey also alluded to electoral bribery as a cause of his defeat:

"The people of my race, unfortunately, were fed on rum, sugar and water and sandwiches, as a reward for their votes, for Mr. Seymour. I was approached to send rum into certain sections of the parish, to give money away and to send provisions etc., which I refused to do. If I could not have gotten the people's votes because of the merit of my policy then they were quite at liberty to vote for Mr. Seymour on the rum, sugar and water and bread that they got. I am only sorry that while the people of my race sold their votes in the hilly regions in this way, the people of Mr. Seymour's race voluntarily went to the polls in the plains without being supplied with vehicles and voted for him." *(DG,* 1 February 1930, 12)

Similar sentiments were expressed in a letter to the *Gleaner* on February 5, 1930 by A. Wesley Atherton who pointed out that it was precisely because of Garvey's programme that he became a marked man:

> ".... the entire plantocracy of the island rallied against him . . . . He has lost in what was almost a rum war; a money scramble. With the bait again dangling before their gaze — the red linen of filthy lucre — Negro sons of African slaves, in this enlightened age voted away their birthright and suffered themselves to be indentured for another five years under conditions that have sucked their vitals to the very bones. They traded on the future happiness of their children, and trampled their manhood into the dust. With the whip of the slave master still cracking in their ears, they followed the steam of molten gold down the hills of St. Andrew to vote against Marcus Garvey. They stabbed him fiercely in the back."

The letter ended by stating that the cause of Garvey was immortal. Atherton's letter expressed the mood of a defeated fighter who had not given up but who knew that he had to lick his wounds and prepare to come back into the ring once more to avenge himself.

The extent of his persecution by the Jamaican press, in particular the *Gleaner,* is revealed by a study of the propaganda campaign against him over a four-month period. Before, during and after his imprisonment in Jamaica, from September 1, 1929 to January 31, 1930 "there were 121 articles which made reference to Garvey" either in editorials, letters to the editor, or news reports. Of these one hundred and twenty-one items, sixty-eight were unfavourable, twenty-one favourable, and thirty-two neutral. Of seventy-four news reports, thirty-four were unfavourable while twenty-five were judged to be neutral. Out of a total of fourteen editorials, twelve were unfavourable, two were thought to be neutral. So that editorial and reportage were both pitched strongly against him. Then, of a total of thirty-three letters, twenty-two were unfavourable and only six

favourable. The study further points out that the most un-
favourable articles and letters were focused around the dates of
Garvey's election to the KSAC in October 1929 and around the
January 1930 legislative election. (Campbell, 19-20)

Garvey himself had lost his seat with nine hundred and fifteen
votes against Seymour Seymour who won with a total of one
thousand six hundred and seventy-seventy votes. A third
candidate, Dillon, obtained only two hundred and sixty votes.
The *Gleaner* was relieved:

> "The lesson to be learnt from the results of the election
> is patent: the vast influence which Mr. Garvey was
> supposed to have exercised over the minds and actions
> of a majority of our people existed only in the imagina-
> tions of those who most dread his propaganda . . . . It was
> known that the wealthier householders in the Plain of
> St. Andrew would support Mr. Seymour to the last man
> and women, but some persons supposed that the
> peasant and the working classes would reply to the last
> man in support of Mr. Garvey." (*DG*, 31 January 1930)

But given the circumstances, Garvey's showing was creditable. He won convincingly in working-class communities like
Jones Pen and the old Pound Road Area, but the enfranchised
population in such areas was considerably less than in the
middle-class areas where Seymour Seymour's winning margins
were greater. Garvey also lost in most of the rural areas, but won
in a few.

Nationally, only three of the twelve candidates who had PPP
support won seats in the Legislative Council. These were R.
Ehrenstein in St. Thomas, Dr. Veitch in Hanover, and Philip
Lightbody, a journalist of long standing who came closest to
sharing Garvey's nationalist views. The *Gleaner* exulted, ". . . .
the people's Political Party with its extremely radical programme and propaganda was signally defeated." (*DG*, 4 February 1930, 12)

Apart from the reasons of voter eligibility and electoral
bribery, yet another reason for the PPP's poor results was that
the party was not really an organized force and had had too little
time to develop. The result was that some of Garvey's candidates were drawn from among men who thought they could

benefit from his mass following and who were not fully supportive of his anti-colonial aspirations as expressed in the PPP programme. In the final analysis they were men of the old pre-party school of colonial politics.

In fact, while Garvey had been critical both of the United Fruit Company monopoly as well as the local oligarchy who predominated in the Jamaica Producers Association, two of the candidates who contested seats with PPP backing were P.H. Lightbody and E. McNeil who ran in the parishes of St. James and St. Catherine respectively. McNeil, in fact, was the United Fruit Company agent in St. Catherine where he was a fairly large landowner and where he had a notorious reputation among agricultural workers. His opponent, T. Cawley, was an executive of the Producers' Association. As such, Garvey's support among the people was not and could not be truly reflected in his choice of candidates because of the stiff property requirements for nomination to the Legislative Council.

The *Gleaner* was quick to catch on to this inconsistency, and in an editorial concerning the PPP candidates pointed out:

> "If we glance over the list of candidates mentioned up to now, we see at once that they are either persons who have already been in the Legislative Council or persons who talked about becoming candidates long before the People's Political Party was ever heard of." (*DG*, 2 October 1929, 12)

With the possible exception of Manasseh Scott who contested the St. Ann seat against D.T. Wint this was true, for the PPP could not have broken through the political stranglehold of independent candidacy. This stranglehold was of such a nature that when J.E. Fractus was invited by the PPP to stand against the old-timer, G. Nash, in Manchester, he refused at once to contest the seat. (*DG*, 9 January 1930, 14) The PPP thus failed to present an alternative political force that could tackle both the British colonizers and the big landowners. Candidates did not even defend their party's manifesto and one, R. Ehrenstein — a naturalized British subject of Czechoslovak origin — owner of the large Serge Island Sugar Estate in St. Thomas, went so far as to publish a manifesto of his own. In the same way,

Garvey's subsequent support for Lewis Ashenheim at the 1935 polls was seen as a continuation of the association that had started with Ehrenstein and McNeil, men who stood to benefit from Garvey's popular following but who did not share his ideas. So much so that on several occasions during the 1935 campaign Garvey was interrupted by hecklers on this score.[5] *(DG,* 26 January 1935, 20) And when Garvey was imprisoned and persecuted, the petitions for clemency did not come from his PPP colleagues but from UNIA members. *(DG,* 10 October 1929, 3)

As such, Garvey's Jamaican work was tinged with bitter frustration which he often contained, but which at other times became impossible for him to suppress. This resentful conclusion made after his 1930 election defeat betrays the depth of his disappointment:

> "From my observation I am forced to conclude that Jamaica is indeed an ignorant community; it is limited in intelligence, narrow in its intellectual concepts, almost to the point where one can honestly say that the country is ridiculous . . . ." *(DG,* 6 February 1930, 14)

Clearly, idealist as he was, he found it extremely difficult to work in Jamaica. But he persisted at a time when political apathy was high, political rights and freedoms were considerably restricted and the political awakening of the late thirties was still a few years away. The ripening process was underway, but Garvey grew despairingly despondent of its fruition, and his decision to leave local politics meant that he was destined not to reap the harvest himself.

In one sense, then, T.A. Marryshow was right when he referred to Jamaica as Garvey's St. Helena, for Harlem was no match for Kingston, the administrative and commercial centre of a small British colony. But in another sense Marryshow was wrong, for the working-class demonstrations and riots of the late thirties showed that Jamaica was no St. Helena. It had gained a social and political dynamism of its own, the education for which had emerged partially from Garveyism and other independent struggles of the oppressed. Those island riots, which Garvey lived to comment on, but from afar, were moreover part of the general crisis of the colonial political system on an international scale.

Chapter Thirteen

Ideological Engagement

Press and Commercial Opposition

Opposition to Garvey cannot be fully appreciated without comment on the class and commercial forces dominant in Jamaican colonial society. The 1930 General Election amply reveals the strong political influence of the large landowners and merchants who were organized in the Jamaica Imperial Association (JIA), and the growth in influence of the medium-sized farmers within the Jamaica Producers' Association (JPA) and the Jamaica Banana Producers Association (JBPA). Although both had many peasant members they were dominated by the big planters. They were not, however, unified as there were differences between those (in these associations) who wanted to preserve their relationship with the American multinational, United Fruit Company, and others who were fighting against the monopoly control of the UFC over the banana trade. The latter were organized in the Jamaica Producers Association.

On the one hand, the JIA was tied up with British sugar interests. Their secretary, H.G. DeLisser, was leader-writer for the *Daily Gleaner* which faithfully reflected this position. Garvey once noted that the difference between DeLisser's two roles was almost imperceptible, as one buttressed the other. *(B,* 19 April 1930, 2)

On the other hand, the JPA represented an unequal alliance between the large landowners and the middle-farmers, the latter represented by teacher-legislators such as D.T. Wint, and teacher produce-inspectors such as H.B. Monteith. Wint and

Monteith had both served as presidents of the Jamaica Union of Teachers.[1] They represented the better-off Blacks who combined their professional teaching work with farming and other business activities. Wint, an executive member of the JPA, published the monthly *West India Critic and Review* of which Monteith was a co-editor.

The main organ of the Jamaica Producers Association was the *Jamaica Mail* which was owned by G. Seymour Seymour. (Post b, 128-131) The political aspirations of the JPA were well known. One correspondent to the press went so far as to state:

> "Although I am a staunch supporter of the Jamaica Producers Association, yet I must lift my voice and pen against this scheme to put men into the Legislative Council only (sic.) who can back up this concern by asking for loans etc. Where will we poor tax-payers find ourselves in a few more years?" *(DG,* 15 Nov. 1929, 12)

The *Gleaner* editorial in an attack on the *Jamaica Mail* had stated:

> ".... the supporters of the Jamaica Producers Association are striving to put into the Council men who they believe will vote for what the Association may wish." *(DG,* 2 Oct. 1929, 12)

And Garvey, for his part, had characterized the JPA as being composed of "a large number of big fish with a larger number of smaller fish," *(B,* 2 April 1929, 1) and had promised: ".... the People's Political Party is going to oppose every candidate of the Jamaica Producers Association because we want no Trust Control of the Legislative." *(B,* 10 July 1929, 1, 2)

But, in the event, the 1930 election was a political victory for organized agricultural interests. The Banana Producers Association gained most of the seats in the Council. (Carnegie, 8) Four of the elected members were executive members of the JPA and the Jamaica Citrus Producers Association. (Jamaica Govt.) T. Cawley, member for St. Catherine, was first Vice-President of the Jamaica Producers Association; G. Seymour Seymour, who defeated Garvey, was second Vice-President of the Jamaica Producers Association; D.T. Wint was an executive member of the Jamaica Producers Association Council; and G. Nash, member for Manchester, an official of the Jamaica Citrus Producers Association. (idem.)

The Cultural Lobby

Partially, but not completely, overlapping these commercial interests was a strong eurocentric cultural lobby. For opposition to Garvey also stemmed from social sectors which disparaged his stress on racial identity and integrity. Colonialism had inculcated a depreciation of Africa, especially among the educated. Furthermore, Garvey's ethnic appeal rallied the sentiments of the most deprived in the society who were, at the same time, Blacks, and such sentiments were perceived as a menace to the authority and security of privileged social groups.

Both the *Gleaner* and the *West India Critic and Review,* therefore, accused Garvey of recreating the 1865 atmosphere in their journalistic assaults. Wint wrote that,

> "Garveyism is spreading with great rapidity throughout the Island; because its votaries are for the most part ignorant and illiterate people and they are thousands." (WICR, January 1939, 7-8)

He went on to advise that "British prestige and constituted authority must be maintained and upheld in Jamaica. Loyal citizens of the Empire must stand by the Empire." (idem.) And in a letter to the *Gleaner* of January 17, 1930, he sounded the alarm of a repetition of 1865:

> "Noxious doctrines are being instilled into the heads of ignorant people. The seeds of disorder and disunion are being sown and unless we join together and rip out these pernicious weeds they will engulf the island. The danger must be stopped and stopped now. Remember the Morant Bay rebellion. Gordon and Paul Bogle did not preach sedition to the people, did not tell them to rebel but they laid the train for the outbreak, by sowing the seeds of unrest and discord among the people. And I tell you that this is being done again today and unless we are careful we are heading for disaster.

> If Mr. Garvey wanted to go to Africa, let him go there
> by all means but it is an insult to every Jamaican to tell
> him that his aim in life is to go back to African savagery."

The population was constantly exposed to 'informed' opinion of the type given by Sir Fiennes Barrett Lennard,[2] a former Chief Justice of Jamaica who had served in the judiciary in Africa:

> "Cruelty is a characteristic of Negroes . . . . contacts
> between Africans and Europeans often result in in-
> fecting the higher race with one or more of the vices of
> the inferior race." (*DG,* 27 Nov., 1934)

Perceiving themselves as having been 'enlightened' by contact with European values and life-style, some educated West Indians wanted to have nothing ,o do with 'inferior' peoples. Interestingly, but not surprisingly, the educated West African readership was treated to views which exalted political dependency and denigrated political independence. In its anti-Garvey campaign, the pro-colonial *Nigerian Pioneer* described Haiti and Santo Domingo as lands of unrests groping in darkness, corruption and fetishism, in contrast to Jamaica where 're-presentative' government existed. (*NP,* 17 December 1920 *in* Olusanya, 147-8)

Thus, Garvey had long encountered hostility from the middle strata and petty bourgeoisie over his international perspective of the black struggle. During his 1921 visit to Jamaica from the United States, a sharp confrontation had taken place between Garvey and the Jamaica League. Garvey had been very critical of the leaders of the League, Rev. Gordon-Somers and Rev. C.A. Wilson, Baptist and Presbyterian ministers respectively.

> "Your Gordon-Somers and your Wilsons and the great
> bunch of Negro preachers are a bunch of hypocrites
> because if they were not hypocrites they would have
> led. They are men with superior education but they have
> no backbone. If they were not cowards they would lead
> you, but they bow and cringe before a man because he is
> white." (*DG,* 26 March 1921, 6, 10)

And a June 2, 1921 letter to the *Gleaner* again criticized colonial parsons:

> "The people of Jamaica want advanced religion now. The religion that will prepare them for heaven by having them live clean, healthy, happy and prosperous lives down here. No hungry man can be a good Christian. No dirty, naked, civilized man can be a good Christian. No shelterless civilized man can be a good Christian for he is bound to have bad wicked thoughts, therefore, it should be the duty of religion to find physical as well as spiritual food for the body of man; so when your preachers ignore the economic condition and moral depravity of the people, they are but serving themselves through preachings and not representing the spirit of God . . . ." *(in* Jacques Garvey a 66)

This was a similar line of argument to the positions espoused today by many radical theologians and Christians. But the press assailed Garvey, for these clergymen had the support of 'educated' opinion on the island. The real cause for this difference lay in the ideological gap between Garveyism which was oriented towards the masses and the colonial mentality of the Jamaica League. For the latter, the idea of anti-colonial struggle was alien, as their political, social and religious activities were based on bettering their condition within the British Empire. And they were sold on the idea that Britain was the 'Mother Country'.

The leaders of the League were defended by the Rev. Ernest Price, a British Baptist missionary, who was President of Calabar Theological College. He argued that the people of Africa did not acknowledge Garvey and suggested that his agitation against European imperialism was futile as Africans were benefitting from the European presence in Africa. He criticized Garvey's failure to pursue his original intention of establishing a Jamaica Tuskegee. To this Garvey countered:

> "Rev. Price referred to my failure in starting a Tuskegee Institute in Jamaica. He suggests that it would have been a good thing to have. I can really understand why Mr. Price draws the line at the present time — he would much prefer to see an industrial school where Negroes

> are taught to plough, hoe, wash plates and clean pots,
> rather than to have Negroes thinking about building
> empires and running big steamships across the ocean.
> Ah! a Tuskegee in Jamaica would be but the carrying
> out of the philosophy of Mr. Price . . . .!" (*DG,* 2 April
> 1921, 10)

People like Price, who were responsible for the training of local parsons and, generally speaking, a local colonial-minded intelligentsia, would have much preferred if Garvey had limited himself to becoming another Booker T. Washington. But Garvey's American experience had radicalized him and he was more outspokenly anti-colonial.

Because it saw the UNIA as a rival with growing support, the Jamaica League organized a meeting during Garvey's visit to declare its own existence. Rev. Gordon-Somers ruled that during this meeting there should be no mention of Garvey's name. However, Rev. Wilson could not measure up to this restraint and indicated that while "Garvey was glancing on the large continent of Africa, his dream was a big one, but the dream of the League was to make Jamaica a paradise, and they felt that Jamaica could only be a paradise by co-operation." (*DG,* 14 April 1921, 13)

This positing of Africa versus Jamaica was, at bottom, a denial of the African-Jamaican realities, and an exaltation of metropolitan paternalism.

Another of Garvey's opponents was the *Jamaica Times,* which was very popular among teachers, civil servants, clergymen, and small-farmers. It stated that Garvey's speeches "aimed at disparaging, declassing, decrying British rule, British officials and British ideals." (*JT,* 18 Sept. 1920, 16) This newspaper (1898-1963) was a weekly founded by an Englishman, Walter Durie, who became a prosperous businessman and engaged in municipal politics. An early editor of this newspaper was the island's first poet-laureate, Thomas Henry Mac-Dermot, better known as Tom Redcam, a Jamaica white. The *Times* was generally regarded as a 'teacher's paper' and reflected in general, the views of educated Blacks. Although the *Jamaica Times* did fairly adequate reporting on Garvey's activities, their leading writers like T.S. Phillips, a black journalist who was also an editor in the thirties, and Major

Caws, a retired British army officer, who was a regular columnist (Ginger) — frequently attacked and ridiculed the UNIA.
(McFarlane, 9, 25-26, 29) The *Times* assessment was eloquent
in showing that Garvey was a staunch critic of British colonialism. The *Times* also printed articles which argued that British
imperialism and the black man's interest coincided. (*JT*, 11
September 1920, 16:2 October 1920, 16) The articles were in
response to the 1920 Madison Square Gardens speech by
Garvey and the successful UNIA Convention of August 1920,
which was widely reported.

During this same Convention, the *Gleaner* had referred to the
young Garvey as "a rabid protagonist" who was "fanning the
flames of race hatred" which they argued in a mixed community
was a matter fraught with serious consequence. (*DG*, 12 August
1920) But the population was not 'evenly mixed', in addition to
which, the social structure bore sharp class and racial antagonisms. In 1921, the racial composition was as follows: Black
and Coloured — 95.3%, East Indian — 2.2%, White — 1.7%,
Chinese — 0.4%, and others — 0.4%. (Eisner, 153) Within each
racial group there were, of course, class divisions, but class and
racial lines generally coincided in a typical colonial pyramid-like
structure of white oppressor and black oppressed. The *Gleaner*
has long been an opponent of all anti-colonial movements,
especially those directed against the British. The *Gleaner*
defended British imperialism in Africa by suggesting that the
"natives of Africa" were satisfied with British rule. (*DG*, 12
August 1920) Referring to Garvey and other black militants
whose activities in New York were making an impact locally, the
editorial stated:

> "Unfortunately, their frothy utterances have trickled
> down to the West Indies, the land of their birth, and
> have caused a good deal of trouble. There is no room for
> race hatred in the British West Indies, and so it has
> become necessary to nip in the bud every effort of those
> leaders of thought (?) in New York.... to stir up strife in
> some of the Caribbean colonies. Not only are certain
> newspapers and magazines controlled by them banned
> in the West Indies, but in various colonies, legislation of
> a drastic nature has been resorted to in order to
> pressure each community from the evil influences that
> are at work in North America." (idem.)

Clearly, the colonial ruling circles in Jamaica were a little more confident of their capacity to contain the spread of Garveyism by means other than those adopted elsewhere in the Empire. In 1922, when the Governor introduced the 'Harmful Publications Prohibition Bill', the *Gleaner* successfully opposed it, contending that such legislation was unnecessary as "Garvey's publications could not do much harm in Jamaica." (*DG,* 2 March 1922) However, three years later, in February 1925, the *Gleaner* made a right-about turn calling for "means of preventing what is fundamentally seditious agitation." (*DG,* 11 February 1925, 10) This editorial was written after Garvey's appeal had been rejected and he was committed to the Atlanta Federal prison for five years with the certainty of being deported after his release.

The *Gleaner's* editorial "Trouble Coming" is well worth quoting as it reveals the lack of confidence now felt within the colony's ruling circles in the face of Garvey's nationalist agitation:

> "Whether Mr. Garvey comes here shortly or five years hence there can be no doubt that he will prove a dangerous element in Jamaica unless it is made unmistakably clear at the very beginning that the authorities are not prepared to tolerate, any nonsense on his part.... His business is agitation along racial lines, and we have recently witnessed something of the effect of his propaganda methods in our own general election.... There are now in Jamaica, societies attached to the Central Society which he formed in America; he has, therefore, already a foundation which he may build upon. But Jamaica is not New York; what makes no impression there might well crack and rupture our very well established social organization." (*DG,* 11 February 1925, 10)

This "very well established social organization" had been built on slavery and colonialism and in the 1920's its sharpest critic was Garvey. The *Gleaner's* extreme reaction was matched by that of A.S. Jelf, the Acting Governor. In a confidential despatch to the Secretary of State for the Colonies, Jelf indicated that the British Government should make representation "to the United States of America against the deportation of

Garvey to Jamaica . . . ." (Jelf) The *Gleaner* and the Acting Governor were both agreed on the necessity of suppressing Garvey because he represented a serious threat to the entire fabric of the Jamaican colonial 'order'.

In order to understand what was responsible for this uncompromising attitude, the post-war unrest must be taken into account. As was the case in the United States, the post-war years in Jamaica were characterized by a great deal of social unrest among the veterans, petty bourgeoisie, the working class and the unemployed, which made them disposed to radical political activity. During June-July 1918, there had been strikes in Kingston, St. Catherine, Portland, St. Thomas, St. Mary, Clarendon, and Manchester. *(DG,* 2-6 July 1918) Dockworkers, railway employees and labourers on sugar and banana estates took strike action. On the Amity Hall sugar estate in Clarendon, the reading of the Riot Act preceded the shooting to death of three workers. (*DG,* 4 July 1918, 1) The workers had resorted not only to strike action but also to the cutting of telephone wires and the burning of canefields. (*DG,* 5 July 1918, 1) These months were in a sense, a prelude to the 1938 strikes. But the actions of 1918 were localized ones, they did not have a national outreach. Still, the strikes among railway workers between 1918 and 1919 exerted pressure on the colonial government to pass legislation in favour of a limited form of trade union representation. (Hart f, 8; Phelps, 420)

In July 1918, there had also been anti-Chinese demonstrations in St. Catherine, which threatened to develop in other parts of the island. In the competition between the black shopkeepers and the Chinese retailers, the latter were winning the battle. As far as access to credit was concerned, the British banks and big importers gave preference to cultivating and encouraging this minority and frustrating black business aspirations. By 1911, one of three Chinese was engaged in retail trade and by 1925, this had increased to one out of every two. (Levy, 14-16) Thus, the Chinese had become a highly visible, prosperous minority based in the towns and rural villages. For damages incurred during these anti-Chinese demonstrations, the colonial government in Kingston had to pay a large bill (*DG,* 2 October 1919, 8)

In October 1919 a number of West Indian and West African seamen who had been repatriated from London reportedly "terrorized a section of the city for two hours." In this protest against a delayed payment at the Immigration Office, they attacked a number of business places and were said to have singled out white people for reprisals, seeking in their own way to avenge racism in England and especially the treatment meted out to black residents during the Liverpool race riots. *(DG,* 11 October 1919, 3)

In addition, in December 1918, there had been a revolt involving black soldiers of the British West Indian Regiments in Taranto, Italy, against racism in the army. (Elkins d, 99) This "prefigured the insurrections that took place in the following year in British Honduras and Trinidad" and also stimulated the development of black nationalism in the British Caribbean (idem.) This influence was also noted by C.L.R. James in his political study of Captain Cipriani, the Trinidadian trade union leader and politician, himself a veteran of Taranto. (James, 101-102) Out of the Taranto revolt came the Caribbean League based on "fifty and sixty sergeants" who had pledged themselves to fight for self-determination. (Elkins d, 101-102) This action had some impact in Jamaica as the Governor attempted to "allay the bitter resentment" of the British West India Regiments by putting into effect legislation "which allowed each soldier to vote in the next election only." (idem.) This sop did not mean much. It made the veterans no better off and their dissatisfacton rankled.

1919 was in fact a critical year for the British colonial authorities in the Caribbean. The British official document of 1919 entitled "Unrest Among Negroes" drew attention to the UNIA's correspondence with "prominent coloured men . . . . in Africa, India, Japan and the West Indies." (Elkins b, 70) This was said to be part of the UNIA's efforts to awaken race consciousness among negroes of the United States and Africa, with the aim of gradually bringing about a unity of purpose of the negro peoples of both continents. (idem.) This report also carried an appendix on Garvey who was singled out as a violent agitator and described as a "strong force among the negroes throughout the East and perhaps he is strongest in Chicago where he associates with the Left Wing and I.W.W. elements." (ibid., 79)

So by 1921, Garveyism had established itself as a banner of anti-colonial struggle. Garvey's speeches in 1921 showed that he understood the connection between the broader struggle for the freedom of Africa and the national struggles, for example, those in Jamaica, whose conditions he was most familiar with. In a letter published in the *Gleaner* on June 2, 1921, he criticized the lack of a national spirit and said that:

> "Everybody in Jamaica seems to be looking to the 'Mother Country' for everything . . . . Jamaicans . . . . worship too much that which comes from abroad, and from anywhere. If a thing, a man, or an animal is imported, it is supposed to be better than the native product. How silly! I recommend that the poorer classes of Jamaica — the working classes — get together and form themselves into unions and organizations and elect their members for the Legislative Council. With few exceptions, the men in the Council are representing themselves and their class. The workers of Jamaica should elect their own representatives . . . ."

These were not revolutionary suggestions, but important democratic measures.

Garvey further called for the payment of legislators by the government. If this was not done then the unions and organizations should do so. But the substance of this letter does not lie so much in the reforms suggested but in the direction of Garvey's thinking — that independent class politics was necessary. This was a theme Garvey was to take up in Jamaica in 1929-34. In a colonial situation where unions were not allowed and politics was for the monied classes, this approach had revolutionary implications. This idea did not simply reflect abstract conceptions but showed Garvey's knowledge that in Europe the working-class movement was developing; so was it also in the United States, and moreover in the Caribbean people were more receptive to ideas for change.

So, the colonial officials had to assess the implications of the growth of the UNIA in Jamaica which after Garvey's 1921 visit had spread to every parish in the island. (Jacques Garvey b) The organization was strongest in the parishes of Kingston and St. Andrew with growing outreach through its branches in the rural parishes.

In June 1924, there had occurred what became known as the Darling Street Riot in Kingston (*DG*, 10 June 1924, 1), which

preceded a very violent strike of banana carriers in Port
Antonio. (*DG*, 21 June 1924) The Darling Street Riot was the
result of a protest march by one thousand road construction
workers and their unemployed supporters to the Public Works
headquarters for an increase in wages. Two people had been
killed and forty injured in clashes with the colonial authorities,
while in Port Antonio one person had, been killed.

This unrest had filtered over into the 1925 electoral campaign where slogans like "Colour for Colour" and "Skin for
Skin" had been popular. (*DG*, 24 February 1925, 8) This had
prompted the *Gleaner* to comment:

> "We have to admit that this class consciousness we
> speak of has been very potent; never has it been so
> powerfully operative as in this instance, and it is
> possible that it may become still more powerfully
> operative in the future." (*DG*, 7 February 1925, 13)

Garvey's 1921 advice that "the poorer classes of Jamaica, the
working classes, get together and form themselves into unions
and organizations and elect their own representative" (*DG*, 2
June 1921, 6), and the flow of militant speeches from New York
had acted as yeast to the anti-colonial movement, particularly
its determined working-class component.

Then there was the Wood Commission of 1921-22, which had
encouraged the formation of pressure group-type political clubs
organized by two legislators, J.A.G. Smith and H.A.L. Simpson.
Smith and Simpson called for moderate constitutional changes.
(Carnegie, 100) S.M. Jones, President of the Jamaica UNIA,
was associated with Smith's platform.

Although these groups were short-lived ad hoc formations,
they attested to the social and political ferment which existed in
the colony.

For all these reasons, then, the call made in February 1925,
for the suppression of Garvey in Jamaica was certainly not
surprising but one made necessary by the growing opposition to
and questioning of British colonialism. Therefore, in April
1924, the *Gleaner* took the view:

> "It is with profound regret that we view the arrival of
> Marcus Garvey in Jamaica. And it is with more than
> profound regret that we picture any leader of thought

and culture in this island associating himself with a
welcome given to him. But Kingston has reached such a
level of degeneracy that there is no knowing what she
will do . . . . A new spirit has passed over the lower
classes which has nothing to commend it except its
ignorance. . . ."

The paper further saw Garvey's return as giving an impetus to
this trend and referred to it as the "dumping upon us of a man
who indeed is Jamaican but for whom the island as a whole or
the more intelligent section of it, has no use." *(in* Edwards, 25-
26)

So in the pre-1925 period, the *Gleaner's* prime tactic, as in the
case with the Bedward movement, was to discredit the Garvey
organization by slandering it. Two of the main targets used were
the Black Star Line enterprise for which Jamaican contributions had come and Garvey's insistence on the paramount
importance of African political emancipation. The *Gleaner*
consistently propagandized against the financial contributions
of Jamaicans and also said they already had a country. (*DG,* 6
September 1922, 8) For them the idea of a "great Negro
Republic" was impossible and those who subscribed to it knew
it was impossible. (idem.) They pointed to the imperial presence in Africa which was considered irremovable and added
that tribal divisions and backwardness of the continent proved
the irrationality of the UNIA's actions. This editorial position
resulted in a great deal of correspondence from Garvey's
enemies and his supporters.

This journalistic propaganda DeLisser of the *Gleaner* continued in the literary field. In the 1925-6 issue of his Literary
journal, aptly named *Planters' Punch,* DeLisser included a
novelette entitled *The Jamaican Nobility or The Story of Sir
Mortimer and Lady Mat* which parodied Garvey and the
Jamaican Garveyites. (*PP,* 1925-26) His preface read in part:

"When Mr. Marcus Garvey constituted himself President of the African Republic, which itself had not yet
been constituted, he bethought him of forming a court
and of creating a nobility to adorn that court. . . ." (ibid.,
9)

He went on to create two fictional Garveyites: one a hotel-worker, the other a railway employee who had been honoured by the UNIA with the titles, "Knight of Nile" and "High Conspicuous Potentate". This novelette described the reactions of the employers who dismissed them from their jobs because of their association with the UNIA. This story enables one to examine some of the prejudices against Garveyites at the time as well as the type of persecution they suffered. But more than this, it reflected the post-1925 tension caused in Jamaican colonial circles by the announcement of Garvey's deportation consequent on his release from prison. Two brief excerpts indicate the tension-ridden prejudices against the UNIA. Before the hotel manager dismisses the Garveyite worker, the following exchange takes place between them:

> "You have been sending money to America to support this propaganda, perhaps?"
> "Yes sir."
> "Then it is clear that you are not sane." (ibid., 22)

With regard to the railway employee, DeLisser writes:

> ". . . . but various spies and talebearers knew that he was one of the Garveyan nobles, and they suggested to those higher up in the Railway hierarchy that a man so intimately connected with Mr. Marcus Garvey must of necessity be at the root of any annoyance or disorder, past, present or to come . . . ." (ibid., 23)

DeLisser's novelette, together with his journalism, offer the main arguments on which colonialist propaganda against Garveyism was based. In fact, his fictional portraits of leading figures in Jamaican history made them all negative symbols.[3]

Garvey's Cultural Programme

Marcus Garvey's cultural programme formed an integral part of his Jamaican activities.

Novelist and critic Sylvia Wynter, in a positive assessment of Garvey, advances the view that

> "What Césaire was in the intellectual and cultural field, Marcus Garvey was in the political-agitational. His great organization based in the United States and his massive plans for a physical return to Africa comprised the corollary of the spiritual and intellectual return of the 'negritude' movement. While his movement failed, it had shaken up the fantasy and stirred up the imagination of millions of black 'folk' in the United States and the Caribbean. His movement awakened an awareness of Africa, a revaluation of Africa and a sense of pride in the past, whose myths had been used to keep black people in servitude and self-contempt. This started the process which has led in a direct line to the Black Power movement." (Wynter, 34)

This analysis, though praiseworthy, belongs to a school of thought which selects as its starting point Garvey's so-called "massive plans for a physical return to Africa." (*See* Editorial *SG*, 31 May 1970)

Beginning from a false interpretation, it ends up by considering Garveyism almost exclusively in the emotional, spiritual, psychological, and even mystical spheres. It is true that he "awakened an awareness of Africa, a revaluation of Africa, and a sense of pride in the past." In fact, his cultural programme bolstered his political-agitational work in this direction. However, his contribution to cultural development and his active promotion of artistes in Jamaica have been neglected areas of attention and appreciation. At the same time, the significance of his movement for the Harlem Renaissance in the 1920's has been evaluated by a number of scholars.[4]

And in respect of Jamaica, Ivy Baxter does not omit to take cognizance of Garvey. In her historical study of the creative arts in Jamaica, Baxter notes that Garvey

> "urged political and cultural activities upon black people and gave a new sense of self-awareness to people who had not had enough opportunity for expression." (Baxter, 83)

This point was made in reference to his work at Edelweiss Park. Edelweiss Park was located at 76 Slipe Pen Road in Cross Roads in the island's capital. It housed various UNIA offices upstairs, entrance to which was gained from stairs at the back, since at the front of the building, a high stage projected onto the front lawn. Over the stage was a dome which helped with acoustics. A section of the ground floor of the house served as a dressing room. The audience was accommodated in a four-tiered amphitheatre while Garvey, his wife and visiting UNIA delegates sat to one side of the stage, Garvey in a rocking-chair. (Patterson)

From 1919, Edelweiss Park became the most significant cultural-political centre for black people in the history of the island at a time when the arts were dominated by expatriates — both local residents and touring drama groups — and when a black face on stage was a curiosity. (Bennett) In April 1931, Garvey launched the Edelweiss Amusement Company. (*CA*, 25 April, 1931, 1) This company formed the organizational foundation for a very varied cultural programme which ranged from dramatic productions, choral singing, elocution contests, vaudeville shows, movies (which had only recently been introduced), to boxing. Dancing took place every night to the music of quadrille players and bands specializing in the Susie-Q and other contemporary North American dances. Garvey himself had described the Park as a centre where people could relax and refresh themselves "after the heat and burden of the day." (Patterson) On the other hand, a non-denominational religious service was conducted by Garvey on Sunday mornings and evenings, during which he lectured, and this was followed by anthems from the choir.

> "The choir was women, about thirty of them, dressed in white. White hats . . . . His wife was in the choir . . . . The men in black caps with white braid around it, the jackets had white braid round the neck, and white braid on the seam of their pants. The choir started to sing and Garvey come up and take his place at the pulpit . . . . Garvey wore a black pants and a white sash with three different colours on it across his chest, and a regalia, a robe, over him. It was yellow. And he had something like a crown — mortar-board — on his head. People felt proud of him. Proud. Anytime he was coming it was a proud meeting . . . . Garvey was stout, big, with a big head and with a commanding voice. He wasn't bad looking. He spoke ordinary, plain talk. You could

understand all that he said . . . .
 That Edelweiss meeting was packed with people . . . .
orderly. Everybody sit down quietly, everybody dress
like a church. It was church . . . . Garvey preached from
the Bible . . . . He talked about how humans should live
to God . . . . In the service he didn't talk about politics. . ."
(Rose, 6, 7)

Another target of the newly formed Edelweiss Amusement
company was the re-publication of the *Blackman* which had
ceased publication in February 1931.
 Two aspects of the Edelweiss Park project are important.
Firstly, Garvey recognized the necessity for artists to be
employed full time at their work. He helped to create conditions
whereby this could become possible. Secondly, much of the
entertainment had roots in the church, school and folk concert
tradition — the tea-meeting — of the post-Emancipation
period, aspects of which can be gleaned from Claude McKay's
portrayal of village life in his novel, *Banana Bottom.* As such,
mock trials and mock weddings were staged. In the latter, the
'bride' would be pinned up on stage in her wedding outfit
without the use of scissors. The 'wedding ceremony' itself
would feature a solo and afterwards the 'reception' would take
place. (Patterson)
 But the importance of Garvey's contribution to the cultural
awakening of the 1930's lay not only in his role as a promoter
but also as a creative artist. Garvey's three dramatic productions dealt with historical and contemporary themes. His
"Slavery — From Hut to Mansion" had a cast of one hundred
and twenty characters and was described as "a revelation of the
horrors of slavery", which it took as its starting point, and ended
with a portrayal of post-Emancipation struggles." (*B*, 9 August
1930, 11; 16 August 1930, 10) "Roaming Jamaicans" depicted
the West Indian diaspora in the Americas. "The Coronation of
an African King" which had scenes in several African, European
and West Indian capitals, was an exposition of the UNIA's work
and the attempts by European and American governments to
stem the tide of the Garvey movement. (*B*, 21 June 1930, 3)
These three plays were produced between June and August
1930, and were very well attended. Another play was entitled
"Ethiopia at the Bar of Justice". Costumes were colourful.
None of the scripts are now available — which means that one

has to take as source the very sketchy reviews and advertisements which were written to promote the plays. It is even possible that the narrative line allowed for improvisations. All the same, the plays contained dialogues, short speeches, and a lot of jokes. Garvey himself "was a good joker," testified Iris Patterson. She herself had acted in one of the plays. She reported that the actors were adaptable and, therefore, rehearsals went without strain.

These efforts mark the beginning of a serious indigenous political theatre which was bold enough to tackle themes and issues of relevance at a time when second-hand British or quasi-European standards and dramatic content prevailed.

Edelweiss Park was also the centre for the development of a number of creative artists. Among them were Gerardo Leon who was in charge of the musical orchestra for the UNIA Follies — a dance troupe; Una Marson, poet/playwright; Granville Campbell, who conducted the one hundred-strong Edelweiss Park Choir; (DG, 28 November 1931, 12), and Randolph Williams, an outstanding comedian of the theatre and radio, who later became as identified with the annual Jamaican pantomime as Louise Bennett, and who died in 1981. As early as October 17 1929, the Blackman had reported that

> "Mr. Ran Williams, our celebrated comedian, who has been largely responsible for the high standard and variety of amusement at the park, will contribute to the programme in his usual comic way."

As indicated. Ranny Williams was also responsible for putting on musical comedies, such as "Blacks Gone Wild" and "She is a Sheba." (B, 22 November 12 December 1929; 15 February 1930) He was a young man at the time, having recently graduated from Kingston College, where he had distinguished himself in elocution. (Patterson) Other popular comedians who distinguished themselves were E.M. Cupidon, and the double-billed artists Kid Harold and Trim, and Racca and Sandy.[5] "The pairs were very good . . . . the public always appreciated them together, but they were good separately all the same." (Patterson) Kid Harold was performing well into the 1930's a veteran tap dancer, Trim died performing in England in the Second World War, but "when he laughed the . . . . corners of his

mouth went back to his ears and his pearly teeth showed."
(Patterson) The comedians performed skits in the Jamaican
dialect. Poems in dialect and Standard English were composed
and recited by Garveyites. Iris Patterson, Stennett Kerr-
Coombs and George McCormack wrote and performed in
Standard English.

The role of the Garvey newspapers in bringing to their
readers constant reports on cultural activities which affected
Black people and critical appreciation of the arts was unpre-
cedented in local journalism. Of significance in this field, were
the contributions of J.A. Rogers, the Jamaican-born writer who
had migrated to the United States and made a name for himself
as an authority on Black History. Rogers' articles were wide-
ranging. He discussed the work of the Cuban revolutionary,
Antonio Maceo, famous African leaders, Afro-American music
and the fortunes of individuals like Paul Robeson and Claude
McKay in Europe,[6] as well as Blacks in antiquity. Most of his
contributions were historical.

Of this kind of material, the Garvey papers were never short
as they dipped into the writings of W.E.B. DuBois and Carter G.
Woodson, who was the founder-editor of the *Journal of Negro
History. (NJ,* 21 February 1933, 5) One of the longest historical
features published in the *New Jamaican* was an anonymous
serial entitled "Fifty Years in Chains or the Life of An American
Slave." (*NJ,* 14 August — 9 September 1933) This serial had
not yet concluded when the *New Jamaican* ceased publication
in September, 1933.

An important Jamaican sculptor whose work the *Blackman*
also encouraged was Alvin Marriott. (*B,* 26 September 1929, 3)
J.E. Clare McFarlane. (*B,* 19 September 1929, 2; 3 May, 1930,
Favourable reviews were devoted to the poetry of Claude
McKay, Arthur Nicholas, Una Marson, Constance Hollar, and
Garvey himself contributed his own verse to the pages of the
Blackman, most of which was written in solitude in Atlanta
Prison.

Garvey's criticism of Paul Robeson and Claude McKay in his
publications reflected his philosophy of the arts. For instance,
while in London he wrote of Robeson:

> "Paul Robeson is a Negro of genius as a singer and he
> has some ability as an actor. Unfortunately he has not

been using his genius as a singer and actor in the thoroughly selective manner of personalities of other races . . . . he cannot be compared to John McCormack or Caruso, who have used the talent of their voices to dignify their respective races, neither has he used his ability as an actor like Garrick,' Irving or Sir Beerbohm Tree to add intellectual lustre to their race. He has used his genius to appear in pictures and plays that tend to dishonour, mimic, discredit and abuse the cultural attainments of the Black Race, such as can be seen in pictures like 'Sanders of the River', 'Emperor Jones', 'Song of Freedom', 'Stevedore'." (*BM*, 19 January 1937, 3)

This, however, cannot be accepted as a valid overall assessment of Robeson but as a telling criticism of his work at certain points in his career. Robeson, himself, for example, was said to have repudiated "Sanders of the River" at its premiere, a fact which indicates self-criticism on similar grounds to those being raised by Garvey. Clearly Garvey felt that Black creative artists should not only identify with the struggle of their own people but that their work should be a direct contribution to this struggle. And certainly, overall, Paul Robeson did not fail that test. In fact, he was a brilliant political fighter and used his art, his artistry, and his prestige in support of his people as well as of other oppressed peoples — a choice for which he was made to suffer political and artistic repression and ostracism. (Dyer)

The criticism of Claude McKay which appeared in the *Blackman* newsaper in 1929, was headlined, "Claude McKay, Jamaican Negro Prostitutes Poetic Ability". The critic, interviewing the novelist in Paris had been mainly intent on censuring McKay for his depiction of the seamy side of Harlem life. McKay dismissed this well-intended piece of prudery by replying that *Home to Harlem* was ahead of its time and he saw "one hope for the Negro and this is for him to tell the truth about himself." (*B*, 29 April 1929) This particular attack on McKay reflected certain of the limitations of cultural criticism from a nationalist viewpoint, that is, a tendency to promote what is perceived as good, to suppress what is perceived as negative, as well as to idealize the past. However, the critique raised questions about McKay's own bohemianism, his rootlessness, and the quality of his relationship to the Black struggle, questions which McKay himself did not answer satisfactorily in his autobiography, *A Long Way From Home.*[7]

All the same, in a discussion of Art at the 1934 Convention in Kingston, Garvey described it as the highest form of human intelligence. (*DG*, 18 August 1934, 27) Having assessed the role of art from the standpoint of the interests of the struggle, Garvey also approached art with a very deep sense of the aesthetic worth of an individual work. For example, Garvey had for a number of years been a collector of ceramics, paintings and antiques. Amy Jacques Garvey recalled that after visiting antique shops and returning with a few treasures

> "he would spend time and patience to place them in the right setting, colour scheme and the most effective lighting . . . . he enjoyed sitting in an easy chair and contemplating the beauty of the setting he had created or the exquisite workmanship of a Satsuma from Japan, a Delph vase from Holland or the delicacy of an eggshell goblet." (Jacques Garvey a, 189; *DG*, 7 February 1930)

Furthermore, in his 1934 address, he pointed to the need for a dynamic concept of Art through which contemporary experience and values could be projected:

> "You can still find in Egypt, lasting monuments of Negro Art which still remain a puzzle to the world. But it is not a credit to us of today. As much as we are trying to develop ourselves in business, religion, politics and so on, we have to build up ourselves in Art." (*DG*, 18 August 1934, 27)

So that while the monuments of the past, the achievements of the African race necessarily had to be projected so as to counter the myths of colonialism which would denigrate our racial heritage,[8] Garvey was also pointing out that the accomplishments of the distant past were no substitute for creativity in the present. His question, "Are we going to build up a civilization without those things that go to make up the culture of the civilization?" is of enduring validity.

Much of Garvey's own journalism and cultural writings were of course geared towards attacking racism. He exposed not only racist attitudes of Whites to Blacks but what was referred to as the "internal prejudices of Negroes", which were themselves a consequence of slavery and colonialism. About this Garvey wrote:

> "In countries where the blacks outnumber the whites, the 'colored' build up a buffer society through financial assistance and patronage of the minority whites. They convince the minority whites that the blacks are dangerous and vicious, and that their only chance of successfully living among them is to elevate to positions of trust, superiority and overseership the 'colored' element who will directly deal with the blacks and exploit them for the general benefit of whites." *(B, 31 January 1930)*

In marriage, Black men who were on their way up, sought to marry women of fair or white complexion. Again, Garvey exposed the basis of these social prejudices and the political and economic function that such social relations played in the colonial framework.

These prejudices were, of course, deeply rooted. Amy Jacques Garvey, herself a mulatto, records that after the birth of her second son, Julius, in 1933, she met an old schoolmate on the main street of Kingston, Jamaica. Her greeting was, "I haven't seen you in ages. What are you doing with this little black baby?" Her comment in *Garvey and Garveyism* was: "The old concept of skin-color distinction and the idea of 'raising one's color' by marriage dies hard with our people." (222-223)

Being the torch-bearer of a progressive cultural policy, Garvey's press naturally came into conflict with H.G. De-Lisser's journal, *Planter's Punch* which was primarily a vehicle for DeLisser's own literary efforts and those of his clique. *Planter's Punch* also featured the work of British and European writers, several of whom wrote about the "exotic tropics" and "peasant life" after brief excursions to the Caribbean. Finally, *Planter's Punch* published the achievements of the local Whites and capitalists whose advertisements kept the literary annual alive. It neither recognized nor published the work of the new talent that was emerging in the 1930's. It remained DeLisser's hobby horse and the vehicle for the work of his "friends and social companions." On this score the *Blackman* of December 10, 1929, felt compelled to editorialize:

"It is our duty to protest against any publication standing in the name of Jamaica, that does not represent Jamaica as it is, giving equal credit to the Negro and White population; but to selfishly put forward a few friends and social companions; that is not only a false representation, but an insult to the seven hundred thousand Negroes of the colony; and sowing the seed of racial antagonism. . . ."

So that the Garvey press, the weekly Liberty Hall meeting, and the *Philosophy and Opinions of Marcus Garvey* — which was second only to the Bible in the homes of many Garveyites — all these were bulwarks of the counter-attack by Garvey in the political and cultural spheres of anti-colonialism.

AMY JACQUES GARVEY, Garvey's second wife.
[Photo courtesy of the National Library of Jamaica]

Chapter Fourteen

People's Representative

KSAC Stewardship

On 24th March 1930, Garvey raised in the Council the issue of the Mayor's refusal to allow him to hold a public meeting at Ward Theatre "in the interest of the labouring and working classes of the island." (KSAC, 24 March 1930) The Mayor replied that it was his prerogative "to grant the free use of the Theatre for Religious, Educational or Charitable purposes, and he did not think that the application in question came under the heads referred to." (idem.) Yet, on other occasions, the Ward Theatre had been rented to Garvey for political meetings. But whenever he was thwarted in this way, Garvey would hold his meetings on the Ward Theatre steps, the Coke Methodist Church Hall steps or at Burnt Ground in Cross Roads, which were traditional public meeting spots. These supplemented Edelweiss Park and the small Liberty Halls in Kingston and St. Andrew.

On this occasion Garvey held the meeting outside Ward Theatre. The meeting was attended by six thousand people. On the platform were Madam M.L.T. DeMena, UNIA International Organizer, Rev. S.M. Jones, J.I. Denniston, S.M. DeLeon, C.D. Johnson, etc.

In his speech, Garvey outlined the economic conditions in graphic language and was sharp in his criticism of DeLisser and Wint. The economic crisis was grave. The root of the problem was that

"The reign of oligarchy in this country must come to a close, and the reign of government and government alone under the constitution must continue (applause). This oligarchy of so called 'influential men' has ridden rough-shod over the rights and privileges of the people and reduced them to misery, disease and early death". (Garvey i, 174)

He continued:

"We have heard a lot of gab, seen written a lot of lies about the prosperity of the country — prosperity judged from the condition of a very limited number of people who have all that they want — money, property, leisure and unrighteous power, they are the limited few. . . . This Sunday afternoon if you were to go into the homes of hundreds of thousands of the people of this island, you would find thousands of Jamaicans who haven't had a meal for their families this Sunday afternoon, who have not put a pot on the fire possibly for days, because they haven't got the money to buy meat and fish and chickens to go with the ground provisions. Year in, year out, they have to eat ground food or bare rice, with a little mackerel or herring sometimes, not enough to nourish their bodies, and the poor little children have pot-bellies and scurvy, yaws and ecze-mas." (175)

This is one of Garvey's finest political speeches on the Jamaican situation. He engages the oligarchy and their spokes-men directly, and puts forward modern approaches to pro-blems. For example, he speaks of the need for scientific statistics by which the conditions of the people can be judged:

"Later on we hope to get those figures, so that the state and the government can realize the condition of the country and its people, and not allow these paid newspaper men to boast that the country is prosperous, when the people are on the verge of starvation. In the absence of statistics, we have to form opinions by the life of the people." (175-176)

He further points out that "one does not judge the prosperity of England, America or Europe by the position of the limited few, but by the *condition of the masses.*" (176)

His proposals to deal with the country's economic problems further imply the involvement of the state in the economy. The proposal for raising a loan of five million pounds from the Imperial government was geared towards the "development of agricultural and general industries.... with the object of finding employment, through such enterprises, for the thousands of unemployed, and at the same time, make such enterprises so productive and profitable as to be a source of revenue to the island." (187)

He also reiterated the need for a minimum wage and the eight-hour day. His consistent defence of the interests of the working masses around a radical programme was influenced in part by similar state interventionist measures that were being proposed and in some cases implemented in the United States and Europe in order to alleviate the effects of the Depression. But Garvey was not simply copying what was being implemented in the imperialist countries; he was breaking with the political traditions of colonial legislatures which hitherto were not concerned with the problems of the country as a whole and with planning at a national level. He made this point in the KSAC:

> "The Legislative Council, instead of tackling our problems at this level, ignore them and continue their individual narrow policy of getting bridges built, a stretch of road repaired or a water tank erected. Let us set them an example in sensible planning and make the people of Kingston and St. Andrew happy.
>
> Some of us will ask where is the money to come from. It is right here in Jamaica. Just recently I read in the newspapers that a man died and left six hundred and fifty thousand pounds. There are many planters. merchants and business men who have made their money here and are wealthy; but alive or dead, they do nothing to benefit the people of their communities. They have no national spirit; but they could be asked to subscribe a loan for development, for which they would be paid interest. This act would

also ease their consciences . . . ." (Jacques Garvey a, 283).

Garvey was then speaking on a motion involving better water supply, better lighting, proper sewage, a Fire Brigade station, and recreation grounds for the Corporate Area. Although he lost the motion, Garvey set an example as to how a representative of the masses should conduct himself in a legislature, limited though it was, by colonial laws.

In 1931, Garvey ended a report on his visit to Europe at Edelweiss Park with an outline of his ideas for a national development plan based on a ten million dollar loan from the British Government. *(DG,* 26 November 1931, 20) He argued that conditions had deteriorated so badly in Jamaica that she was on the verge of a violent outbreak because no attention had been paid to certain pressing economic problems. From Edelweiss Park, he carried his ideas to the KSAC as he had been re-elected to that body in absentia.[1] But the fact that Seymour had also been returned as Mayor made it all the more difficult for reform measures to be taken up in the Council. Garvey pressed for increased wages to the employees of the KSAC and a scheme for civic improvement which included better housing in slum areas, the establishment of Race Course as a National Park, the building of a Town Hall and a School of Domestic Science. This plan he considered moderate enough for the Municipal Council to undertake after it had approached the central government to secure the floating of a loan of one million dollars. (KSAC, 14 December 1931) This bill, however, was never accepted. Opposed and shelved by reactionary Council members, several of these same reforms were later to be incorporated in the recommendations of the Moyne Commission instituted by the British Government after the 1937-1938 riots throughout the West Indies.

Labour Agitation

Garvey was not only sharply critical of propertied vested interests in Jamaica, but also agitated on behalf of the working class.

For instance, by the end of May 1929, the *Blackman* found itself playing the role of chief representative of Kingston's banana loaders before the May 24th and 27th strike demonstrations occurred. The newspaper was well prepared for this role as it had been waging a systematic onslaught against the bad conditions under which these workers loaded the boats. For example, on May 14, 1929 Garvey wrote in his column under the caption 'Brutal Men' about the maltreatment of a young loader:

> "A poor black boy trying to earn a living by running task in carrying bananas for the Jamaica Fruit Company at the No. 3 Pier was beaten up a couple days ago by the Assistant Wharfinger."

On the other hand, the newspaper representing the local agents of American banana imperialism, *The Jamaica Mail,* accused the *Blackman* of creating unrest among the workers which occurred later that May. In reply to charges of incitement by the *Jamaica Mail,* the *Blackman* of May 27th replied:

> "The *Blackman* has exposed many acts on the waterfront, acts amounting to a form of slavery and oppression, but neither the *Mail* nor anyone can positively say that recent dissatisfaction is indirectly traceable to our remarks. For what we know, it might have been a mere coincidence. The proletariat . . . . are an indispensable asset to any country and the flood of light which the twentieth century has brought with it, sweeps along in one grand 'Universal Urge' pointing these same 'lower classes' to their rights on the labour market. In England, in America and other places, the cry of the labourer has gone up 'into the ears of the Lord of Sabaoth' and the comments of the *Blackman* form only a part of the great cry for justice."

This front page article was headlined 'A Moderate Reply to the *Jamaica Mail's* comment on Saturday'.

The battle between the *Jamaica Mail* and the *Blackman* concerned the strike action that the workers had taken on the Friday night, 24th May and on Monday, May 27th. The reporter for the *Blackman* wrote up the Friday story in detail. On Monday there was a demonstration with five hundred labourers walking off the job, so leaving about fifteen thousand stems of bananas on the wharf to be loaded on the Elders & Fyffes ship, the "S.S. Carare." This boat had docked on Monday morning and was scheduled to sail in the afternoon. But the workers demanded a wage of 4/-2 per one hundred bunches instead of 1/-9, the same pay on Sunday, and double-time on holidays and during the night.

The manager of the United Fruit Company in Kingston, speaking to a small group of female carriers, said that they were not going to pay a farthing more and that the workers ought to realise that the Company could get machines to load the ship. The United Fruit Company had not only the *Mail* and *Gleaner* editorials on its side but also the police and the Governor. The workers were fired.

In order to understand Garvey's role, it is necessary to trace the action of the banana loaders on May 27th. The *Gleaner* on May 28th reported that in the afternoon the strikers had marched with an "improvised red banner . . . . waving green branches and wild red flowers" up to the UNIA Liberty Hall on upper King Street and then to Edelweiss Park, Headquarters of the UNIA on Slipe Pen Road. The headlines of the *Blackman*, May 28th, 1929 the following day read:

> "FIVE HUNDRED LABOURERS WALKED OUT
> LABOUR UNREST DELAYS WORK
> STRIKERS SEEK ADVICE OF THE HON.
> MARCUS GARVEY".

The workers called on Garvey "to make an appeal on their behalf to the United Fruit Company for better wages." (*B,* 28 May 1929) Garvey addressed them:

> "You are unfortunate enough as not to control any large amount of capital. You are therefore labourers. The people who control capital, who own property are regarded as the most substantial of our citizenry, and at all times their demands and their requests receive careful consideration and quicker attention than those of the citizenry who do not represent wealth nor property. Because of this peculiar situation, a large number of your people, my people, our race form the unemployed element in this country . . . . Unfortunately, you of the Labouring Classes have never organized

yourselves into a Union through which you could barter
with those who employ you for the kind of wage that you
desire. In the absence of individual wealth, the greatest
weapon for bargaining is organization. In that you are
not individually wealthy your only strength of resistance
would be through organization, through union, through
co-operation. That you have not got. You in Jamaica
have no organization . . . . and therefore you are at the
mercy of the capitalist. In the absence of that I do not
want you to lose your position; because the people who
employ you have no sympathy for you. They will just
transfer you for another group of Negroes." (idem.)

He negotiated on their behalf but the UFC had already taken
action against the strikers. But Garvey's connection with the
daily struggles of the masses won him their support and respect.
It also strengthened the resolve of his class enemies that he
should not make any political headway. The wealthy owners of
the UFC bribed Garvey's political opponents and some of his
adherents in order to achieve this objective.

In January 1930, Garvey petitioned the Olivier Sugar
Commission which was then visiting the West Indies. *(B,* 9
January 1930; 7). This petition called for: "a minimum wage,
definite hours of work, housing accommodation for those
compelled to live on the estates, prohibition of labour for
children of schoolable age and assurance against accident or
failing health in all cases of those employed in the industry." *(B,*
11 January 1930, 2) Several public meetings, explaining this
petition, were held. *(B,* 10 January 1930, 2) Garvey emphasized that the landowners were prepared and ready to give their
side of the picture to the Commission and it was up to the
workers to prevent this one-sided view from dominating the
investigation by advancing their side. These meetings were
followed by a deputation to the Governor. Garvey argued that
the Olivier Commission was inadequate and called for a Royal
Commission to "make a thorough investigation of the condition
of the working classes in Jamaica." *(B,* 26 April 1930, 3).

Shortly after this, the formation of the Jamaica Workers and
Labourers Association was announced. (idem.) Garvey was
elected Chairman, A. Aikman, Vice-Chairman, and S.M. De-
Leon, Secretary.[2] DeLeon had also been a Garveyite and had

served the UNIA in several capacities. The Jamaica Workers and Labourers Association set about pursuing the aims of the January petition and repeated the call for an investigatory Royal Commission. But the political pressure was not great enough for Whitehall to act accordingly.

Again, on February 27, 1930, Garvey wrote a lengthy letter to Phillip Snowdon who was then Chancellor of the Exchequer, in which he set out the conditions facing the masses in the small British colony. He summed up the situation as follows:

> "Jamaica is a British colony with a population of nearly one million people, of this number, more than 850,000 are black people. There are 15,000 white and the rest are offsprings of white and black — coloured people. In this population there is a social arrangement whereby all positions of influence are held by a minority class. The bulk of the black people are kept in conditions bordering on serfdom, they are made up generally of the labouring class who receive but a pittance of a wage, ranging from six-pence for women a day to a 9d., and for men from 1/- a day to 2/-. Because of this low scale of wages among the people, crime is rife, our poor houses are filled, our lunatic asylums are overcrowded; to say nothing of the hundreds of thousands who live next door to poverty day by day in the island.
>
> In the midst of this distress of the black majority we have a prosperous minority of white, coloured and a few black persons who have been taken under the patronage of the privileged minority." (Garvey c)

On the surface, it would seem that Garvey was appealing against Caesar to Caesar but this would be to underestimate the significance of mobilizing liberal and democratic opinion in England as a result of an investigatory commission. Moreover, colonial officers were quite mindful of the implications of letters such as these for their career prospects. The letters that Garvey wrote to the Colonial Office were followed by others to Members of Parliament and to public figures as a means of internationalizing the struggle.

In 1930, when the Depression was making itself felt through-out the capitalist world and thousands of West Indian migrant

workers in the Americas had been laid off, Garvey spoke up on
behalf of their deteriorating circumstances and their immediate
threat of repatriation in a speech at the Ward Theatre:

> "To talk about prosperity when Cuba spits upon our
> labourers, when Costa Rica and other nearby Latin
> American countries are preventing our sons and daugh-
> ters from entering their borders. Prosperity! When in
> Bocas-del-Toro our people are chopped and robbed by
> the natives at week-ends. When Guatemala insults our
> labourers and reduces them lower than the level of dogs.
> When Nicaragua and Spanish Honduras close their
> doors to our people. The great country of the United
> States of America, which has given work and sheltered
> so many of our people, has turned her doors of oppor-
> tunity by adopting a quota system, which reduces our
> entry to a minimum." (Garvey i, 190)

So grave was the crisis that the *Gleaner* itself had to come out
strongly against the hostility to Jamaicans in Panama, Cuba and
Costa Rica as they were being treated as "undesirable aliens".
(*DG*, 20 November 1931, 11). The colonial government had
taken very limited action since the late 1920s when a Secretary
for Immigration had been put in charge of repatriating Jamaicans. But this was now inadequate to meet the flood.

By 1937, their plight had worsened, and from London Garvey
wrote a Memorandum to the Colonial Secretary, a memorandum which was also published in *Plain Talk* (Jamaica) and in
a number of other West Indian newspapers and in the *Panama
Tribune* whose editor was a Garveyite. (*PT*, 8 May 1937, 23)

> "Several years ago, owing to the very bad economic
> conditions then prevailing in certain of the British West
> Indian islands, namely, Jamaica, Barbados, Trinidad,
> the Windward Islands, Leeward Islands, a large number
> of British West Indian Negroes were forced to leave
> their respective countries for the Republic of Cuba
> where there was a boom in the sugar and banana
> industries." (idem.)

After discussing the exploitation of West Indian workers in
Cuba and the Central American Republics, he concluded:

"The different West Indian islands from which these immigrants hail have resources sufficient within them to guarantee proper employment to these people if they should be returned, but the Government of these resources must be undertaken not by private ownership which is always selfish but under government direction without prejudices to the class of people who need consideration and assistance." (idem.)

During that same year and again the following year, the West Indian labour scene had exploded in a series of riots.

Garvey's Memorandum to the West Indian Royal Commission of September 24, 1938, spelt out the situation which had led to the upheavals. He advised that a

"commission going out to the West Indies should seek to get information from the lowest classes of the population on their own account and not in any way by the arranged information that would be given by the aristocracy or their agents . . . . the revolt of the West Indian masses is not due to any propaganda other than their feeling terribly the strain of life, due to the peculiar arrangement that keeps them in a society with an economic system, that is far above their realizations and appreciating them only when they can live up to that system, which is impossible." (Garvey, d)

He also said that

"the labouring condition in Jamaica and all other West Indian Islands has been arranged by the original employers, who desire to get the people as near to the condition of slavery as possible." (idem.)

And in the *Black Man* of July 1938, in commenting on the Jamaican riots, he used less diplomatic language than in the Memorandum, alleging that "the labouring classes of Jamaica have never had anything to be loyal about." To this 'disloyalty' he had made a great contribution.

But whereas in this 1938 Memorandum Garvey was putting forward proposals for social and economic reforms as he had been doing throughout the thirties, the labour situation in the Caribbean had now reached a point where the masses were prepared to act and had done so. From the distance of London, and in days when communications were slow and wireless was still in its infancy, Garvey did not appreciate the depth of this change. Indeed, the series of riots in the Caribbean were part of a crisis in the British colonial empire which was manifesting itself especially in India and the Caribbean. At this point the masses were in greater demand of practical leadership than of petitions to the Colonial Office. So in a sense Garvey was to find himself upstaged by events and in a position similar to that of Cipriani in Trinidad who had been replaced as the real leader of the Trinidadian masses by Tubal Uriah 'Buzz' Butler.

Indeed, Garvey had not ever been truly in the heat of labour agitation and organization to the extent that he had been a UNIA political activist and organizer. Despite his founding of the Jamaica Labourers and Workers Asociation in 1930, he was to act as an inspirer and catalyst in working class causes rather than as an effective organizational head, and it was left to his aides to pursue the day-to-day formulation of labour strategy and organization.

By 1937, a Garveyite, A.G.S. Coombs, had launched the Jamaica Workers and Tradesmen Union; and R.E. Rumble — the Poor Man's Improvement Association, a poor peasant organization in the parish of Clarendon. Rumble was constantly agitating against the oppressive conditions of the workers and peasants, publishing sixteen letters in *Plain Talk* between 1937 and 1938.

Plain Talk newspaper (1935-38) was the main forum for pro-labour agitation. Its proprietor, T. Kitchener, was a Garveyite and its editor, A Mends, had been associated with the UNIA in the early twenties. *Plain Talk* had started out with a moderate political stance, supporting progressive legislators, but eventually it got caught up in the militant movement of the working class struggle. During its existence, *Plain Talk* published over forty letters by Alexander Bustamante, who emerged as the leader of the island's largest trade union. Bustamante later became the first Prime Minister of independent Jamaica and a National Hero.

By 1937, several of the labour organizers around Bustamante like A.G.S. Coombs, Hugh Buchanan, J.A.G. Edwards, Stennet Kerr Coombs, St. William Grant and L.W.J. Rose, were either Garveyites or had at some time in the past been connected with the UNIA.

Garvey and the 1937-38 Labour Crises

Plain Talk itself was recognized by Captain Arthur Cipriani's Trinidad Labour Party as its mouthpiece in Jamaica and its editor dubbed as 'Minister of Propaganda'. *(PT,* 4 June 1938, 3) The basis of this contact lay in the fact that the working class movement had developed in Jamaica and Trinidad under the same impetus and through similar catalysts. As in Jamaica, ex-World War I soldiers in Trinidad had played a very important role in working class agitation especially during strikes in 1919. These strikes, initiated by the dockworkers, were said to have "sparked a wave of uprisings throughout the island against the common oppressors — white racists, prinicipally merchants, planters and officials." (Elkins c, 71) The stevedores were represented by the Trinidad Workingman's Association whose leaders were "Garvey's most important disciplines on the island." (72) At meetings of the TWA speakers were said to have used verbatim quotations from the *Negro World* and the writings of Garvey. (Elkins e, 10)

Captain Arthur Andrew Cipriani, a Trinidad white of Corsican origin, was head of the TWA and was partial to Garvey. W.H. Bishop, the editor-proprietor of the radical *Labour Leader* and General Secretary of the TWA, was equally said "to be ever ready to give a fair chance in publishing Garveyism and its activities." *(B,* 15 February 1930, 12) The *Blackman* reciprocated this journalistic relationship by publishing relevant articles from the *Labour Leader.* (B, 20 January 1930, 4)

In Barbados too, Herbert Seale, who later became General Secretary of the Barbados Progressive League, had earlier on been a Garveyite (Hoyos, 86), and his countryman, Clennel Wickham, editor of the *Weekly Herald,* supported Garveyism. *(NW,* 27 October 1923, 4) In British Honduras, Hubert Cain, editor of the progressive *Independent* was also Treasurer of the Belize division of the UNIA *(B,* 27 April 1929, 10) Garvey in turn closely followed the activities of Marryshow and Cipriani whom he termed "the bull-dogs of West Indian politics". *(NJ,* 23 August 1932, 2)

It is not, therefore, surprising that Garvey envisaged in 1927-8 the prospect of organizing the UNIA divisions in these territories into mass political parties, and also that he was a proponent of a West Indian federation. The *Blackman* on May

16, 1929 proposed that the West Indian colonies form a geographical, social and economic entity within the tropics, as in these respects their outlook was one and the same.

> "Their history has advanced along one general line indicated by slavery, emancipation, failure of sugar crops and prices, disasters of nature, neglect by the Motherland." (Garvey i, 166)

A follow-up to this editorial put the view that "one Central Government is a sine qua non of Federation. Yes, and it must be a Central Government that gives full Dominion status to the West Indies." (168)

But in Trinidad the pattern of colonial-minded opposition to Garvey was in evidence, and mobilized itself against a projected Garvey visit in 1928. The *Trinidad Teachers' Journal* stated:

> "We share the opinion with the Guardian that no good purpose will result from the Government allowing Mr. Garvey to land in Trinidad. His presence will simply upset the peace and harmony which at present obtain among the various races in the colony, a visit of this kind will be the means of depleting the coffers of the poorer people of the small savings they have been able to make. We West Indians have no desire to dominate Africa. What we want is a larger share in the economic assets of the country in which we live". (*in Herald,* 25 February 1928, 17).

Barred then in 1928, Garvey was however allowed to land in Trinidad in 1937,[3] only three months after the island had been rocked by labour riots in which fourteen people had been killed, fifty-nine wounded and hundreds arrested. (Ramdin, 106) But at this time, Garvey's political star was on the wane, and he was conceded this visit only after energetic petitions to the Governor on his behalf by Captain Cipriani. But, reported the *Trinidad Guardian* of October 20, 1937,

> "Mr. Marcus Garvey, President General of the Universal Negro Improvement Association lands in the colony this morning under certain restrictions according to authoritative information received yesterday. His landing is on the expressed condition that there will be no

open air meeting, and in respect of indoor meetings he will not be allowed to speak on matters political or on matters which are likely to cause ill-feeling or disaffection. Government is anxious to stop meetings of a seditious and scurrilous nature in open spaces and parks in the city under the control of the Port of Spain City Council."

So the Mayor, Alfred Richards, was 'asked' to call off the meeting scheduled for Woodford Square.

Garvey was however met by an "enthusiastic crowd" as he disembarked from the 'Lady Nelson'. He was then driven up to a packed Globe Theatre "in a car draped with red, green and black flags, the colours of the UNIA and ACL." *(TG,* 21 October 1937, 2). Among those on the platform were Mr. Joshua Douglas, Mr. Frederick and Mr. Atkinson and Micea Smith of La Brea; Mr. Thomas and Mr. Savary of Pointe-à-Pierre, Mr. Nelson of St. Madeleine, Alderman Ogierally, Mr. Creece and Mr. Murdock of San Fernando, Mrs. Byer, Mr. Martin and Mr. Giroux of Port of Spain, and Mr. Smith of Tobago. The provenance of those on the platform suggests that Garveyites were active in the oil, asphalt and sugar areas of the colony and likely to be therefore active in the trade unions.

Cipriani welcomed Garvey as

> "one of the greatest leaders in present-day history . . . . it is the first occasion in which we've met . . . . but it is not the man or the individual, it is the work and the word that will stand through the long ages that are yet to be (applause). And when you and I are dead and gone the grateful and ungrateful shall come to the little spot of earth which marks our last resting place and it is then that we will know if it is impossible for those who cross the great divide ever to know what those on the other side think of the work done and the achievements accomplished (applause)." *POSG,* 21 October 1937, 13).

It would not be far-fetched to suggest that Cipriani's prophetic remarks, directed at the then restive masses as well as the colonial authorities, mirrored Garvey's own sentiments and betrayed the feelings of political leaders who felt themselves being left behind by their own followers.

Given the fact that Cipriani had had to wage a struggle with the authorities to allow Garvey to address the public at all, Cipriani may have advised Garvey to confine his remarks to abstract and morally edifying themes such as "The Power of the Mind" and "The Equality of Man". (*TG*, 24 October 1937, 21)

Similarly, when Garvey went on to Grenada he spoke on "Man's Rise to Greatness". He was well feted in St. George's, Grenada, paid an official call on the Governor and was entertained at the Hotel St. James. He also visited British Guiana and on his return to Trinidad was given a civic reception by the Port of Spain City Council. He also toured the South — the industrial belt of Trinidad and Tobago. There he contended that "it is the mind of man that keeps him down and sends him up" and, to his detriment in the eyes of his admirers, ignored the concrete conditions of colonialism, the oil-field owners, sugar planters — the entire oligarchy which sat like deadweight on the people. Not that Garvey did not know these facts, not that he himself had not educated an entire generation against colonialism, but at the moment that the workers were in rebellion against patent exploitation of their labour, Garvey probably saw this as another skirmish that would be crushed and that the workers, in their self-assertion, would be victimized as he himself had been. He was therefore cautious and content to preserve what remained of his organization and to tone down his sharp reactions.

Wherever he visited, people turned out in large numbers to see and hear him. But among the more militant there was deep disappointment tantamount to disillusion.

The basis for this disillusionment stemmed from the fact that Garvey's evasion of controversial labour issues in his West Indian tour speeches appeared to confirm remarks he had made a few months earlier in London regarding the Trinidad labour disturbances.

At a meeting in Hyde Park on August 8, 1937, Garvey had been heckled by the Trinidadians, C.L.R. James and George Padmore, who called upon him to declare his stand on the working class struggle in Trinidad which had erupted in strikes and violence on a national scale in June that year. He at first replied that that was not the theme of his speech. Further goaded, Garvey declared in an interview reported in the *Trinidad Guardian* of August 29, 1937 that:

"though he had no doubt that the strikers had some
grievances which demanded looking into, yet they had
been misled during the absence in Europe of Captain
Cipriani by agitators. The Colonial Office had now
appointed a commission and there was no point in an
organization in London trying to keep the troubles
going."

This latter remark was intended as a personal rebuff to
C.L.R. James and George Padmore, who were Marxists and
who were young leaders of the International African Service
Bureau, one of the two other London-based organizations
rivalling Garvey's UNIA. Garvey then allowed anger and
personalities to get the better of him and launched into an anti-
communist barrage. Such views suited the right-wing and the
colonial authorities so the *Trinidad Guardian* correspondent in
London hastened to interview him on the subject and then gave
front-page coverage to this interview with the intention of
discrediting the resistance of the people and alienating Garvey
from his followers. Garvey played into their hands, for in his
interview he depicted the Trinidad workers as having been
manipulated by, of all people, the IASB in London! He also
adopted a partisan position vis-à-vis Cipriani and Butler. He
sided with Cipriani. Such an analysis was a gross underestima-
tion of the local and genuine socio-economic problems in the
West Indies, and on the other hand, a failure to appreciate the
shift of working class power from the Trinidad capital, Port of
Spain, and the Trinidad Workingmen's Association to the oil
and sugar belts in the south of the island, then mobilized around
Butler's trade union-cum-political party, the British Empire
Workers and Citizens' Home Rule Party.
    Butler, a Grenadian war veteran and migrant worker on the
Trinidad oilfields, had been a member of the Trinidad Labour
Party headed by Cipriani, who had converted the Trinidad
Workingmen's Association into a political party "which steered
well clear of any serious involvement with trade union activities,
and more particularly, the use of strikes." (Ramdin, 96) ". . . .
being white and a liberal, Cipriani had a charismatic quality that
appealed to the black masses who believed that a white man
was best suited to deal with the white colonizers." (93-4) But
Butler was also charismatic. "A natural agitator" and "deeply

religious", he advanced a combined messianic and militant approach to alleviate poverty. (95) On August 1, 1936, Butler formed his own party because of dissatisfaction with Cipriani's "somersaults and back-pedalling tactics", as he put it (96), having already in 1935 led a march of unemployed men from the south to the capital of the island.

Because of this polarization of the Trinidad labour leadership, Garvey's remarks in his interview constituted an attack on the militancy of the Butler movement. He said:

> "I am, of course, not hostile to the workers of Trinidad, but it grieves me to see them being misled. This organization called the International African Service Bureau is nothing but a political body and a communist one at that, which is using the Trinidad workers for its own end, sending out inflammatory literature and in every way trying to keep the pot of trouble boiling. Why should the Trinidad workers risk their employment for the sake of these agitators in London who have nothing to lose. It is a shame. I have worked for the negro peoples all my life and nobody will say I am siding with the capitalists, but it grieves me when I see ordinary, decent workers being used as pawns in the political game. Undoubtedly the workers had grievances that needed looking into, but in the absence of Captain Cipriani they got themselves into the hands of people who had no claim to lead them. And now let me warn them. They are still being used. Though peace has been restored and the government has promised an inquiry, trouble is still being served up from London. There is a reason for that which I will give them: it is that this African Service Bureau, though posing as a progressive movement among Africans, is in fact a communist organization and I have no time for such a body which busies itself making industrial strife instead of aiming at industrial peace." (SG, 29 August 1937, 1)

Criticism of these views preceded Garvey's arrival in the West Indies, and contrary to his assertion, he was being regarded by some as a stooge of the capitalists. Leo Darlington, writing in the Trinidad left-wing paper, *The People,* expressed "surprise and disappointment" at Garvey, saying that "his language smacks strongly of the capitalists . . . . one is left to wonder whether the Negro leader attempting to conceal under the guise of service for his race" did not realize that he was "gnawing away at the confidence of not a few of his supporters." Cipriani was also branded as a "deserter of the working class". Darlington contended: "a person has only to open his mouth on behalf of an oppressed wage earner and forthwith he is branded communist." *(People,* 4 September 1937) Which was true. In 1921, Cipriani's demands for an eight-hour day, revision of salaries, vacation for clerks, and support for co-operatives, were denounced as tantamount to Communism and Bolshevism. *(POSG,* 30 March 1921)

A further reaction to Garvey's rightist assessment was a letter signed by a depressed worker who expressed the view that Garvey should have maintained "an attitude of neutrality." *(People,* 4 September 1937) Even Mr. E.M. Mitchell, President of the Port of Spain UNIA felt that Garvey had made an "unjustified, a serious blunder . . . . due to misinformation and ignorance of local conditions". (ibid.) This meant that the local UNIA did not endorse Garvey's views.

After his tour he was still not forgiven. Indeed, Garvey was a past-master at expressing himself in such a manner that he could escape the charge of sedition even while his audience understood his revolutionary message. His 1927 arrival speech in Jamaica is one such example. But apart from his desire to avoid confrontation with the colonial hawks, the cautious tenor of his 1937 Caribbean speeches seems to reflect reformism rather than militancy as his approach and, in the Trinidad context, partisanship towards his host, Cipriani, as against the popular mass leader, Butler.

There was criticism of this moderate line from St. Lucia. The Grenada *West Indian* was scathing. It reported that Garvey's speeches amounted to "unscientific, half-baked speculations of a madly rushing man whose mind is unchastened by educational reflections." *(People,* 27 November 1937) In London, Wallace Johnson, the Sierra Leone nationalist who served as General Secretary of the IASB, was critical of Garvey, pointing out that while the UNIA had been an important "stepping stone" of the anti-colonial movement, Garvey had outlived his usefulness. *(People,* 13 November 1937, 8, 9)

Garvey denied that he had said that communism was at the root of labour struggles in the West Indies and expressed surprise at the conditions of labour that he had seen. *(People,* 20 November 1937, 9) But the damage had already been done.

Recognition of Garvey's Trade Union and Political Legacy

The 1937 criticisms were among the sharpest made against Garvey. But they did not affect his reputation in any profound way. A few months before his death on June 10, 1940, Hugh Buchanan, Jamaica's first Marxist who had been General Secretary of the Bustamante Industrial Trade Union, and who had parted ways with the authoritarian leadership of Alexander Bustamante in the trade union movement, made this assessment in the *Worker and Peasant,* journal of the Negro Workers' Educational League:

> "Since the days of the nineteen twenties and early thirties many of those who sat at his feet have gone into active service, fully imbued with the cardinal principles for which Garvey stood, and their work has not been without its good results." (*WP,* 11 April 1940, 5, 13. This publication was soon banned.)

And after Garvey's death, at a mass meeting of dockworkers and banana carriers, Bustamante gave priority to a discussion of Garvey's work, acknowledging his pioneer efforts in agitating for progressive labour legislation. (*DG,* 22 June 1940, 8)

Public Opinion, the organ of Jamaica's nationalist intelligentsia, reflected the views of the People's National Party. In its obituary on 15 June 1940 *Public Opinion* wrote:

> "No Jamaican, except perhaps Bustamante, has exercised so astonishig an influence over the masses as the late Marcus Garvey. That influence was not always wisely exercised, and the most superb showmanship could not prevent this from being seen. None the less Garvey never lost his hold. Even when he was four thousand miles away, his name still had power. With this knack of attracting and holding loyalty, Mr. Garvey combined more solid qualities which were never put to

their full use. He remained too much of the adventurer.
The political backwardness of the people whom he
wished to help prevented him from ever climbing into
that effective power which mellows the adventurer and
knocks off the sharp corners of his personality".

Garvey was a figure with undoubted national appeal and no
one can tell the course Jamaican politics would have taken had
he continued to function politically in the land of his birth. For
several of the leading UNIA members, including Amy Jacques
Garvey herself, were identified with the predominantly middle-
class-led People's National Party which carried a social democratic programme. Amy Jacques Garvey maintained good
relations with P.N.P. leaders, particularly those like Dudley
Thompson,[4] who were interested in the question of African
liberation. Furthermore, she actively campaigned for Norman
Manley in 1944. For despite his judgement against Garvey in
the matter of his municipal council seat in 1930, Manley later
subsidised the *New Negro Voice,* a Garveyite organ. (Personal
communication from Patricia Anderson, Research Assistant to
N.W. Manley)

However, so protean had been Garvey's activities and so
broadly based his movement, that his influence was felt in
Africa, the United States and the Caribbean. Garvey's legacy is
essentially one of a fight against racism and colonialism. His
determination, optimism, intellectual abilities and oratorical
skills constitute a legacy from which fighters against racism and
neo-colonialism of other generations can draw upon.

Conclusion

My main concern has been to look at the Garvey Movement as an anti-colonial force reflecting the struggles of Black people for civil and political rights in the post-World War I years. Special emphasis has been placed on Garvey's Caribbean years. These years still tend to be neglected in the literature on Marcus Garvey or are relegated to a postscript. Yet his work, especially in Jamaica, enables us to understand the dialectical inter-connection between the struggle to liberate the ancestral homeland from colonialism and the efforts to gain civil and political freedom in the diaspora. These two apparently con-tradictory ideas were embodied in the slogan "Africa for the Africans, those at home and those abroad" as well as in his statement "to fight for African Redemption does not mean that we must give up our domestic fights for political justice and industrial rights." (Garvey h, 35) This latter position expressed by Garvey in an article written in 1923 sums up his political strategy and that approach has guided this study.

Although the classical colonial system has been defeated, insufficient attention has been paid to the movements which contributed to its demise, particularly those active in the inter-war years. These movements, with all their contradictions, uncertainties, strengths and weaknesses, functioned at a time when most people felt that colonialism would last for centuries more. These early stirrings laid a foundation for the post-World War II liberation movements.

Racist attitudes were prevalent not only within the colonial establishment which maintained an iron rule but also within liberal as well as left-wing forces who felt that colonialism had been a civilizing force and that national liberation would be given to the colonial peoples by the European working-class. On this issue, Lenin distinguished himself from many other communists, as he saw the storm clouds that were gathering in the far-flung European Empires and fully recognized their great potential in the struggle against imperialism.

Garvey's contribution is now much better documented, thereby facilitating a deeper study of the specific forms of the anti-colonial and civil rights movement he led.

The Garvey legacy is extraordinarily rich and has not yet been really mined. There is much in his work for political scientists, cultural analysts, historians, journalists, theologians, philosophers, etc.

In dealing with this legacy researchers and writers will encounter a great deal of prejudice in the academic and journalistic literature. Neo-colonialist ideology draws on this and uses it to undermine the popular recognition of Garvey or to cast him in a mould of a utopian, a buffoon, an unprincipled character, a thief or even a con-man. But we know that this has been the lot of those who have stood up for fundamental change.

This study has not been concerned, however, to make a case for Garvey or to disprove views based on prejudice but to gain a better grasp of the positions he took and the mass support he built in the early decades of the twentieth century.

Footnotes

Chapter One

Origins

1. Hill d 1, cx, suggests that around 1904 Garvey went to work in Port Maria at a printery established by Alfred Burrowes.

Chapter Two

Turn-of-Century Ambience

1. A biographical sketch of Dr. Robert Love appears in Roberts a. Roberts is wrong on Love's date of birth which he has as 1839 when it was more likely to have been 1835. Roberts further dates his death in 1913 when it should have been 1914. For confirmation of this cf. *JT*, 28 November 1914, 10. Nevertheless, Roberts provides useful biographical information on Love. See also *Daily Chronicle*, November 23, 1914, 3. Students of this period anxiously await the work of Mrs. Joy Lumsden, postgraduate researcher in the Department of History, University of the West Indies, who is doing a doctoral thesis on Robert Love.

2. See *JA*, 8 May 1901, 7. Cf. also *DG*, March-May 1901 *passim* for reports of meetings.

3. See 1897 *JA*, 20 March, 2, 3; 27 March, 2, 3; 3 April, 3; 24, April; 15, May, 3.

4. In an autobiographical essay, Theodore Sealy, former Editor-in-Chief of the *Gleaner*, wrote, "I succeeded Herbert George DeLisser who was Leader Writer, not Editor.

Indeed he did not work at the *Gleaner* but was Secretary of the Jamaica Imperial Association, who kept him living a great life as permanent lodger at the posh Myrtle Bank Hotel from which he would come chauffeur-driven to the *Gleaner* . . . . to read his proofs while smoking cigars." (*SGM,* 25 November 1984, 3)

Chapter Three

Initial Political Involvement

1.   See *JG,* 16 December 1908, 2. For a discussion of this strike and the early trade union movement in Jamaica, see Hart e, 60.

2.   There is as yet no evidence of collaboration between Cox and Love. The latter was still active in his seventies but was not eligible for membership in the Club as this was based on Jamaican birth.

3.   There are discrepancies about the precise number of the address. See Hill d I, 54 fn. 2.

5.   One such is T.H. Duncanson, first Baptist Minister to hold a theological degree from Morehouse College, Atlanta. (Oral evidence from Rev. Horace Russell, 1975)

6.   Marcus Garvey to Major Moton, 29 February 1916, in personal papers of Amy Jacques Garvey.

Chapter Six

The Art of the Word

1.   *B,* 13 April 1929. There is a report in this about a vendor of the newspaper having been arrested by the police.

Chapter Seven

The UNIA in Cuba and Central America

1.   Ryan left Montserrat for Cuba in 1921.

2. Quoted from *La Défense — Revista de Emigrados Poliíticos Antillanos,* Santiago de Cuba, 1921.

3. Mitchell migrated to Cuba from Happy Hill, St. Georges, Grenada in 1920.

4. See the introduction to the selection of Nicolás Guillén's poetry by Robert Marquez and David Arthur Mc-Murray. The authority on Guillén is the Cuban poet Nancy Morejón. Following in the *negrismo* fashion imported from Europe, and out of the social liberal ideal, several white and mulatto Cuban and Puerto Rican poets of the 1920's and 30's had taken to depicting Blacks in their writings but always with a stress on the exotic and sensual. Cf. Coulthard, Chapters 5 and 7.

5. Cf. also the character Manuel in Jacques Roumain's Haitian novel, *Masters of the Dew.* Manuel becomes politically and technologically alert through his experience of working in Cuba and on return to his Haitian village assumes a leadership role in his community.

6. 1 *arroba* = approx. 25 lbs.

7. Cf. Nicolás Guillén's "Elegía a Jesús Menéndez" in the collection, *Man-Making Words.*

8. In this article Garvey is said to have made a recent visit to Cuba but Jacques Garvey b denied this.

9. For a comprehensive account of West Indian migration to Panama, see Newton.

10. See also Biesanz, 23.

11. Hector-Connor died in February 1971, aged 70.

Chapter Eight

Communism and the Garvey Movement

1. For further discussion of this problem see Fedoseyev, 540.

2.   An "international revolutionary proletarian organization
      (1919-1943) uniting the Communist Parties of different
      countries." (Bogoslovsky, p. 22, fn).

3.   John Reed was one of the founders of the Communist Party
      of the United States and is best known as author of the
      famous book on the Russian Revolution, *Ten Days That
      Shook the World.*

4.   Claude McKay was a Jamaican poet and novelist who came
      to prominence in the U.S. in the 1920's.

5.   Ho Chi Minh, the Vietnamese Communist Leader and later
      founding father of the socialist nation, signed on behalf
      of the Indo-China colonies under his name, Nguyen-Ai-
      Quoc. Cf. George Jackson, 69, fn. In *NW,* 7 Nov. 1925,
      10 the printer's devil mis-spelt 'Quoc' as 'Quack'!

6.   Reference to Indian and Egyptian bourgeois nationalist
      parties.

7.   Cyril Briggs, originally from St. Kitts, became editor of the
      Crusader magazine in New York and in 1919 founded
      the socialist-nationalist African Blood Brotherhood in
      Harlem and later became editor of the *Harlem Libera-
      tor,* weekly organ of the Harlem branch of the Com-
      munist Party in the early 1930's. For a discussion of the
      complex relationship between Garvey and individuals
      in the socialist groups in New York, see Vincent b. For
      biographical sketches of Briggs (1887-1966) and Dom-
      ingo (1889-1968) see Hill d I, 521-531. Cf. also Dom-
      ingo.

8.   Quoted from the Chamber of Mines, 32nd Annual Report,
      219-221.

9.   For other positive references by Garvey on Lenin and the
      Russian Revolution, see Hill d I, 354, 376; II, 617.

10.   Among the contributors were George Padmore, J.W. Ford,
      Langston Hughes, W.E.B. DuBois, Franklin Frazier,
      Nnamdi Azikiwe, Alain Locke, Countee Cullen and
      Arthur Schomburg.

Chapter Nine

Contribution to African
Liberation Struggles

1. See Hughes, 129, fn. 2. Evidence of Rev. A.W. Wilkie, 1920 correspondence. Cf. also C.O. 583/109/281/28194 of 27.2.22.

2. Conditions for West Indians employed in missionary and technical capacities in West Africa during the early part of the century were obtained from interviews between Maureen Warner-Lewis and Martha Warner and Irene Cleghorn (Trinidad), May Foster, Rowena Douglas (Jamaica).

3. Asante, 126 reports that the Nigerian colonial administration was criticized over its stance toward the Italo-Ethiopian War by "Mrs G.S. Wynter Shackleford, an influential woman of Ebute Meta, Lagos. The Shackleford family appeared to be ardently Pan-Africanist in outlook and activity, having played a prominent role in the local branch of the UNIA in the early twenties. West Indian by birth, Amos Stanley Wynter Shackleford 'The Bread King of Nigeria' came to Nigeria as a railway clerk in 1913, became an entrepreneur in 1917 and in 1921 entered the bread trade in Lagos." It is instructive that his independent trading activity was undertaken at the same time as his involvement with the UNIA. See Okonkwo.

4. Nwezeh 1978 however perceives Maran as ambivalent towards African culture.

5. Dahomeyan penalties included the death sentence for possession of Garveyite literature. See Langley a.

6. See Willan. For an analysis of Plaatje's literary work, see Ogungbesan.

7. See also Odinga, Chapter 4.

8. See, for example, Armah, 89.

9.   Sir Hugh Springer is currently Governor-General of Barbados, having previously worked in an administrative capacity at the University of the West Indies, Jamaica Campus and at the Commonwealth Secretariat in London. A.A. Thompson and world renowned cricketer, Sir Learie Constantine, both held ministerial positions in the 50's and 60's in the Trinidad and Tobago government, with Thompson serving as Attorney-General. Sir Learie later became Trinidad and Tobago High Commissioner to London.

10.   Jacques Garvey b reported that she knew and corresponded with Solanke. See also Garique *in* Coleman, 458.

Chapter Ten
Persecution and Setbacks

1.   N.W. Manley, later founder and leader of the People's National Party, appeared on behalf of G.O. Marke. See Reid, 66-7.

2.   See Ramchand and Martin e.

3.   See DuBois, 175-7.

Chapter Eleven

Choice Between Local and International Politics

1.   See back cover of Jacques Garvey a.

2.   *JT*, 3 Nov. 1928 reported that Garvey also addressed the Handsworth (Rookery Road) Brotherhood.

Chapter Twelve

Garvey's Jamaican Commitments

1.   See *B*, 20 December 1929. See however Garvey c where he claims to have been incarcerated from September 25 to December 23.

Footnotes 283

2. Quoted in letter from King's House to Colonial Secretary, C.O. 318/399 041476, 30 June 1930.

3.Idem.

4.The *Blackman* had mounted a vigorous registration campaign to muster all the possible votes, stating the necessary tax and income requirements. A centre was set up at Edelweiss Park for this purpose. See *Blackman,* 19 November 1929.

5. Although contradictory, the electoral connection with Ehrenstein and later Ashenheim seemed to have been politically pragmatic,, Cf. Wilmot who shows that a political alliance between Jewish businessmen and the Black peasantry/petty bourgeoisie had been in evidence since 1836, and continued throughout the nineteenth century. Electoral support for Jewish merchants by Blacks was clearly an anti-planter gesture since Jews consistently gained Black support where a Jew opposed a member of the plantocracy for a seat. Besides, Blacks had credit relations with Jewish merchants, which created one form of the client relationship which has come to distinguish the Jamaican electoral process. Furthermore some Jewish candidates are known to have opposed taxes in support of the Established Church and other oppressive taxation measures as well as to have agitated against immigration from Europe and Asia and Africa — financed by the government. Imported labour of course depressed local wages.

The Black peasantry and petty bourgeoisie looked up to and respected mulattos and whites. Individuals from these classes who won popular support were called 'people's men'. (Patterson) Wilmot cites one Jewish legislator as being titled the 'people's friend'.

Chapter Thirteen

Ideological Engagement

1. For Wint's work as teacher-legislator see Mills, 65-66. For obituary of Monteith, see *DG* 23 June 1970, 1.

2. Sir Fiennes Barrett Lennard was also the trial judge in the case brought against Garvey by Marke.

3.   See the portrait of the slave Sam Sharpe, leader of the 1832
      Montego Bay Rebellion in DeLisser's novel *Psyche,*
      London, 1952; also that of Paul Bogle in *Revenge: A Tale
      of Old Jamaica,* Kingston, 1919.

4.   For treatment of this theme see Clarke d; Martin e.

5.   For discussion of some of these figures, see Baxter. See also
      Arthur Kitchin, "Cupidon — the Greatest Entertainer of
      All" in *SGM,* August 5, 1979, and "Ranny Williams —
      Crowd Favourite," *SGM,* August 19, 1979.

6.   For a selection of his articles see *B,* 11 May and 10, 11 Oct.
      1929; 17, 18, 19 February; 1 March and 10 May, 1930;
      NJ, 22 October and 5, 15 November 1932.

7.   For a more appreciative review of McKay's work see Eric
      Waldron's review of *Banjo, DG,* 17 August 1929, 8.
      Waldron's review followed DeLisser's attack on the
      novel where he argued that *Banjo* was pamphleterring
      because "Ray, an educated man delivered long speech-
      es again and again on the race question." See DeLisser's
      column 'Random Jottings,' *DG,* 4 July 1929.

8.   Scientific research into the dominant role of Blacks in
      Pharonic Egypt has been shunted aside by mainstream
      European writings on Ancient Egypt. But Diop and Van
      Sertima have done much to correct this racist bias. See
      also *Journal of African Civilizations,* Sept. 1980.

Chapter Fourteen

People's Representative

1.   On 26 September 1930 the Council of the KSAC was
      dissolved by the Acting Governor due to corruption. Sir
      William Morrison was appointed to administer its
      affairs until an election was called in September 1931.
      See *Handbook of Jamaica 1931,* 351.

2.   In personal communicastion December 24, 1985 Richard
      Hart writes that DeLeon visited Moscow in "1920, after

attending the Conference of the Red International of Trade Unions in Hamburg. The Anglophone Caribbean delegation to this conference had been arranged by Otto Huiswoud field organizer of the National Negro Labour Congress, who was in Jamaica in 1929. That delegation consisted of S.M. DeLeon (Jamaica), Hubert N. Critchlow (British Guiana) and Vivian Henry (Trinidad)."

3.   This seems to have been Garvey's second visit to Trinidad as he had stopped there in 1914 on his way back from England.

4.   Thompson served in the Cabinet of Michael Manley's People's National Party government in the 1970's.

BIG TIME FOR THE PEOPLE

OF BOSTON

HEAR

HON. MARCUS GARVEY

The World's Greatest Negro Orator, President-General of the
Universal Negro Improvement Association and President of
the Black Star Line Steamship Corporation

He Will Speak at

THE PEOPLE'S BAPTIST CHURCH

Tremont and Camden Streets
MONDAY and TUESDAY NIGHTS, MARCH 1 and 2
at 8 o'clock sharp

Ebenezer Baptist Church	Zion M. E. Church
West Springfield Street	Northampton St. & Columbus Ave.
Wednesday and Thursday	
Nights, March 3 and 4	**Friday Night, March 5**
at 8 o'clock sharp	at 8 o'clock sharp

Hear This Great Man in One of His Wonderful Speeches on

"THE LIBERATION OF OUR RACE"

THE BLACK STAR LINE

Has Startled the World and He Will Tell You All About It
Many Other Prominent Speakers   Big Musical Program
Come Prepared to BUY Your SHARES in

*"The Black Star Line Steamship Corporation" and the "Negro
Factories Corporation"*

You May Buy From 1 to 200 Shares at $5.00 Each

Be Early to Get Seats and Avoid the Rush   All Seats Free

SIGNED, UNIVERSAL NEGRO IMPROVEMENT ASSOCIATION

Bibliography

African National Congress (ANC) *Unity in Action—a Photographic History of the African National Congress, South Africa, 1912-82*, ANC, London, 1982

Allen, C.H. and Johnson, R.W. eds. *African Perspectives,* Cambridge University Press, New York, 1970

Armah, Ayi Kwei *The Beautyful Ones Are Not Yet Born,* Heinemann, London, 1971 reprint

Arthur, Clarisse Interview wtih R. Lewis, Colón, Panama, 1977

Asante, S.K.B. *Pan-African Protest—West Africa and the Italo-Ethiopian Crisis, 1934-41* Longman, London, 1977

Ashwood Garvey, Amy "The birth of the Universal Negro Improvement Association" *in* Martin c, 219-226

Ashdown, Peter "Marcus Garvey—the UNIA and the Black cause in British Honduras, 1914-49" *Journal of Caribbean History* 15, 1981, 41-55

Ayearst, Morley *The British West Indies—the Search for Self-Government,* Allen & Unwin, London, 1960

Batson, J.M. "Negroes of Togoland want Garvey to lead" *in NW,* 30 May 1931

Baxter, Ivy *The Arts of An Island—the Development of the Folk and Creative Arts in Jamaica, 1494-62,* Scarecrow Press, New Jersey, 1970

Beecher, John Coleman, comp. *Jamaica Cricket 1863-1926, a Book of Information on Cricket in Jamaica, the West Indies, England and Australia,* Gleaner Co., Kingston, 1926

Bennett, Wycliffe Illustrated talk on "The development of the Jamaican Theatre", Little Theatre, Kingston, June 1982; see also "The Jamaica theatre", *Jamaica Journal* 8:2/3, Summer 1974, 3-9

Biesanz, John "Race Relations in the Canal Zone", *Phylon* 1, 1950

Bogolovsky, V. *et al The October Revolution and Africa,* Progress Publishers, Moscow, 1983

Bose, Dilip "Mahatma Gandhi—an evaluation", *Party Life* (fortnightly journal of the Communist Party of India) 19:3, 7 February 1983, 15-28

Braithwaite, Lloyd "Social Stratification in Trinidad", *Social and Economic Studies* 1:4, Kingston, October 1983

Britain Report no. 232 (S), M.I.I.C. New York, 7 Jan. 1920 on 'Negro Agitation', P.R.O., F.I. 371/4567 (1920)

Brooks, A.A. *History of Bedwardism or the Jamaica Native Baptist Free Church,* Gleaner Co. Ltd., Kingston, 1917

Campbell, Orville "Response of the Gleaner to Marcus Garvey between September 1929—January 1930", Caribbean Studies Paper, Institute of Mass Communications, University of the West Indies, Jamaica, 1981

Carnegie, James "Some Aspects of Jamaica's Politics, 1918-38", MA thesis, University of the West Indies, 1969

Chevannes, Barry "Social Origins of the Rastafarian Movement", Institute of Social and Economic Research, University of the West Indies, Kingston, 1978 (mimeo)

Clarke, John Henrik, ed. a. *Harlem: A Community in Transition,* Citadel Press, New York, 1964

_____ ed, b. *Marcus Garvey and the Vision of Africa,* Vintage Books, Random House, New York, 1974

_____ c. "The Caribbean antecedents of Marcus Garvey" *in* Clarke b, 14-28

_____ d. "The neglected dimensions of the Harlem Renaissance", *Black World,* November 1970

Cohen, Victor G. Letter to Jacques Garvey, February 9, 1970

Coleman, James *Nigeria—Background to Nationalism,* UCLA Press, California, 1958

1866 Commission Report of the Jamaica Royal Commission, Part II, HMSO, London, 1866

Cooke, Mercer *Five French Negro Authors,* Associated Publishers, Washington, 1943

Cooper, Wayne, ed. *The Passion of Claude McKay: Selected Prose and Poetry, 1912-1948,* Schocken Books, New York, 1973

Craig, Susan, ed. *Contemporary Caribbean: A Sociological Reader,* Susan Craig, Trinidad, Vol. I: 1981, Vol. II: 1982

Cronon, E.D. *Black Moses: The Story of Marcus Garvey and the*

Universal Negro Improvement Association, University of
Wisconsin Press, 1968
_____ *Marcus Garvey* Prentice Hall, New Jersey, 1973
Coulthard, George Robert *Race and Colour in Caribbean
Literature,* Oxford University Press, London, 1962
Cunard, Nancy, ed. *Negro Anthology,* Wishart & Co., London,
1934
Curtin, Phillip D. *Two Jamaicas: The Role of Ideas in a Tropical
Colony, 1830-65,* Harvard University Press, Cambridge,
Massachusetts, 1955
Dange, *et al The Mahatma—Marxist Evaluation,* People's
Publishing House, New Delhi, 1977
Davidson, Basil *The Africans—an Entry to Cultural History,*
London, 1969
Degras, Jane ed. a. *The Communist International, 1919-1943:
Selected Documents I, 1919-1922,* Frank Cass, London, 1971
_____ b. *The Communist International, 1919-1943: Selected
Documents II, 1923-28,* Frank Cass, London, 1971
DeLisser, H.G. *In Cuba and Jamaica,* Gleaner, Kingston, 1910
Diop, Chiekh Anta *Black Africa—the Economic and Cultural
Basis for a Federated State,* Lawrence Hill, Connecticut,
1978
Domingo, W.A. "Testimony", Noel White ed., typescript, n.d.
DuBois, W.E.B. *An ABC of Colour—Selections from Over a Half
Century of the Writings of W.E.B. DuBois,* Seven Seas Books,
Berlin, 1963
Dyer, Richard "Paul Robeson: militant humanism", *Marxism
Today,* September 1983, 39
Edwards, Adolph *Marcus Garvey, 1887-1940,* New Beacon
Books, London, 1972
Eisner, Gisela *Jamaica, 1830-1930: a Study in Economic
Growth,* Manchester University Press, 1961
Eisenberg, Bernard and Miller, Kelly "The Negro leader as a
marginal man", *Journal of Negro History* 45:3, July 1960
Elkins, W.F. a. "The influence of Marcus Garvey on Africa—a
British Report of 1922", *Science and Society,* Summer 1968
_____ b. "Unrest among the negroes—a British document of
1919", *Science and Society,* Winter 1968
_____ c. "Black Power in the British West Indies—the Trinidad
Longshoremen's strike of 1919", *Science and Society,* Winter
1969; also *in Jamaica Journal* 3 & 4, March 1978, 76-77
_____ d. "A source of Black nationalism in the Caribbean: The
revolt of the British West Indies Regiment at Taranto",

Science and Society, Spring 1970; also *in Jamaica Journal*
11:3 &4, March 1978, 73-5

_____ e. "Marcus Garvey the *Negro World* and the British West
Indies, 1919-1920", *In* Lewis & Lewis b, 36-51

Essien-Udom, E.U. *Black Nationalism—a Search for an Indentity in America,* University of Chicago Press, 1962

Ethiopia, Ministry of Information *The Italo-Ethiopian War, 1935-41: Genesis, Ordeal, Victory,* Addis Ababa, 1975

Fedoseyev, P.N. *Leninism and the National Question,* Progress Publishers, Moscow, 1977

Foner, Phillip a. "The I.W.W. and the Black worker", *Journal of Negro History,* 55:1, 19??

_____ b. *Antonio Maceo—'the Bronze Titan' of Cuba's Struggle for Independence,* Monthly Review Press, New York, 1977

Foster, William *The History of the Communist Party of the United States,* International Publishers, New York, 1952

Fryer, Peter *Staying Power—the History of Black People in Britain,* Pluto Press, London, 1984

Franco, José Luciano "Martí y Juan Gualberto Gomez" *Revolutión y Cultura 95,* July 1980, 10-13

Galló, Caspar Jorge Garcia *Esbozo biográfico de Jesús Menendez,* Editora Politica, Havana, 1978

Garique, Phillip "The West African Students Union", *Africa* 23, January 1953

Garvey, Amy Ashwood (*See* Ashwood)

Garvey, Amy Jacques (*See* Jacques Garvey)

Garvey, Marcus a. "Minutes of Proceedings of the speech by the Honourable Marcus Garvey at the Century Theatre, Archer St., Westbourne Grove, London", 2 September 1928, UNIA, London.

_____ b. "Minutes of proceedings of meeting held at Ward Theatre, Kingston Jamaica, under the auspices of the People's Political Party on December 13, 1928 to expose the *Daily Gleaner*", Blackman Publishing Co., Kingston.

_____ c. Programme enclosed in "Letters to Rt. Honourable Philip Snowdon" February 27—11 March 1930, CO. 318/399 041476, PPO, London.

_____ d. Memorandum to the West Indian Royal Commission, 24 Sept. 1938, CO 950/44, PRO London.

_____ e. "Instruction for Mrs. Garvey, Mr. McIntyre, Miss Whyte, Miss Brooks", 1938 (pages not numbered) in Jacques Garvey's personal papers, Kingston.

_____ f. "The case of the Negro to international racial adjustment", Poets and Painters' Press, London, 1968.

⸱ ___ g. "A journey of selfdiscovery" *in* Clarke b, 71-76

___ h. *Philosophy and Opinions of Marcus Garvey* Vols. I and II, Amy Jacques Garvey, ed., Atheneum, New York, 1969.

___ i. *More Philosophy and Opinions*, Vol. III. Amy Jacques Garvey and E.U. Essien Udom, eds., Frank Cass, London, 1977.

Geiss, Immanuel "Notes on the development of Pan-Africanism", *Journal of the Historical Society of Nigeria,* 3:4, June 1967.

Guillén, Nicolás *Man-making Words, Selected Poems of Nicolás Guillén* trans. by Robert Marquéz and David Arthur McMurray, Editorial de Arte y Literatura, La Habana, 1973.

Harding, Chester "Memorandum to A.L. Flint", Sept. 22, 1919, *in* Hill d II, 22.

Hart, Richard a. "The life and resurrection of Marcus Garvey" *Race* 9:2, 1967.

___ b. Letter *in Race,* April 1968, 528

___ c. Letter to Rupert Lewis, August 12, 1970.

___ d. Interviews with Trevor Munore, September 1972.

___ d. "Trade unionism in the English-speaking Caribbean: the formative years and the Caribbean Labour Congress *in* Craig II. 59-91

___ f. *Freedom Now,* Kingston, n.d.

Hill, Robert a. "The first English years and after, 1912-16" *in* Clarke b 38-70

___ comp, b. *The Black Man—A Monthly Magazine of Negro Thought and Opinion, 1933-39,* Kraus-Thompson, New York, 1975

___ c. "Leonard P. Howell and millenarian visitions in early Rastafari", *Jamaica Journal* 16:1, February 1983, 24-39

___ d. *The Marcus Garvey and Universal Negro Improvement Association Papers, Vol. I, 1826—August 1919; Vol. II, August 27, 1919-31 August 1920,* University of California Press, Los Angeles, 1983; Vol. IV, 1 September 1921—2 September 1922, UCLA Press, 1985

Ho Chi Minh *Ho Chi Minh and Africa,* Foreign Languages Publishing House, Hanoi, 1980

Hooker, James R. *Black Revolutionary: George Padmore's Path from Communism to Pan-Africanism,* Pall Mall Press, London, 1967

Hoover, J. Edgar Memorandum for Mr. Ridgely, 11 Oct. 1919, National Archives, Washington, D.C., RG 60, File 198940

Howe, Russell Warren "Twilight of the One-party state in Africa", *Daily Gleaner,* 28 May 1971

Hoyos, F.A. *The Rise of West Indian Democracy—the Life and*

Times of Sir Grantley Adams, Advocate Press, Barbados, 1963

Huggins, George "Marcus Garvey and the League of Nations, 1921-31 an episode in the international relations of the UNIA", *in* Lewis & Lewis b, 152-164

Hughes, Arnold "Africa and the Garvey Movement in the Interwar years", *in* Lewis & Lewis b, 111-135

Jackson Jnr. George D. *Comintern and Peasant in East Europe 1919-1930,* Columbia University Press, New York, 1966

Jackson, James *Report to the Black Liberation Commission,* Communist Party of the U.S.A. January 1957.

_____ b. "On the theory of Black Liberation in the USA", *Political Affairs,* March 1968

_____ c. *Revolutionary Tracings in World Politics and Black Liberation,* International Publishers, New York, 1974.

Jamaica Government *Handbook of Jamaica for 1930,* Kingston

JHS "The Second Arrest of Bedward", *Jamaica Historical Society Bulletin* 11:15, Sept. 1960, 245-8

James, C.L.R. *The Life of Captain Cipriani,* Lancashire, 1932

Jacques Garvey, Amy a. *Garvey and Garveyism,* Collier Books, Macmillan, New York, 1970

_____ b. Interviews with Rupert Lewis, 1969, 1970

_____ c. "The Early Years of Marcus Garvey" *in* Clarke b, 29-37

_____ d. *"The Political Activities of Marcus Garvey in Jamaica" in* Clarke b, 276-283

Jelf, A.S. Letter to L.C.M.S. Amery, Colonial Secretary, March 31, 1926, E.O. 115/3120

Jenkins, David *Black Zion: The Return of Afro-Americans and West Indians to Africa,* Wildwood House, London, 1975

Jones, David "Report to Executive of the 1919 Third Communist International on behalf of the International and Socialist League of South Africa" *in* South African Communist Party, 41-56

King, Kenneth "Early Pan-African politicians in East Africa", *Mawazo* 2:1, June 1969

KSAC Minutes Kingston and St. Andrew Corporation Minutes 1929-30, Jamaica

Knox, Graham "Political change in Jamaica (1866-1906) and the local reaction to the policies of the Crown Colony Government" *in Caribbean in Transition,* F.M. Andic & T.G. Matthews, eds., Institute of Caribbean Studies, Puerto Rico, 1965

Kotane, Moses Letter to Johannesburg District Party Committee, 23 February 1934 *in* South African Communist Party, 120-2

Kafeber, Walter *The Panama Canal: the Crisis in Historical Perspective,* OUP, New York, 1978

La Guerre, John *The Social and Cultural Thought of the Colonial Intelligentsia,* Institute of Social and Economic Research, University of the West Indies, Kingston, 1982

Lamming, George *In the Castle of my Skin,* Longman Drumbeat, London, 1979

Langley, J. Ayodele a. "Garveyism and African nationalism", *Race* 10:2, Oct. 1969, also *in* Clarke b, 405-13

_____ b. "Pan-Africanism in Paris, 1924-36", *Journal of Modern African Studies* 7:1, 1969, 69-84

Lenin, V.I. a. "The question of nationalities or 'autonomization' ", *in The National Question—Proletarian Internationalism,* Novosti Press, Moscow, 1969, 142-146

_____ b. *Collected Works,* Vol 31 (April-December 1920), Progress Publishers, Moscow, 1966

_____ c. "Thesis for a report on the tactics of the R(ussian) C(ommunist) P(arty)" *in Collected Works,* Vol. 32, Progress Publishers, Moscow, 1973, 453-96

Lerumo, A. *Fifty Fighting Years—the South African Communist Party, 1921-72,* Inkululeko Publishers, London, rev. ed., 1980

Levy, Jacqueline "The Economic role of the Chinese in Jamaica: the grocery retail trade," Seminar paper, Dept. of History, University of the West Indies, Jamaica, 1967.

Lewis, Rupert "A Political Study of Garveyism in Jamaica and London, 1914-40", MSc thesis, University of the West Indies, Jamaica, 1971

_____ b. "Political aspects of Garvey's work in Jamaica, 1929-35", *Jamaica Journal,* March/June 1973, 30-5

_____ c. "Garvey in Jamaica" *in* Cronon b, 154-60

_____ d. "Amy Jacques Garvey—a Political Portrait" *Xaymaca (Sunday Jamaica Daily News),* July 29, 1973

_____ e. "The last London years, 1935-40" *in* Clarke b, 330-41

_____ f. "Hugh Clifford Buchanan—Jamaica's first Marxist", *Socialism!,* December 6, 1974, 19-28

_____ g. "Robert Love—a democrat in colonial Jamaica", *Jamaica Journal,* August 1977, 59-63

_____ i. "Garvey and the Press", *Daily News,* September 8, 1978

_____ j. "Garvey 50 years Ago", *Xaymaca, (Sunday Sun),* 19 August, 1979

_____ k. "Garveyism, Communism and the Jamaican Struggle", *Jamaica Daily News,* August 18, 1980, 10-11

_____ l. "El nacionalismo anticolonial en el pensamiento de Marcus Garvey", *Anals del Caribe* I, Casa de las Américas, Havana, 1981, 99-113; also *in El Caribe Contemporáneo* 7, October 1983, 99-112

Lewis, Rupert & Maureen a. "Claude McKay's Jamaica", *Caribbean Quarterly,* June/September 1977; 23:2 & 3, 38-51

_____ eds. b. *Garvey, Africa, Europe, the Americas,* Institute of Social and Economic Research, University of the West Indies, Jamaica, 1986

Makonnen, Ras *Pan Africanism from Within* (Kenneth King, ed.), Oxford University Press, London, 1973

Martin, Tony a. *Race First: The Ideological and Organizational Struggles of Marcus Garvey and the Universal Negro Improvement Association,* Greenwood Press, Connecticut, 1976

_____ b. *Marcus Garvey, hero—a First Biography,* Majority Press, Massachusetts, 1983

_____ c. *The Pan-African Connection—from Slavery to Garvey and Beyond,* Schenkman Pub. Co., Massachusetts, 1983

_____ d. *The Political Works of Marcus Garvey,* Majority Press, Massachusetts, 1983

_____ e. *Literary Garveyism: Garvey, Black Arts and the Harlem Renaissance,* Majority Press, Massachusetts, 1983

Martyshin, O.V., "The Comintern and the problem of a united anti-imperialist front in India" *in* Ulyanovsky ed., 421-65

McFarlane, Basil "The rise and fall of the times", *The Warfare Reporter* 22:1, February 1963, 9, 25-6, 29

Mills, J.J. *His Own Accout of His Life and Times,* R.N. Murray ed., Collins and Sangster, Jamaica, 1969

Mitchell, Charles Interview with Rupert Lewis, Marianao, Havana, Cuba, 1978

Moore, Richard B. "Africa-conscious Harlem" *in* Clarke a

Mozlov, Victor & Cheboksarov, Nokolai "Races and ethnoses" *in Racism and the Struggle Against it in the Contemporary World,* Social Sciences Today, Moscow, 1982, 19-55

Navas, Luis *El Movimiento Obrero en Panama 1980-1914,* Editorial Universitaria, Panama, 1974

Neame-Jahn, Sylvia "The dual role of Garveyite influence in the Industrial and Commercial Workers Union", ms.

Nembhard, L.S. *Trials and Triumphs of Marcus Garvey,* Jamaica Times Press, Kingston, 1953

Newton, Velma *The Silver Men— West Indian Labour Migration* to *Panama, 1850-1914,* Institute of Social and Economic Research, University of the West Indies, Jamaica, 1984

Nwezeh, E.C. *Africa in French and German Fiction,* University of Ife Press, Nigeria, 1978

Odinga, Ajuma Oginga *Not yet Uhuru—the autobiography of Oginga Odinga,* Heinemann, London, 1967

Ogungbesan, Kolawole "The long eye of history in *Mhudi*" *Caribbean Journal of African Studies* 1, 1979, 27-42

Okonkwo, Rina. "A Jamaican export to Nigeria! The life of Amos Stanley Wynter Shackleford", *Caribbean Quarterly* 30:2, June 1984, 48-59

Olusanya, Gabriel O. "Garvey and Nigeria" *in* Lewis & Lewis, b, 136-151

Padmore, George a. *American Imperialism Enslaves Liberia,* Centrizdat, Moscow, 1931

_____ b. *The Life and Struggles of Negro Toilers,* International Trade Union Committee of Negro Workers, London, 1931

_____ c. *Pan-Africanism or Communism?—The Coming Struggle for Africa,* Dennis Dobson, London, 1956

Panama Canal Information Officer "Panama Canal and the Canal Zone" (brochure) Canal Zone, n.d.

Patterson, Iris Interview with Maureen Warner-Lewis, Kingston, 1978

Pedro, Alberto a. "El nacionalismo negro", *Cultura* 64:18, June, 1965

_____ b. Interview with Rupert Lewis, Havana, Cuba, 1978

Perez de la Riva, Juan "La república necolonial" *in Anuario de estudios cubanos,* Editorial de Ciencias Sociales, Havana, 1973

Phelps, O.W. "Rise of the labour movement in Jamaica", *Social and Economic Studies* 9:4, December 1960, 417-68

Pierson, Roscoe M. "Alexander Bedward and the Jamaica Native Baptist Free Church", *Lexington Theological Quarterly* 4:13, 1969, 65-76

Post, Ken a. "The bible as ideology: Ethiopianism in Jamaica, 1930-38" *in* Allen & Johnson

_____ b. *Arise Ye Starvelings—the Jamaican Labour Rebellion of 1938 and its Aftermath,* Martinus Nijhoff, the Hague, 1978

_____ c. *Strike the Iron—a Colony at War: Jamaica, 1939-1945,* Vols. I and II, Humanities Press, New Jersey, 1981

Prescott, Reginald Interview with Rupert Lewis, Colón, Panama, 1977

Primelles, León "Menocal y la Liga Nacional, Zayas y Crowder.

. . . " in *Crónica Cubana, 1919-1922,* Editorial Lex, Havana, 1957

Proudfoot, Malcolm *Population Movements in the Caribbean,* Central Secretariat, Caribbean Commission, 1950; also Negro Universities Press, New York, 1970 (reprint)

Rose, Issac Interview with Wenty Bowen, *Jamaica Daily News,* 19 October 1975, 3-7

Ramchand, Kenneth "The writer who ran away—Eric Walrond and *Tropic Death", Savacou,* September 1970, 67-75

Ramdin, Ron *From Chattel Slave to Wage Earner,* Martin Brian O'Keefe, London, 1982

Reid, Victor Stafford *The Horses of the Morning: About the Right Excellent N. W. Manley, Q. C. National Hero of Jamaica—An Understanding,* Caribbean Authors Publishing Co., Kingston, 1985

Ricketts, F.S. Address to 1920 Convention *in* Hill d II, 512-3

Roberts, W. Adolphe a. *Six Great Jamaicans,* Pioneer Press, Kingston, 1957

_____ b. "Bedward", *Sunday Gleaner,* 31 January 1960

Rosenstone, Robert A. *Romantic Revolutionary—a Biography of John Reed,* Knopf, New York, 1975

Ryan, James Interview with Rupert Lewis, Marianao, Havana, 1978

Samad, Marianne Interview with Maureen Warner-Lewis, Kingston, 1978

Sardesai, S.G. "Gandhi and the CPT" *in* Dange *et al*

Scarlett, Z. Monroe Interview with Rupert Lewis, Kingston, 1975

Scholes, T.E.S. *The British Empire and Alliance, or Britain's Duty to Her Colonies and Subject Races,* E. Stock, London, 1899

Senior, Olive a. "The Colón People" (Pt. 1) *Jamaica Journal* 11:3/4, March 1978, 62-71; (Pt. 2) *Jamaica Journal,* 42, Sept. 1978 87-103

_____ b. "The Panama Railway corollary—the Chinese who came from Panama", *Jamaica Journal* 44, n.d., 67-79

Simons, H.J. & R.E. *Class and Colour in South Africa, 1850-1950,* Penguin African Library, 1969

Smilowitz, Erica "Una Marson: woman before her time", *Jamaica Journal,* May 1983, 61-8

Smith, M.C. Augier, R. & Nettleford, R. "The Rastafari Movement in Kingston", *Caribbean Quarterly* 13:3, September 1967

South African Communist Party (SACP) *South African Communists Speak, 1915—1980—Documents from the History of the South African Communist Party,* Inkululeko Publishers, London, 1981

Souza Dário, Rubén *et al Panama, 1903-1970,* Sofia Press, n.d.

Spitzer, Leo *The Creoles of Sierra Leone—Responses to Colonialism, 1870-1945,* University of Wisconsin Press, 1974

Taylor, Godfrey "Slim and Sam—Jamaican street singers" *Jamaica Journal* 16:4, August 1983, 39-45

Thomas, Herbert *The Story of a West Indian Policeman,* Gleaner Co., Kingston, 1927

Thompson, V.B. *Africa and Unity: The Evolution of Pan Africanism,* Longman, London, 1969

Tolbert, Emory *The UNIA and Black Los Angeles,* Center for Afro-American Studies, UCLA, 1980

Ulyanovsky, R.A., ed. *The Comintern and the East—the Struggle for the Leninist Strategy and Tactics in National Liberation Movements,* Progress Publishers, Moscow, 1979

Universal Negro Improvement Association (UNIA) a. Booklet of Information and Instructions to Presidents of UNIA Divisions, Kingston, 1929

_____ b. Official Minutes of Eighth International Convention UNIA, Community Hall, 355 College St., Toronto, Canada, August 1-7 1938

Valdés, Nelson "Ideological roots of the Cuban revolutionary movement" *in* Craig II, 211-242

Van Sertima, Ivan *They Came Before Columbus,* Random House, New York, 1979

Vincent, Theodore a. *Black Power and the Garvey Movement,* Ramparts Press, California, 1971

_____ b. "The evolution of the split between the Garvey movement and the organized left in the United States, 1917-1933" *in* Lewis & Lewis b, 165-199

Weisbord, Robert G. a. "Marcus Garvey—Pan-Negroist: the view from Whitehall" *Race* 11:4, April 1970, 419-429: also *in* Clarke b, 421-7

_____ b. "British West Indian reaction to the Italo-Ethiopian War—an episode in Pan-Africanism", *Caribbean Studies* 10:1

Willan, Brian *Sol Plaatje—South African Nationalist,* 1876-1932, Heinemann, 1984.

Williams, Daniel T. *The Perilous Road of Marcus Garvey—a Bibliography,* Tuskegee Inst., Alabama, 1969.

Williams, Eric *From Columbus to Castro—the History of the Caribbean, 1492-1969,* Deutsch, London, 1970.

Willis, A.N. Address to the 1920 UNIA convention *in* Hill d II, 5-6

Wilmot, Swithin "Jewish politicians and Black voters in free Jamaica", *Social History Project Newsletter, Dept. of History,* Univ. of the West Indies, Jamaica 9 June 1984, 6-10

Wilson, William J. *The Declining Significance of Race and Changing American Institutions,* University of Chicago Press, Chicago, 1980.

Workers Party of Jamaica (WPJ) Programme of the Workers Party of Jamaica, Vanguard Press, Kingston, 1978.

Wynter, Sylvia "Jonkonnu in Jamaica—towards the interpretation of folk dance as a cultural process", *Jamaica Journal* 4:2, June 1970, 34-48

Zipser, Arthur *Working Class Giant—the Life of William Z. Foster,* International Publishers, New York, 1981.

Index